WHAT DO I COOK NOW?

Tami A. Ross, RDN, LD, CDCES, MLDE, FADCES

Recipes by **Nancy S. Hughes**

American Diabetes Association.

Director, Book Operations, Victor Van Beuren; *Managing Editor, Books,* John Clark; *Associate Director, Book Marketing*, Annette Reape; *Acquisitions Editor*, Jaclyn Konich; *Editor,* Wendy Martin-Shuma; *Composition*, Circle Graphics; *Cover Design*, Jenn French Designs; *Printer*, Versa Press.

Printed in the United States of America
1 3 5 7 9 10 8 6 4 2

The suggestions and information contained in this publication are generally consistent with the *Standards of Medical Care in Diabetes* and other policies of the American Diabetes Association, but they do not represent the policy or position of the Association or any of its boards or committees. Reasonable steps have been taken to ensure the accuracy of the information presented. However, the American Diabetes Association cannot ensure the safety or efficacy of any product or service described in this publication. Individuals are advised to consult a physician or other appropriate health care professional before undertaking any diet or exercise program or taking any medication referred to in this publication. Professionals must use and apply their own professional judgment, experience, and training and should not rely solely on the information contained in this publication before prescribing any diet, exercise, or medication. The American Diabetes Association—its officers, directors, employees, volunteers, and members—assumes no responsibility or liability for personal or other injury, loss, or damage that may result from the suggestions or information in this publication.

Shamera Robinson and Madelyn L. Wheeler conducted the internal review of this book to ensure that it meets American Diabetes Association guidelines.

♾ The paper in this publication meets the requirements of the ANSI Standard Z39.48-1992 (permanence of paper).

ADA titles may be purchased for business or promotional use or for special sales. To purchase more than 50 copies of this book at a discount, or for custom editions of this book with your logo, contact the American Diabetes Association at the address below or at booksales@diabetes.org.

American Diabetes Association
2451 Crystal Drive, Suite 900
Arlington, VA 22202

DOI: 10.2337/9781580407601

Library of Congress Control Number (LCCN): 2020951922

Dedications

To my husband, Mike—my encourager, support, and #1 fan. And in memory of Patti Bazel Geil, my longtime friend, and coauthor of *What Do I Eat Now?*, 1st and 2nd editions. Remembering all of the fun and writing projects we cooked up together.

– Tami

This book is dedicated to YOU, the readers. I normally write a dedication to my husband and my children, but this time, it's to you. I've written 13 books now for the American Diabetes Association. These books and the pages here were written *solely* with you in mind . . . every recipe, every day . . . so go out and start enjoying my time in the kitchen . . . in your kitchen. And have fun with it. I did! Enjoy!

– Nancy

Table of Contents

Recipe Index

Beverages

Breakfast

Snacks, Dips, and Appetizers

Salads, Soups, and Stews

Entrées

Seafood

Poultry

Meat

Vegetarian

Introduction

WHAT DO I EAT NOW?
ALSO, WHAT DO I COOK NOW?

What you eat is a powerful tool in managing blood glucose. In fact, "What can I eat?" is the #1 question asked when people learn they have diabetes. Whether you have recently learned that you have type 2 diabetes or pre-diabetes, or have a newfound interest in self-care, you'll quickly discover that healthy eating is fundamental to taking good care of yourself and feeling your best. You can learn much more about this topic in *What Do I Eat Now?*, 3rd edition, the companion book to this cookbook.

Following close behind, "What do I eat now?" is the question, "What do I *cook* now?" We want you to know that eating doesn't have to be bland or boring. Food and eating should be pleasurable and help you to live your best life!

HOW THIS BOOK CAN HELP YOU

Throughout this book, you'll find the latest science and evidence translated in a way that's understandable and actionable. We provide easy to follow steps that *you can do*. In Chapter 3, you will learn a variety of eating patterns and approaches that will help you maintain a healthy lifestyle. And you'll find a multitude of practical examples, illustrations, and recipes. It's good to have options. Everyone is different. The end goal is finding what works for you to keep your blood glucose in range, and then doing more of that.

How This Book Works

- Each chapter focuses on a different topic related to healthy eating with diabetes (or prediabetes). In each chapter the content is broken down into sections, making it easy to jump around and focus on what you want to learn more about.
- Interspersed throughout the book, you'll find close to 100 wholesome recipes complete with nutrition breakdown. You'll also find tried-and-true tips to keep the recipes as quick and easy as possible.
- Along with each recipe, there's a brief description and a notation of the different eating patterns (such as low- or very-low-carbohydrate, DASH, Mediterranean, etc.) in which the recipe can fit. You can learn about the seven eating patterns beneficial in managing blood glucose in Chapter 3 and determine which may work best for you.
- In Chapter 6, you'll find several menus with accompanying recipes for breakfast, lunch, dinner, and snacks. The sample menus contain approximately 45 g carbohydrate per meal. That amount of carbohydrate is intended to be a starting point and is a significant reduction for many people. (You'll learn more about carbohydrate and how it affects blood glucose on page 17.) Your diabetes health-care team may recommend a higher or lower carbohydrate goal based on a number of factors. You can see if what you're doing is working for you based on whether your blood glucose is in range or out of range.
- The sample menus include information on how the meal fills a healthy plate following the Diabetes Plate Method (described and discussed in Chapter 3) along with swift, simple tips for preparing the meal.

A Note on the Nutrition Information for Recipes

Many of the recipes Nancy developed for this book include pointers, tips, and techniques for improving the recipe or making preparation easier. Many also include **Cook's Swaps**, which are helpful ways to make a recipe friendlier to certain eating patterns (vegetarian, low-carbohydrate, etc.) or simply change up the flavor profile. Keep in mind that many of these **Swaps** will also change the nutrition information listed on the recipe, sometimes dramatically. We've made sure all of the recipes remain diabetes-friendly and in line with the nutrition guidelines of the American Diabetes Association, but they may have a different nutrition profile. Enjoy!

We hope that you find many recipes and menus that suit your tastes to add to your personal collection. We encourage you to work with your registered dietitian nutritionist (RDN) and diabetes health-care team to determine which menus, recipes, and tips are right for you. Then when the question pops up— "What do I eat now?" or "What do I cook now?"—you'll have options ready to use.

The Authors

The nutrition and meal planning portions of this book, along with the sample menus and recipes in Chapter 6, were written by Tami Ross and complement the guidance in *What Do I Eat Now?*, 3rd edition.

The other original recipes, with a couple of noted exceptions, were written and developed for this book by Nancy S. Hughes.

How Lifestyle Changes Help Type 2 Diabetes and Prediabetes

Prediabetes and type 2 diabetes are progressive conditions that can be managed. Adopting a healthy lifestyle is a significant part of that.

IF YOU HAVE PREDIABETES . . .

Having prediabetes means that you are at risk for developing type 2 diabetes. Taking action now can help hold off or prevent type 2 diabetes. Substantial evidence has shown the following three lifestyle changes can significantly reduce the incidence of going on to develop type 2 diabetes:

- **Lifestyle change #1:** Improve eating habits and food quality
- **Lifestyle change # 2:** Maintain a 7–10% weight loss (if overweight)
- **Lifestyle change #3:** Get at least 150 minutes of moderate-intensity physical activity per week

This book is rich in recipes, menu ideas, and tips to help you with the first two lifestyle changes. If fitting in physical activity is a challenge for you, *The I "Hate to Exercise" Book for People with Diabetes*, 3rd edition, by Charlotte Hayes (American Diabetes Association), may be a practical, helpful resource for you.

In addition to the lifestyle changes, some health-care professionals may recommend a medication called metformin to help *prevent* type 2 diabetes. Although not approved by the U.S. Food and Drug Administration specifically for diabetes prevention, metformin has a strong evidence base and demonstrated long-term safety as a medication therapy for diabetes prevention. Metformin is also prescribed to help *manage* type 2 diabetes. It is inexpensive, effective, and does not cause weight gain. In fact, many notice modest weight loss when taking metformin. So if your health-care team recommends metformin, it does not mean things are "in really bad shape." It's just another option to help hold off type 2 diabetes. If you have prediabetes, we encourage you to join a Diabetes Prevention Program (DPP) in your area or online. This lifestyle-change program is built on the lifestyle changes noted as effective in the large Diabetes Prevention Program study. Health insurance plans often cover the DPP for people at risk of developing type 2 diabetes, so it may be available to you at low or no cost. Locate one near you at https://nccd.cdc.gov/DDT_DPRP/Programs.aspx or by typing "DPP near me" into a search engine.

IF YOU HAVE TYPE 2 DIABETES . . .

Healthy eating, reaching and maintaining a healthy weight, and getting at least 150 minutes per week of physical activity spread over at least 3 days per week, with no more than 2 consecutive days without activity, are equally essential in managing blood glucose. It's also important to understand that, over time, your insulin-producing cells gradually lose their ability to function well. However, this occurrence does not mean that your diabetes is getting "worse." Don't blame yourself. *Would*

you blame yourself if you needed stronger glasses because your eyesight changed? Treatments such as oral medications, injectable medications, or both may be needed to manage blood glucose as an add-on to healthy eating, physical activity, and changing lifestyle behaviors. If your health-care team recommends starting, changing, or adding a medication (or two or three medications) to help manage blood glucose, it does not mean your best efforts at healthy eating and lifestyle change have failed.

. . . .

Would you blame yourself if you needed stronger glasses because your eyesight changed?

. . . .

Healthy eating remains a core part of diabetes management across your lifetime. As time goes on, your eating habits may need tweaks, too.

HOW IS FOOD RELATED TO RAISING BLOOD GLUCOSE?

What you eat or drink, and how much, can have a big effect on your blood glucose. To put it simply, here's what happens: when you eat food or drink beverages that have carbohydrate, your body breaks down the carbohydrate into a sugar called glucose. Glucose is then absorbed into the bloodstream, where it is called "blood glucose" (or "blood sugar"). This glucose is then escorted out of the blood by insulin (a hormone made by your pancreas) into the body cells, where it's used to fuel your body. With prediabetes or type 2 diabetes, basically either insulin isn't working well to move sugar out of the blood, or your body stops making enough insulin to do the job.

Other Factors that Affect Blood Glucose

Aside from what you eat and drink, there are actually over 40 identified factors that can affect blood glucose. You can learn much more about the food-related factors in the companion book to this cookbook, *What Do I Eat Now?*, 3rd edition. Other things that broadly affect blood glucose include the following:

- **Physical activity** (including type of activity, fitness level, time of day, and food and medication timing)
- **Medication** if any (dose, timing, interactions, and type)
- **Biological factors** (including sleep, stress, illness, hypoglycemia, blood glucose overnight, allergies, menstruation, and tobacco use)
- **Environmental factors** (including temperature, sunburn, and altitude)
- **Behavioral/decision making** (including issues with family relationships and social pressures).

There are lots of opportunities to make small changes to help manage blood glucose.

SUMMARY OF THE NUTRITION GUIDELINES FOR DIABETES

To help answer the question, "What do I eat now?" we've provided a quick summary of the general nutrition guidelines for managing blood glucose based on the latest science and research (Table 1.1). You will find an additional explanation in Chapter 2 and a much greater explanation and practical how-to's in *What Do I Eat Now?*, 3rd edition, the companion publication to this book.

We encourage you to meet with an RDN to develop an individualized, personalized eating plan based on your needs, goals, and personal food preferences.

What Does It Mean When a Food Is "Nutrient-Rich"?

You will see the term "nutrient-rich" used to describe foods that are low in sugar, sodium, starches, and unhealthy fats. These foods contain a lot of vitamins and minerals and generally few calories.

TABLE 1.1 NUTRIENT GUIDELINES FOR DIABETES

Nutrient	Nutrition guidelines for diabetes
Calories	You may need to reduce the number of calories you eat to lower your blood glucose and promote weight loss. Reducing just 500 calories from your daily intake could mean a weight loss of 1 lb each week.
Carbohydrate	The amount (in grams) of carbohydrate and available insulin have a strong influence on the way your blood glucose reacts after you eat. Aim for nutrient-dense, fiber-rich, minimally processed carbohydrate sources over highly processed ones. Reducing carbohydrate can be a key strategy to improve blood glucose and may be implemented through a variety of eating patterns.
Fiber and whole grains	Your fiber and whole grain goals should be the same amount recommended for the other members of the family: about 25 g fiber each day for adult women and 38 g fiber each day for adult men. Another way to think about fiber is to aim to get at least 14 g for every 1,000 calories consumed. At least half of all the grains you eat should be whole grains.
Protein	If you have normal kidney function, your intake of protein foods (meats, poultry, seafood, dairy foods, beans, peas, tofu, tempeh and other soy foods, nuts, and seeds) should be the same as that of the general public. That portion would cover about 1/4 of a 9-inch plate.
Fat	There is no proven ideal quantity of fat recommended for people with diabetes; however, quality or type of fat is important for heart health. Foods higher in unsaturated fats (liquid fats) are healthier than solid saturated and trans fats. An RDN can help you learn more about heart-healthy unsaturated fats and how to avoid saturated and trans fats, as well as identify the right amount of fat for you. Lower fat intake can also translate into lower calorie intake, which may help you maintain a healthy body weight.
Vitamins, minerals, and herbal supplements	The American Diabetes Association does not recommend any special vitamins, minerals, or herbal supplements as a general rule for individuals with diabetes. Vitamin B12 levels should be monitored in individuals taking metformin.

(continued)

TABLE 1.1	NUTRIENT GUIDELINES FOR DIABETES *(continued)*
Nutrient	**Nutrition guidelines for diabetes**
Alcohol	If you choose to drink alcohol, use it in moderation: one drink or fewer per day if you're a woman or two drinks or fewer per day if you're a man. Alcohol may increase risk for hypoglycemia.
Sodium	Sodium recommendations for people with diabetes are similar to recommendations for the general population: <2,300 mg per day. If you have high blood pressure, your doctor may recommend an even lower sodium goal.
Sweeteners	A number of zero-calorie and reduced-calorie sweeteners are approved for use in the U.S. People with diabetes are advised to limit or avoid sugar-sweetened beverages to reduce the risk of weight gain and cardiovascular disease. Sugar-sweetened beverages can also cause rapid spikes in blood glucose.

Source: Evert AB, Dennison M, Gardner CD, et al. Nutrition therapy for adults with diabetes or prediabetes: a consensus report. *Diabetes Care* 2019;42:731–754.

TIPS TO IMPROVE YOUR EATING HABITS AND FOOD QUALITY

Let's turn and focus now on what it means to improve your eating habits and food quality. Making healthy choices in what you eat and drink can play a big role in managing blood glucose. Overall, the goal is to build your eating around foods rich in nutrients, vitamins, minerals, and fiber—that means foods that are less processed and closer to nature (instead of foods laden with fat, sugar, or sodium). These high-quality foods include vegetables, fruits, beans, legumes, low-fat milk and dairy, lean protein, nuts, seeds, and whole grains. There's much more to come on all of this.

8 Tips to Guide You in the Quest to Find Your Healthy Eating Style and Maintain It for a Lifetime

1. Know that everything you eat and drink day-to-day throughout your life matters. The right mix can help keep you healthier now and in the future.

2. Focus on including a variety of foods and colors at each meal to get a variety of flavors and nutrients.

3. Manage portions to help manage weight and blood glucose.

4. Start with small changes or swaps to build a healthier eating style, instead of going for a total overhaul from the start, which may feel overwhelming.

5. Take it one meal, one day at a time. Healthy eating doesn't mean always being perfect. There will be days when things go as planned and days that they just don't, for any number of reasons.

6. The foods that are good for you are good for everyone in the family.

7. Team up with someone to help you stay on track, whether it's a friend, family member, your health-care team, online support, or another form of support.

8. Celebrate each positive change or success as you build healthy eating habits.

Are You Eating Healthy? 14 Questions You Can Ask Yourself to Find Out

To help you begin to get in touch with how your eating habits measure up, answer the following questions. Any questions that you answer as "no" or "sometimes" show opportunities for positive change.

1. Do you eat a variety of vegetables?
2. Do you eat vegetables and/or fruit at most meals?
3. Do you eat at least 1 1/2 cups of vegetables a day?
4. Do you eat more nonstarchy vegetables than the starchy variety? (See a listing on page 136 that shows which is which.)
5. Do you eat 1 cup of fruit a day?
6. Do you choose whole fruit more often than fruit juice?
7. Do you eat at least three small servings of whole grains each day?
8. Do you use lower-fat dairy (skim, 1%, or 2% milk; reduced-fat or fat-free cheese), if you use dairy foods?
9. Do you eat protein-rich foods like fish, poultry, meat, soy foods, legumes (e.g., beans and lentils), dairy, nuts or nut butters, or eggs at most meals?
10. Do you eat naturally fatty fish like tuna, salmon, sardines, lake trout, and herring at least twice a week?
11. Do you limit solid fats (like butter or coconut oil), animal fats, and fatty cuts of meat?
12. Do you use liquid oils like olive oil more often than butter and solid spreads?
13. Do you avoid sugary drinks like regular soda, sweet tea, sweetened coffee beverages, fruit punch, and regular lemonade?
14. Do you choose foods reduced in or naturally low in sodium?

3 Small Changes that Create a Healthier Eating Style

1. **Brighten up your plate with vegetables that are red, orange, yellow, and dark green.** Eating different-colored vegetables ensures a variety of nutrients.
2. **Choose whole fruit instead of juice.** Whole fruit has more fiber, is more satisfying, and will not raise blood glucose as quickly as fruit juice.
3. **Choose bread, tortillas, crackers, cereals, rice, or pasta that are whole grain.** Look for the words "100% whole wheat" or "100% whole grain" on the label. The goal is that at least half the grains you eat are whole grains. Whole grains have more fiber and nutrients than processed grains like white flour or white rice.

4 Swaps to Improve Your Food Quality Throughout the Day

1. **At breakfast:** Rather than eating a processed cereal, work in a whole grain by swapping in oats. Don't like mushy quick oats? Then try steel-cut oats, which have a hearty, chewier texture. (Try the recipe for Cinnamon Steel-Cut Oats on page 265). Steel-cut oats take longer to cook, so cook a larger batch and freeze in muffin tins to pop out for a perfectly portioned, ready-to-microwave breakfast.
2. **At lunch:** Rather than chips or pretzels, swap in carrots for crunch.
3. **At dinner:** Rather than white rice, swap in quinoa, which is a whole grain. Or expand your horizons with nutty-tasting millet or farrow. There are frozen and microwavable forms of these foods to keep dinner prep simple.
4. **At snacks:** Rather than a cookie or other sweet treat, grab a small piece of fruit that doesn't need to be prepped. For instance, start with a clementine or plum.

ENERGY BALANCE IS IMPORTANT

Balancing energy intake (calories from food and beverages) with energy expenditure (calories burnt off through physical activity) leads to weight maintenance. To achieve weight loss means altering that balance—in other words, burn off more calories than you eat or drink.

The amount of calories you need is based on a number of things including your age, sex, height, weight, and physical activity.

6 Small Changes and Swaps that Can Cut Calories

Small changes cut calories and add up. Make all of the small swaps below and save over 1,000 calories!

1. **Switch in water or other zero-calorie beverage** instead of a regular soda, sweet tea, lemonade, or juice drink. This swap cuts out about 250 calories for each 20-oz drink swap.

2. **Go for foods that aren't fried.** The calorie and fat savings can be dramatic. Enjoy 5 oz grilled fish instead of fried and save 234 calories.

3. **Use reduced-fat (light) or fat-free versions** of high-fat foods, such as sour cream, cream cheese, mayonnaise, cheese, and salad dressing. Use buttery spray on veggies instead of margarine or butter and save 65 calories per tablespoon. Replace mayonnaise with creamy Dijon mustard and save 75 calories per tablespoon.

4. **Swap in whole grains.** Substitute whole-wheat pasta, brown rice, and whole-wheat bread for the more refined white versions.

The fiber will help you feel full, so you will likely be satisfied with smaller portions.

5. **Chew, don't drink.** Enjoy a crunchy 4-oz apple instead of 12 oz of natural apple juice and save 122 calories. Plus, you may get more satisfaction from chewing, and the fiber will help you feel full longer.

6. **Swap in nonstarchy vegetables.** Pump up the flavor in an omelet with 1/4 cup bell pepper and onions instead of 1/4 cup shredded cheese to save 200 calories. Swap in mashed cauliflower for mashed potatoes and save 100 calories per cup.

4 More Simple Swaps to Cut Calories

1. **Swap beverages.** Swap in a zero-calorie beverage in place of a 20-oz sweet tea or cola and save 250 calories. Do that twice a day and you've trimmed the 500 calories! Do that every day for a week and you've trimmed 3,500 calories. *That one change can lead to weight loss.* Swap in a zero-calorie black coffee with low-calorie sweetener in place of a 12-oz ("tall") caramel macchiato with whole milk and save 240 calories. Do that every day for a week and you've trimmed nearly 1,700 calories! Again, over time that one change can lead to weight loss.

2. **Swap vegetables.** Swap in 1 cup green salad (nonstarchy vegetables) in place of 1 cup mashed potatoes (a starchy vegetable) and save 25 g carbohydrate and 190 calories (see page 136 for a list

The 3 Things You Need to Know to Lose Weight

The rule of thumb is that burning 3,500 calories more than you consume can lead to 1 lb of weight loss. We also know that aiming to lose 1 lb a week is generally a sustainable goal. With that in mind, remember the following:

1. Trimming 500–750 calories off each day will usually lead to weight loss.

2. Women can often lose weight by reducing calories to around 1,200–1,500 per day.

3. Men can often lose weight by reducing calories to around 1,500–1,800 per day.

of which is which). Or another way to think about it is that you could eat nearly 5 cups salad for the calories you'd get in 1 cup mashed potatoes! Vegetables that are not starchy are a good thing to fill up on and won't raise blood glucose much.

3. **Swap meats.** Swap a 3-oz serving of grilled whitefish (80 calories) in place of a 3-oz serving of grilled rib eye steak (225 calories). This switch saves 145 calories. Make this change once a week and you'll cut over 7,500 calories in a year! That is enough calorie savings to lose about 2 lb. Or swap in a 3-oz grilled skinless chicken breast (140 calories, 3 grams fat) in place of a 3-oz grilled pork chop (176 calories, 8 grams fat). This switch saves 36 calories and 5 g fat! Choosing lean meat over fattier meat is the way to go, and meat won't raise blood glucose much, if any.

4. **Swap spreads.** Swap in 2 Tbsp mashed avocado (45 calories) in place of 2 Tbsp mayonnaise (180 calories) on a sandwich. The avocado has one-fourth the calories and has healthy fats, much less sodium, and more nutrition. Make this change once a week and you'll save over 7,000 calories in a year. Again, that one swap can save enough calories to lose about 2 lb!

USING THE INTERNET IN THE QUEST TO LEARN MORE

In the quest to learn more, if you turn to the Internet for information, there are a few things to keep in mind.

Internet Insight: Reliable Diabetes and Healthy-Eating Information

A seemingly endless amount of diabetes information is available on the Internet. The problem is figuring out whether this information is safe and reliable. Be skeptical. *Anyone* can post to websites and social media, and everyone is fighting for attention. Things that sound too good to be true often are.

To find the best health resources, ask these 5 questions:

1. Who sponsors the website you are browsing? Is it a reputable source? Look for an "About Us" page. Are ads and sponsored content clearly labeled?
2. Is the site trying to sell you something, like an expensive "diet program" or "miracle supplement"?
3. What are the credentials of the individuals who provide information for the site? Does the site have an editorial board?
4. When was the site last updated? Health information is constantly changing.
5. What does your diabetes health-care team think about the information you've found? Information you find on a website does not replace your healthcare team's advice.

An Experience with Unreliable Internet Information: "White Foods Are Bad."

Many times throughout Tami's years in practice, she's had clients come in voicing the belief that "white foods are bad for diabetes" based on a story they read online. The belief that people with diabetes should avoid all white foods is false. The idea of avoiding anything white seems to have blossomed out of the focus on reducing carbohydrate. The phrase "white foods are bad" is an oversimplification and a source of confusion. While originally the intent of this phrase was related to avoiding refined grains, many have taken it literally over the years and avoided good-for-you white foods that are part of a healthy eating pattern, such as low-fat milk or yogurt, white beans, onions, cauliflower, and bananas.

Takeaway

Just because you read information online or on social media does not mean it's true. Ask yourself the five questions mentioned on page 13 and talk it over with your healthcare team.

WEBSITES WITH VALUABLE AND RELIABLE INFORMATION ABOUT DIABETES AND HEALTHY EATING

Diabetes

American Diabetes Association
www.diabetes.org

JDRF (formerly Juvenile Diabetes Research Foundation)
www.jdrf.org

National Diabetes Education Program (NDEP)
www.ndep.nih.gov

National Institutes of Health—MedlinePlus
www.medlineplus.gov

Healthy Eating

Academy of Nutrition and Dietetics
www.eatright.org

ChooseMyPlate (USDA)
www.choosemyplate.gov

Dietary Guidelines for Americans
www.health.gov/dietaryguidelines

U.S. Department of Agriculture (USDA)
www.nutrition.gov

Notable Nutrients and Tips to Renew Recipes

When considering, "What do I cook now?" it's important and helpful to understand the impact of some key nutrients on diabetes and how to tweak recipes to make them healthier. We'll focus first on the three basic energy-containing building blocks that make up food (the nutrients that give food calories):

- Carbohydrates
- Proteins
- Fats

Then we'll turn to three other notable nutrients:

- Fiber
- Sodium
- Potassium

And we'll close out with a few words about alcohol, how to incorporate it in a safe manner if you choose to drink, and share a couple of "mocktail" recipes as nonalcoholic options.

3 THINGS YOU NEED TO KNOW ABOUT THE BUILDING BLOCKS OF FOOD

Carbohydrate, protein, and fat each supply calories to fuel and nourish your body. You need all three to be healthy.

1. **Carbohydrate gets the most attention when it comes to diabetes because it is most directly responsible for the rise in blood glucose after eating.** But keep in mind that carbohydrate is also your body's preferred fuel. It is a ready-to-use energy source. Carbohydrate is found in grains, beans, and other starchy foods; fruit; milk/dairy and milk substitutes; nonstarchy vegetables (in much lesser amounts); sweetened beverages; and sweet treats. You'll learn more about carbohydrate a little later in this chapter and will learn how to renew recipes to reduce carbohydrate.

2. **Protein and fat do not affect blood glucose rise after eating (known as postprandial blood glucose) to anywhere near the extent that carbohydrate does,** particularly in people with type 2 diabetes and prediabetes. Protein-rich foods include meat, poultry, fish, seafood, soy proteins, and eggs. You'll learn more about protein foods later in this chapter and in Chapter 3. You'll also learn how to choose healthy sources of protein and fats and make simple swaps in ingredients and cooking methods to make recipes healthier.

3. **Fat is highest in calories**, providing more than twice the calories of protein or carbohydrate. If you want to lose weight, you can cut a lot of calories simply by eating less fat and fatty foods. However, not all fat is considered unhealthy. Learn more about the "healthy fats" and "unhealthy fats" on page 54.

HEALTH-IFY RECIPES WITH SIMPLE SWAPS

Throughout this chapter, we'll share recipes that illustrate how small swaps and tweaks, whether in ingredients or cooking method, can yield both healthy and delicious dishes. Given that healthy food choices for you are healthy for people around you as well, all can benefit from and enjoy renewed recipes! If you want to give some favorite recipes a healthy makeover, ask yourself these two questions:

- *Could you make recipes healthier by swapping an ingredient or two in each?* These changes might include a swap to reduce carbohydrate, a swap to a leaner protein, or a swap to a healthier fat.

The Calorie Impact of a Swap that Reduces Fat

Swap 1 Tbsp spicy mustard in place of 1 Tbsp mayonnaise on a sandwich.

That swap saves 90 calories and 15 g fat. Make that swap twice a week and save 9,360 calories and 1,560 g of fat in one year! That's a savings equal to 13 sticks of butter!

- *Or could you make the recipes healthier by using a different cooking method?* You could make a swap to grilled fish instead of deep-fried fish, or a swap to oven-roasted chicken instead of fried chicken.

If you feel that swapping out a recipe is the best method, look at each ingredient in the recipe and ask yourself three further questions:

- *What is that ingredient's function? Is it there to add texture? Will the food fall apart if it's not included? Is it there to add color or promote browning? Or is it just a garnish?* If you're not sure, you can learn a little more about the function of different ingredients in recipes as you read through this chapter.
- *Is there more than one swap you could make to "health-ify" the recipe?* You'll get lots of ideas for swaps as you read on.
- *What one swap do you want to start with?* When modifying a recipe, it's important to make only one change at a time so you can note the impact on the recipe's taste, texture, and appearance and decide if it "worked."

CARBOHYDRATE: WHERE DOES IT COME FROM, WHY DOES IT MATTER, AND HOW CAN YOU REDUCE THE AMOUNT DURING COOKING?

Let's get started! First, let's learn a little bit about carbohydrate, what foods and beverages have it (see Table 2.1), and how to make swaps to reduce carbohydrate in cooking.

TABLE 2.1 WHAT FOOD GROUPS CONTAIN CARBOHYDRATE AND HOW MUCH DO THEY HAVE?	
Contain Carbohydrate (Will Raise Blood Glucose)	Amount of Carbohydrate per Serving (g)
Starch/grains • 1/2 cup cooked cereal, grain, or starchy vegetable • 1/3 cup cooked rice or pasta • 1 oz (slice of) bread or 6-inch tortilla • 3/4 to 1 oz crackers or grain-based snack foods	15

(continued)

TABLE 2.1   WHAT FOOD GROUPS CONTAIN CARBOHYDRATE AND HOW MUCH DO THEY HAVE? *(continued)*

Contain Carbohydrate (Will Raise Blood Glucose)	Amount of Carbohydrate per Serving (g)
Fruit • 1 small fresh fruit (about 2 1/2 inches in diameter) • 1/2 cup canned or frozen fruit • 1/2 cup (4 fluid ounces) 100% fruit juice • 2 Tbsp dried fruit	15
Milk/dairy/milk substitutes • 1 cup milk, plain soymilk • 2/3 cup plain yogurt	12
Nonstarchy vegetables • 1 cup raw • 1/2 cup cooked • 3 cups green salad or leafy greens • 1/2 cup (4 fluid ounces) vegetable juice	5
Plant-based proteins • 1/2 cup beans, lentils, or peas • 1/3 cup hummus	15
Sweetened beverages **Sweet treats** **Alcohol**	Varies (check labels if possible)
Do Not Contain Carbohydrate (have little impact on blood glucose) • Animal-based meat/proteins • Fats	

Source: Academy of Nutrition and Dietetics, American Diabetes Association. *Choose Your Foods: Food Lists for Diabetes.* Chicago, IL, Academy of Nutrition and Dietetics, American Diabetes Association, 2019.

Much of the carbohydrate advice you've heard from well-intentioned family members, friends, and acquaintances is likely NOT TRUE when it comes to healthy eating for diabetes.

"Sugar-Free" Doesn't Necessarily Mean "Carbohydrate-Free."

Many people are surprised to see that sugar-free pudding, for instance, has carbohydrate. The carbohydrate comes from the milk and thickener in the sugar-free pudding. However, sugar-free pudding does have considerably less carbohydrate than regular pudding. When in doubt, check the label!

Separating Myths from Facts

Have you heard any of the following advice from well-intentioned family members, friends, or acquaintances?

- "You can't eat sugar or sweets anymore."
- "Avoid bananas and oranges because they'll make your blood glucose levels too high."
- "No more potatoes or carrots."
- "Skip the bread and pasta."

The good news is that these recommendations are actually **NOT TRUE** when it comes to healthy eating with diabetes.

While some foods, like honey, are pure carbohydrate, many foods contain a combination of carbohydrate, protein, and/or fat. For instance, milk and peanut butter are a mix of all three nutrients, while chicken is primarily protein with a little fat. For good health, try to include a variety of nutrient-rich carbohydrate-containing foods at meals and snacks each day, such as dairy, naturally fiber-rich vegetables, fruits, legumes, and whole grains.

Carbohydrate at Work in Your Body

As briefly reviewed in Chapter 1, when you eat foods or drink beverages that contain carbohydrate, your body breaks that carbohydrate down into glucose (a type of sugar), which then raises the level of glucose in your blood to fuel your body. Eating too much carbohydrate may raise your blood glucose too high. Eating too little carbohydrate may cause your blood glucose to drop too low, especially if you take diabetes medicines that lower blood glucose. It's important to learn how to manage carbohydrate to effectively manage your blood glucose. This process is a bit of a balancing act.

Carbohydrate begins to raise blood glucose levels within 15–20 minutes of eating. Maybe you've already noticed that you feel "different" a few minutes after you eat. This feeling may be due to your blood glucose level rising. Before you had diabetes, after eating a meal or snack, your body could sense the glucose coming on board from the carbohydrate you ate and would automatically regulate the amount of glucose in your bloodstream. Now that you have type 2 diabetes (or prediabetes), your body no longer automatically keeps the right amount of glucose in your bloodstream, so the more carbohydrate you eat, the higher your blood glucose level may rise (unless you take action to change it). Blood glucose levels peak about 1 1/2 to 2 hours after you begin eating. Then they should begin to fall. Managing your carbohydrate intake helps reduce that after-meal blood glucose peak, with the goal of keeping your blood glucose in your target range (if you're not sure what your personal target range is, ask your diabetes health-care team).

Blood Glucose Targets

Here are general blood glucose targets as recommended by the American Diabetes Association. Talk with your diabetes health-care team to determine what blood glucose targets are safest for you.

- Before eating: 80–130 mg/dL
- 1–2 hours after the start of the meal: <180 mg/dL

If you use a continuous glucose monitor (CGM) to follow your blood glucose, the reports that can be generated can help you and your diabetes health-care team assess your time in range (TIR) as well as highs, lows, and blood glucose variability.

Monitoring how much carbohydrate you eat and noting your blood glucose response are key steps to improving your blood glucose after eating. If your blood glucose is above target 1 1/2 to 2 hours after eating, you may be able to bring your levels into range by reducing the amount of carbohydrate you eat and choosing more foods with a lower glycemic index and glycemic load. (See page 25 for more on the glycemic index.)

Try the above and note the impact. If it works for you, do more of that. If you are managing carbohydrate and blood glucose is still out of range after eating, you may need a diabetes medication added or the amount adjusted if you take one already. Talk to your diabetes health-care team about what plan is best for you.

The Type or Quality of Carbohydrate Foods You Eat Matters

All carbohydrate foods do not affect blood glucose the same. The goal is to choose high-quality carbohydrate foods, which means picking foods rich in fiber, vitamins, and minerals and low in added sugars, fats, and sodium. Think unrefined, unprocessed, "close-to-nature" foods. Examples of high-quality carbohydrate foods include vegetables, fruits, whole grains, beans, and low-fat dairy. Try to swap out low-quality carbohydrate foods, which are refined, processed, and have added sugars (think sugar-sweetened beverages and desserts). By making healthy swaps, you will likely start seeing your blood glucose spend more time in range. Small changes add up.

The Amount of Carbohydrate Matters, Too

Individualization is important: no one size fits all carbohydrate goals

Having diabetes does *not* mean that you have to totally avoid carbohydrate foods, although many find blood glucose easier to manage and keep in range when eating less carbohydrate. Figuring out how much carbohydrate and which carbohydrate foods to eat are important decisions you'll need to make every day.

Stick Close to Nature: Choose Whole Foods Over Processed Foods

Let's look at an example: baked sweet potato versus sweet potato chips.

A baked sweet potato with the skin on is unrefined and "close to nature." Even though the chips are essentially made of the "same thing," the unprocessed sweet potato has more fiber and less fat, calories, and sodium than processed sweet potato chips.

Are Sweet Treats Off Limits?

While sweets are not totally off limits, they generally are not considered high-quality carbohydrates. As such, it's recommended that *everyone* eat fewer foods with added sugar that might replace healthier, more nutrient-dense food choices. The same is true for people with diabetes as for the general public—less sugar is better, and it's particularly important to avoid displacing nutrient-dense foods with empty calories from sweets. This healthy recommendation is for anyone, whether or not they have diabetes or prediabetes.

If you have a sweet tooth, you will most likely find that you can work small, portion-controlled amounts of sweets into your eating plan. Sweet treats are high in refined carbohydrate and calories, so you'll want to eat them in moderation and include the carbohydrate in your count (we'll cover this more later in this chapter). Check your blood glucose 1 1/2–2 hours after eating and note the effect. If your blood glucose is in range, then what you did worked.

Managing Carbohydrate Can Be Accomplished in Several Different Ways:

- Embrace the Diabetes Plate Method. (See Chapter 3 to learn more about the Diabetes Plate Method.)
- Eat roughly the same amounts of carbohydrate at meals and snacks each day.
- Count carbohydrates by counting grams or by using carbohydrate choices/servings. **How does that work? One Carbohydrate choice/serving = 15 grams carbohydrate.** An example would be if you ate a sandwich with two slices of whole-wheat bread. You see on the Nutrition Facts food label that each slice contains 15 g carbohydrate. You could choose to count that

bread as contributing 30 g carbohydrate or count it as 2 carbohydrate choices/servings. Both options accomplish the same end goal.

For more guidance on carb counts and amounts, we encourage you to meet with a registered dietitian nutritionist (RDN). An RDN can provide personalized guidance on optimizing food and beverage choices and meal timing in coordination with physical activity and any diabetes medication.

Basic Carbohydrate Goals for Meals and Snacks

People need differing amounts of calories and carbohydrate based on whether they're male or female, their height, their activity level, and a number of other factors. Based on studies, a low-carbohydrate diet is typically one that is 26–45% carbohydrate. And a very-low-carbohydrate diet is typically less than 26% carbohydrate. Don't get too caught up in the percentages. The main thing to know if that both "low" carbohydrate and "very low" carbohydrate eating patterns have been shown to lower A1C (estimated average blood glucose), manage blood glucose, and achieve weight loss. A "very low" carbohydrate approach has been shown to achieve weight loss faster. However, this approach can be harder to stick with, and studies show that long-term results are likely to be similar to a low-carb or low-fat approach. Let's look at what those carbohydrate goals would be for different calorie levels (see Table 2.2).

Be Mindful of Your Glucose Response to Meals

Glucose response to meals that are high in protein and/or fat along with carbohydrate (think pizza) may differ among people, causing a rise in blood glucose 3 hours or more after eating. Checking glucose 3 hours after eating these types of foods can help you see how they affect you. Then talk with your diabetes health-care team about any adjustments to make when eating these types of foods, particularly if you use mealtime insulin.

TABLE 2.2 CARBOHYDRATE GOALS FOR DIFFERENT CALORIE LEVELS		
Calories	Goals on a low-carbohydrate diet (g/day)	Goals on a very-low-carbohydrate diet (g/day)
1,200	135	75
1,500	169	94
1,800	203	113
2,000	225	125
2,500	281	156
3,000	338	188

Let's look at the 1,800-calorie carbohydrate goals

If we use 1,800 calories as an example, since it's an average calorie level, and divide the carbohydrate evenly over three meals and one snack for consistency, for both a low-carbohydrate eating approach and a very-low-carbohydrate approach, here's what it would look like:

Low carbohydrate =
203 g carbohydrate/day

This is **63 g carbohydrate** for each of **3 meals** + a **15-gram carbohydrate snack**

- So for simplicity, you might go with 60 g carbohydrate for each meal + 15 g carbohydrate for one snack. **This amount can be a good starting point for many men, or active women.**
- If instead of counting grams of carbohydrate you're counting carbohydrate choices or servings (where 1 choice/serving = 15 g carbohydrate), that would translate into 4 carbohydrate choices/servings for each meal + 1 carbohydrate choice/serving for one snack.

Very low carbohydrate =
113 g carbohydrate/day

This is **33 g carbohydrate** for each of **3 meals** + a **15-g carbohydrate snack**

- So for simplicity, you might go with 30 g carbohydrate for each meal + 15 g carbohydrate for one snack.
- If you're counting choices or servings (where 1 choice/serving = 15 g carbohydrate), that would translate into 2 carbohydrate choices/servings for each meal + 1 carbohydrate choice/serving for one snack.

- A carbohydrate reduction to this level may help you lose weight faster in the short-term and lower A1C more quickly.

· ·

A very-low-carbohydrate diet may help you lose weight faster and lower A1C more quickly, but studies show that weight loss over the long term is similar to other diets.

· ·

4 Swaps to Reduce Carbohydrate

1. Choose a whole-wheat bagel "flat" or "thin" over a regular whole-wheat bagel. Save over 40 g carbohydrate!
2. Choose unsweetened almond milk over dairy milk. Save 10–11 g carbohydrate per cup.
3. Choose cooked spaghetti squash or zucchini spirals over spaghetti noodles. Save 35 g carbohydrate per cup.
4. Choose two grilled portobello mushroom caps as a bun for your burger over a hamburger bun. Save 24 g carbohydrate.

Evidence confirms that reducing overall carbohydrate results in lower blood glucose and greater reduction in A1C. This step may be applied through a variety of eating patterns, not just "low carb."

For people with prediabetes, a variety of eating patterns are acceptable, including a low-carbohydrate eating plan, which shows the potential to improve blood glucose and lipids for up to 1 year. The trick is in maintaining this eating plan, since long-term sustainability can be challenging.

Adopting a very-low-carbohydrate eating plan can initially cause increased urine production and swift reduction in blood glucose. Consult with your diabetes health-care team before launching into a very-low-carbohydrate approach. Your doctor may want to adjust your diabetes medication doses to prevent dangerously low blood glucose (hypoglycemia). Keep a close watch on your blood glucose and note effects. If blood glucose is close to or within range, then you know this level of carbohydrate is working. If blood glucose is still above range, you may benefit from further carbohydrate reduction. If you experience frequent low blood glucose (under 70 mg/dL), consult with your diabetes care team to adjust your medications.

Managing Carbohydrate Is Like Using a Checking Account

Counting carbohydrate through meal and snack carbohydrate goals is somewhat like using a checking account. At each meal, let's say your goal is 45 g carbohydrate (which is a significant carbohydrate reduction for many): So you have 45 g in your account to "spend." You can spend these grams on whichever carbohydrate-containing foods you wish. While not the healthiest choice, you could even have an occasional splurge, like a chocolate donut, if you plan ahead and allocate grams of carbohydrate to spend on it. Although, keep in mind that you may see a higher spike in blood glucose from the refined, sugary food even with the same allocated carbohydrate. While the occasional blood glucose spike may not be harmful by itself, frequent spikes will result in higher A1C. So, the goal is to spend the majority of your carbohydrate on a variety of healthy foods. You may find that you end up eating smaller portions of certain foods and eating some foods less often.

If you "overdraw" your account, the "penalty" is that your blood glucose will run higher after the meal. The same rules apply for snacks.

There is no "savings account"—this method does not allow reserving or saving carbohydrate from one meal or snack to "spend" on a later meal or snack. It's best to eat a consistent amount of carbs at each meal every day, especially if you take glucose-lowering medications and/or use basal insulin. Spend your carbohydrate wisely!

All Carbohydrate Foods Do Not Affect Blood Glucose the Same—Glycemic Index and Glycemic Load

Foods containing carbohydrate have varying amounts of sugars, starches, fiber, protein, and fat, causing them to have varying effects on blood glucose. Some result in an extended rise and slow fall in blood glucose. Others result in a rapid rise in blood glucose followed by a rapid fall. (We'll cover more about fiber and fiber-rich foods later in this chapter.)

You may have read about glycemic index (GI) and glycemic load (GL), or seen an advertisement touting the benefits of low-GI/GL foods. Glycemic index and glycemic load rank foods according to their effect on blood glucose and continue to be topics of interest. Research shows that GI and GL in relation to diabetes are complex because blood glucose response to a particular food varies among individuals and can be affected by a number of factors. There's no clear-cut answer as to whether GI and GL are of significant help. Evidence currently points to no impact on A1C, with mixed results in regard to impact on fasting blood glucose. Still, it's worth understanding how GI and GL work, so let's look a little closer at each.

Glycemic index (GI)

The glycemic index is a method that ranks carbohydrates on a scale of 0–100 according to how the carbohydrates raise blood glucose after eating. Basically, GI predicts the peak blood glucose response:

- **Low-GI foods** (55 or less) produce gradual rises in blood glucose levels because they are slowly digested and absorbed. You may hear these foods called "slow carbs."

4 Tips to Help Count Carbohydrate in Combination Foods

Foods that contain a combination of ingredients can be tricky to figure out how to count, especially if they don't come with a Nutrition Facts label. Examples are things like salads, pizza, casseroles, soups, and burritos. This will also require a bit of guesswork, but here are four tips to help estimate carbohydrate count:

1. **Calculate pizza by crust thickness.** For thin crust, estimate 30 g carbohydrate per slice (1/4 of 12-inch pizza); for regular crust, 37.5 g carbohydrate per slice (1/8 of 12-inch pizza).

2. **Count salad by the ingredients other than salad greens and veggies.** Identify the toppings and ingredients in your salad that contain carbohydrates. Estimate about 15 g carbohydrate per 1/2 cup carb-containing ingredients such as croutons, grains, beans, fruit, corn, and sweet potato. Dried fruit contains about 15 g carbohydrate per 2 Tbsp. Keep in mind that "loaded" salads may bring a "load" of calories and carbohydrate! A fast food taco salad tips in at about 600–800 calories and 60–70 g carbohydrate. A fried chicken strip salad (depending on the size and before dressing is added) runs 600–800 calories and 40 or more grams of carbohydrate. The point is, just because "it's a salad" and "it has chicken" does not always mean it's a healthy choice.

3. **Count combination entrée by the cup.** For an entrée that has meat/protein and vegetables in a savory sauce, such as stews, soups, and Asian-style dishes, estimate each cup as 15 g carbohydrate. For dishes made with rice, pasta, or grains, such as noodle bowls, lasagna, spaghetti with meatballs, chicken and rice, or chili with beans, estimate 30 g carbohydrate per cup.

4. **Count the breading on battered or breaded meats.** Estimate 15 g carbohydrate for a portion around the size of a fried chicken fillet, two to three chicken tenders, or six chicken nuggets. For larger portions, like a fried pork chop or battered fish fillet, estimate 30 g carbohydrate.

- **High-GI foods** (70 or above) are rapidly digested and absorbed and lead to marked elevations in blood glucose.

Keep in mind that two foods that contain the same amount of carbohydrates may have differing GI rankings.

Two foods that contain the same amount of carbohydrates may have differing GI rankings.

If some of your favorite foods are high GI, you may be able to swap them for lower-GI versions. See the examples in Table 2.3.

To complicate matters further, the GI of a specific food can change based on a number of factors, including:

- What else is eaten during the meal or with the food
- How the food is processed and prepared
- Acidity
- Fat content
- Fiber content
- Factors unrelated to the food, including time of day, mealtime blood glucose level, stress, and physical fitness

So while GI may be helpful and may guide you in choosing heathier choices that have a lower impact on your blood glucose levels in the short term, it's not a perfect tool.

TABLE 2.3	SWAP OUT HIGH-GI FOODS FOR LOW-GI FOODS
High-GI favorites	**Lower-GI swap**
Baked white potato, no skin: GI = 98	Boiled yam, no skin: GI = 35
Pretzels: GI = 83	Popcorn: GI = 55
French bread: GI = 81	Stoneground whole-wheat bread: GI = 59

Comparing GI Rankings

Let's look at an example: jelly beans versus kidney beans.

If you have 15 small jelly beans and 1/2 cup kidney beans, and both portions have the same 15 g carbohydrate, the jelly beans will be digested more rapidly and raise blood glucose more than kidney beans. In other words, jelly beans have a higher GI than kidney beans.

Glycemic load

"But what about portion size?" you may ask. "What if I'm eating a bite of apple pie, not a whole slice? Does that matter?" The GI of a food does not change whether you eat a bite of apple pie or an entire slice. However, eating a larger amount of a carbohydrate-containing food (such as a slice of apple pie) will certainly raise your blood glucose more than eating a smaller amount (a bite of apple pie, for example). That's where glycemic load (GL) comes into the picture. GL takes into account the portion size and potential impact on blood

Learn More

Do you want to know the GI of a favorite food? Check out the online database at: ***www.glycemicindex.com***

glucose. Substituting low-GL foods for higher-GL foods may modestly improve blood glucose control. A searchable GL database is available at www.glycemicindex.com.

The takeaway on GI and GL

If you are interested in pursuing the approach of tracking GI and GL, it won't hurt to choose lower-GI and -GL foods more often, but monitoring GI and GL is not recommended as a stand-alone meal-planning method. Swap in lower-GI and lower-GL foods, when possible, while still being mindful of the portions you eat. Keep in mind that a food's effect on blood glucose may vary from person to person.

What About Sugar Substitutes?

Blue, pink, yellow, green, orange—such is the rainbow of packaging colors for the variety of low-calorie sweeteners available today. The

8 Available Sugar Substitutes in the U.S. (late 2020):

1. Acesulfame potassium
2. Advantame
3. Aspartame
4. Luo han guo (monk fruit extracts)
5. Neotame
6. Saccharin
7. Steviol glycosides (stevia)
8. Sucralose

term "sugar substitutes" refers to high-intensity sweeteners, artificial sweeteners, nonnutritive sweeteners, and other low-calorie sweeteners. Only a relatively small amount of a low-calorie sweetener is needed because these substitutes are several hundred to several thousand times sweeter than sugar.

The U.S. Food and Drug Administration (FDA) has reviewed a number of sugar substitutes for safety and approved them safe for consumption by the general public, including people with diabetes. The low-calorie sweeteners listed below are commonly used as "sugar substitutes" because they are *many times sweeter than sugar*, but contribute few to no calories and carbohydrate when added to foods.

While replacing sugars with sugar substitutes *could* decrease intake of carbohydrate and calories (which in turn could benefit blood glucose, weight, lipids, and blood pressure), there's not currently enough evidence to determine whether use leads to long-term reduction in weight, blood glucose, or other factors that affect hearth health (such as lipids and blood pressure).

The way to think about it, using sugar substitutes does not make an unhealthy food choice *healthy*, but may make it less *unhealthy* because you are cutting calories and carbohydrate. However, using artificial sweeteners will only help with weight loss as long as you don't compensate with intake of additional calories (or carbohydrate) from other food or beverages later on.

Sugar substitutes: a personal preference

Navigating the maze of low-calorie sweetener options may seem confusing. Here are 4 considerations to help choose the right sugar substitute for you, if you choose to use one.

1. **Functionality.** What do you want to use it for? Are you using the substitute to just to sweeten coffee or tea, or do you plan to cook and bake with it? Some substitutes perform better in high heat and in cooking and baking.
2. **Taste.** Do you like the taste? They all taste differently. If you don't like the taste of the first one you try, switch to another.
3. **Potential effects.** Are you concerned about potential effects? (For instance, individuals with a rare health condition called phenylketonuria [PKU] have a difficult time metabolizing phenylalanine, a component of aspartame).
4. **Cost.** Does it fit in your budget? Sugar substitutes are priced at different price points.

Table 2.4 provides a brief summary of cooking properties for the available sugar substitutes at the time of printing. In cooking and baking, sugar substitutes may change the taste, color, and texture of the final product and may affect cooking time when compared to sugar. To see how one type of sugar substitute bakes as an ingredient, check out our *Apple-Raisin Crumble with Oat-Crumb Topping* recipe (page 32).

TABLE 2.4 COOKING CONSIDERATIONS WITH SUGAR SUBSTITUTES		
Sugar substitute sweetener	**Select brand names containing the sweetener**	**Cooking Considerations**
Acesulfame potassium (Ace-K)	Sweet One Sunette	• 200 times sweeter than table sugar • Stays sweet at high temperatures during baking • Can replace all of the sugar in sauces and beverages, but recipe adjustments may be needed for baked goods
Advantame	(Not sold directly to consumers)	• 20,000 times sweeter than table sugar

(continued)

TABLE 2.4   COOKING CONSIDERATIONS WITH SUGAR SUBSTITUTES *(continued)*

Sugar substitute sweetener	Select brand names containing the sweetener	Cooking Considerations
Aspartame	Nutrasweet Equal Sugar Twin	• 200 times sweeter than table sugar • Loses sweetness when heated • Won't provide bulk or tenderness in baked goods so recipe adjustments may be needed
Luo han guo (monk fruit extracts)	Monk Fruit in the Raw PureLo	• 100–250 times sweeter than table sugar • Is heat stable, so it's suitable for cooking and baking • In baked goods, substitute for up to half of the sugar in the recipe • Works well in beverages, smoothies, sauces, and dressings
Neotame	Newtame	• 7,000–13,000 times sweeter than sugar • Can be used in both hot and cold mixtures, as well as for baking
Saccharin	Sweet'N Low Sweet Twin NectaSweet	• 200–700 times sweeter than sugar • Is heat stable and can be used in baked goods • Works well in dessert toppings, beverages, and salad dressings

(continued)

TABLE 2.4	COOKING CONSIDERATIONS WITH SUGAR SUBSTITUTES *(continued)*	
Sugar substitute sweetener	**Select brand names containing the sweetener**	**Cooking Considerations**
Steviol glycosides (stevia)	Truvia PureVia ENLITEN	• 200–400 times sweeter than sugar • Stevia-based sweeteners are suitable for baking; however, most can't replace sugar cup for cup in recipes. It's best to leave at least 1/4 cup of sugar in the recipe to help with browning and provide texture. • You likely will need to use a lower baking temperature and increase the baking time
Sucralose	Splenda	• 600 times sweeter than sugar • Retains its sweet taste in a wide variety of temperatures and cooking times • A granulated version measures and pours like sugar and can be used in a variety of ways, including cooking, baking, beverages, sauces, dressings, and frozen desserts • Also comes in blends mixed with white sugar or brown sugar

APPLE-RAISIN CRUMBLE WITH OAT-CRUMB TOPPING

Apples, raisins, sweet spices, and oats are the key ingredients in this warm and comforting sweet treat. Refrigerate the leftovers up to 7 days and enjoy it as part of your carbohydrate foods. The natural sweetness of the fruit and vanilla is enhanced by adding stevia, making this dessert sweet enough to satisfy your sweet tooth, without added sugar.

THIS RECIPE CAN FIT IN THE FOLLOWING EATING PATTERNS*: vegetarian, low-fat, low-carbohydrate, DASH.

NUMBER OF SERVINGS: 8 | **SERVING SIZE:** About 1/2 cup per serving
PREP TIME: 15 minutes | **COOK TIME:** 1 hour

INGREDIENTS

Filling:

- 2 lbs honey crisp or Granny Smith apples, halved, cored, and chopped
- 1/4 cup raisins
- 4 individual packets stevia
- 1 Tbsp apple pie spice
- 1 Tbsp cornstarch
- 1 Tbsp fresh lemon juice
- 1 tsp vanilla
- 2 Tbsp light butter with canola oil

Topping:

- 3/4 cup quick-cooking oats
- 4 individual packets stevia
- 1/2 tsp apple pie spice
- 1/8 tsp salt
- 2 Tbsp canola oil

INSTRUCTIONS

1. Preheat oven to 375°F.
2. Coat an 8 × 8-inch baking pan with nonstick cooking spray.
3. In a large bowl, combine filling, except for light butter. Place in baking pan and dot with light butter.
4. In the same bowl used to combine filling, combine the topping ingredients, except for the oil. Toss until well blended. Drizzle oil over all and toss until well blended. Sprinkle evenly over apple mixture.
5. Bake 1–1 1/4 hours or until apples are tender when pierced with a fork. Remove from oven and let stand 20 minutes to absorb flavors. Cool completely. Cover and refrigerate any leftovers up to 4 days.

*An occasional sweet treat can be incorporated into most eating patterns, in moderation.

CHOICES: 1/2 Starch, 1 Fruit, 1 Fat

BASIC NUTRITIONAL VALUES: Calories 150 | Calories from Fat 50 | **Total Fat** 6.0 g | Saturated Fat 0.9 g | Trans Fat 0.0 g | **Cholesterol** 6 mg | **Sodium** 60 mg | **Potassium** 180 mg | **Total Carbohydrate** 25 g | Dietary Fiber 4 g | Sugars 14 g | Added Sugars 0 g | **Protein** 2 g | **Phosphorus** 50 mg

COOK'S SWAP

- For a vegan dessert, sub a plant-based, nondairy butter for the butter.

Trick

- No need to peel the apples. The peel adds to the body of the dish as well as a bit more fiber, while saving on the prep!

POINTERS

- For more crunch in the topping, add 2 oz chopped pecans to topping mixture.
- For an extra layer of flavor, top with a drizzle of fat-free half-and-half.
- Reheat leftovers in microwave to bring out the rich flavors. Place a single serving in a microwave-safe bowl and microwave on high for 30–45 seconds or until heated through.

What Are Sugar Alcohols?

Sugar alcohols are another category of sweeteners that can be used as a substitute for sugar. Sugar alcohols are not digested the same as other carbohydrates. So even though they count toward the total carbohydrate in a product, they do not raise blood glucose in the same way.

Sugar alcohols have fewer calories than sugar, but are not as sweet, so larger amounts are needed to match the sweetness of sugar. This means that the calorie content of foods sweetened with sugar alcohols may be similar to the sugar-sweetened version.

The following are familiar sugar alcohols approved by the FDA for consumption by the general public as well as people with diabetes; however, there is little evidence on benefits. Many of the names, as you see here, end in the letters –ol, as does sugar "alcohol", which can be helpful to quickly spot them on package ingredient lists.

- Erythritol
- Lactitol
- Maltitol
- Mannitol
- Sorbitol
- Xylitol

Sugar alcohols are not widely used in home food preparation, although at the time of printing, xylitol and erythritol have gained popularity among those choosing to follow a very-low-carbohydrate ("keto") eating style. Sugar alcohols can be found in many commercial products labeled "sugar-free," including "sugar-free" chewing gum, candy, ice cream, fruit spreads, mouthwash, toothpaste, and cough lozenges/syrups. If a product is labeled "diet" or "sugar-free," it may contain sugar alcohols. **Take note, these "sugar-free "products are not necessarily carbohydrate- and calorie-free!** You can quickly check the Nutrition Facts label for any sugar alcohol content. There would be an entry for Sugar Alcohols under Total Carbohydrate. (See Figure 2-1.) If the product does contain sugar alcohols, you can then scan the ingredient list to see which ones.

Sugar alcohols do not promote tooth decay and may not cause as sudden of an increase in blood glucose as other sweeteners. However, some people may experience gas, bloating, and gastrointestinal upset when consuming products sweetened with sugar alcohols. As with sugar substitutes, choosing to use products with sugar alcohols is an individual decision based on your personal preferences, blood glucose goals, and factoring in the potential side effects. Your RDN or diabetes health-care team can help you decide if including any type of sugar substitutes in your eating plan is the best choice for you.

What about Other "Natural" Sweeteners?

There is a common misconception that "natural" sweeteners do not affect blood glucose as much as refined white sugar. However, natural sweeteners *do* have carbohydrate that can raise blood glucose. They *do* have calories. And thus they *do* need to be counted in. Here are some examples of natural sweeteners:

FIGURE 2.1 SUGAR ALCOHOLS ON THE NUTRITION FACTS LABEL

Nutrition Facts

1 serving per container

Serving size	**1 bar (60g)**

Amount per serving

Calories 232

	% Daily Value*
Total Fat 12g	20%
Saturated Fat 7g	60%
Trans Fat 0g	
Cholesterol 13mg	4%
Sodium 50mg	2%
Total Carbohydrate 29g	8%
Dietary Fiber 0g	0%
Total Sugars 0g	
Sugar Alcohol 18g	
Protein 2g	
Vitamin D 0mcg	0%
Calcium 78mg	6%
Iron 1.4mg	8%
Potassium 0mg	0%

*The % Daily Value (DV) tells you how much a nutrient in a serving of food contributes to a daily diet. 2000 calories a day is used for general nutrition advice.

- Agave
- Fructose
- Honey
- Maple syrup
- Molasses
- Sugar in the raw

Cut Carbohydrate by Replacing Sugar-Sweetened Beverages with Water as Often as Possible

Do you want an easy rule for cutting sugar and carbohydrates to help promote weight loss? Here it is: ***Don't drink your calories.*** Table 2.5 lists the sugar and carbohydrate content of popular beverages for a 12-oz serving. Keep in mind that serving sizes at restaurants, fast food eateries, and convenient stores are typically much higher than this—sometimes as much as four to five times higher than this! Water is the drink of choice.

Infused water: A flavorful zero-calorie alternative to help you drink more water

Infused water is water that takes on the flavor of any combination of fruits, vegetables, and herbs immersed in the water for 2–4 hours. This beverage does not have any calories or carbohydrate to count. There's a multitude of combinations you could enjoy mixing and matching. Come up with your own combinations to suit your taste preferences. The box "9 Favorite Infused Water Flavor Combinations" lists, you guessed it, some of our favorite flavor combinations. Find two more combinations in Tami's recipes for ***Lemony Spa Water*** (page 37) and ***Watermelon Rosemary Refresher*** (page 38).

Fortunately, flavorful infused water is incredibly simple to make:

"Sugar-free" isn't "carbohydrate-free"

Foods labeled "sugar-free" may not be carbohydrate-free. In fact, the total carbohydrate may be the same, or even higher (as you see in the example below). As always, check blood glucose 1 1/2–2 hours after eating a food that contains sugar alcohol to note the effect.

Butterscotch hard candy (round disc-shaped)	Carbohydrate (g)
1 piece regular	4.8
1 piece sugar-free	5.7
Chocolate ice cream	**Carbohydrate (g)**
1/2 cup regular	18
1/2 cup fat-free, no-sugar-added	26

1. Put ingredients in a pitcher or large mason jar.
2. Fill with ice cubes.
3. Add water to the top. (You could also use unsweetened tea instead of water.)
4. Chill in the refrigerator 2–4 hours.

9 Favorite Infused Water Flavor Combinations

1. Blueberries and orange slices
2. Tangerine, lemon, and lime slices
3. Lime or orange slices and mint
4. Cucumber slices, lime slices, and mint
5. Cranberries and orange slices
6. Raspberries and lime slices
7. Blackberries and sage
8. Pineapple chunks and mint
9. Sliced strawberries and cucumber

Keep the following tips in mind:

- Flavors will intensify the longer the water sits, so remove flavoring ingredients when desired flavor is reached.
- Store leftover infused water in the refrigerator. Remove the flavoring ingredients, since the ingredients may become mushy and spoil.
- Try infusing smaller amounts of water on-the-go with an infuser water bottle that has a small center compartment to hold the fruit or other ingredients. This special compartment will keep the flavoring ingredients from floating up and blocking the drinking hole.

TABLE 2.5   BUILD AWARENESS ABOUT BEVERAGES

Beverage	Average teaspoons of sugar (grams of carbohydrate)
12 oz lemonade	11 (46 g carbohydrate)
12-oz can regular soda	10 (42 g carbohydrate)
12 oz sweet tea	8 (34 g carbohydrate)
12 oz coconut water	3 (13 g carbohydrate)
12-oz can diet soda	0
12 oz water	0
12 oz black coffee or unsweetened tea	0

LEMONY SPA WATER

This recipe from Tami is a refreshing, low-calorie drink for a hot day—or any time you feel like pampering yourself.

THIS RECIPE CAN FIT IN THE FOLLOWING EATING PATTERNS: All

NUMBER OF SERVINGS: 8 | **SERVING SIZE:** 8 oz
PREP TIME: 5 minutes | **CHILLING TIME:** 2–4 hours

INGREDIENTS

- 1 lemon, thinly sliced
- 1/2 cucumber, thinly sliced
- 1 handful fresh mint leaves
- Ice cubes
- Water (ice and water combined to yield 2 quarts)

INSTRUCTIONS

1. Place lemon and cucumber slices in a 2- to 3-quart pitcher. Gently crush the mint in your hands to release the flavor and aroma, and then add to the pitcher.
2. Fill pitcher with ice cubes.
3. Add water to the top of the pitcher.
4. Cover and chill for 2–4 hours, and then enjoy.
5. To store leftovers, remove lemon, cucumber, and mint. Cover water and refrigerate for up to 3 days.

POINTERS

- You can use tap water, although we like to use spring water or filtered water for best taste.

CHOICES: None
BASIC NUTRITIONAL VALUES: Calories 0 | Calories from Fat 0 | **Total Fat** 0.0 g | Saturated Fat 0.0 g | Trans Fat 0.0 g | **Cholesterol** 0 mg | **Sodium** 10 mg | **Potassium** 0 mg | **Total Carbohydrate** 0 g | Dietary Fiber 0 g | Sugars 0 g | Added Sugars 0 g | **Protein** 0 g | **Phosphorus** 0 mg

WATERMELON ROSEMARY REFRESHER

Another infused water recipe from Tami, which is perfect for summer when watermelons are in season and reaching peak flavor.

THIS RECIPE CAN FIT IN THE FOLLOWING EATING PATTERNS: All

NUMBER OF SERVINGS: 8 | **SERVING SIZE:** 8 oz
PREP TIME: 5 minutes | **CHILLING TIME:** 2–4 hours

INGREDIENTS

- 2 cups cubed watermelon
- 1 sprig fresh rosemary
- Ice cubes
- Water (ice and water combined to yield 2 quarts)

INSTRUCTIONS

1. Place watermelon in a 2- to 3-quart pitcher. Gently crush the rosemary in your hands to release the flavor and aroma, and then add to the pitcher.
2. Fill pitcher with ice cubes.
3. Add water to the top of the pitcher.
4. Cover and chill for 2–4 hours, and then enjoy.
5. To store leftovers, remove watermelon and rosemary. Cover water and refrigerate for up to 3 days.

PREP TIP

- You can use tap water, although spring water or filtered water produces the best taste.

CHOICES: None

BASIC NUTRITIONAL VALUES: Calories 5 | Calories from Fat 0 | **Total Fat** 0.0 g | Saturated Fat 0.0 g | Trans Fat 0.0 g | **Cholesterol** 0 mg | **Sodium** 10 mg | **Potassium** 10 mg | **Total Carbohydrate** 1 g | Dietary Fiber 0 g | Sugars 1 g | Added Sugars 0 g | **Protein** 0 g | **Phosphorus** 0 mg

Recipe Renewal: How to Swap Out Sugar to Reduce Carbohdyrate

As you look to limit sugar and manage your carbohydrate intake, there will be a tendency to simply eliminate granulated sugar from every recipe you cook. However, granulated sugar does play a significant role in some recipes (particularly baked goods), and it can't always be fully replaced with another sweetener. Here's what granulated sugar does in cooking:

- **Sugar adds texture, color, and bulk to baked goods.** Substituting other ingredients for sugar in baked goods can cause your cakes, cookies, pies, and candy to turn out very differently than expected. (That's why you'll see baking blends used in the ***Chocolate Chip, Almond Chip Cookies*** on page 41 and ***Banana Oat Muffins*** on page 79.)
- **Sugar helps yeast bread rise by providing food for the yeast.** As the yeast grows and multiplies, it uses the sugar and releases carbon dioxide and alcohol, which gives bread its characteristic airy texture and flavor.
- **Sugar provides the light brown color and crisp feel** to the tops of baked goods, such as muffins and cakes.

Cook's Notes: 3 Strategies to Cut Sugar

1. **How to reduce sugar.** In most cases, you can cut back on the added sugar in your recipe by one-fourth to one-third without a difference in the finished product. If a recipe calls for 1 cup sugar, for instance, try it with 3/4 cup and note the result. In foods like baked goods, where sugar is used to impart texture, refrain from the urge to totally eliminate sugar or totally replace it with a sugar substitute because your baked goods will not turn out as expected. Some sugar substitutes are not heat-stable, meaning they lose their sweetness when heated, so check the sweetener's label to make sure it can withstand heat. (See more about the sugar substitutes on page 28.)
2. **Enhance sweetness and flavor with extracts.** You may be familiar with vanilla extract. There is actually a multitude of extracts on the grocery shelves ranging in flavors from butter to nuts, fruits, liquors, and herbals. Check out the ***Hint of Maple Dip*** on page 311, which incorporates maple and almond extracts.
3. **Impart a sweet taste with sweet flavored spices.** Sweet spices include allspice, anise, caraway, cardamom, cinnamon, chervil, cloves, fennel, nutmeg, and star anise. They add sweet flavor without adding carbohydrate.

Sometimes the craving for something sweet strikes, and a chocolate chip cookie would hit the spot. Table 2.6 gives you some swaps that can reduce sugar, carbohydrate, and calories and increase fiber and flavor. Make only one swap at a time so you can note the effect.

TABLE 2.6   SWAPS TO CHANGE UP CHOCOLATE CHIP COOKIES

Use this . . .	Instead of this . . .	And you get . . .
Dark chocolate chips or mini chocolate chips in 1/2–3/4 the amount	Regular-size chocolate chips	Reduced sugar, carbohydrate, fat, and calories
Uncooked quick oats	Part of the white flour	Increased fiber
Bran cereal (not flakes)	Part of the white flour	Increased fiber
1/4 cup liquid egg substitute	Whole egg	Reduced fat and calories
3/4 cup sugar	1 cup sugar	Reduced sugar, carbohydrate, and calories
3/4 cup sugar + 1/4 cup powdered milk	1 cup sugar	Reduced sugar
Granulated sugar substitute or sugar baking blend	Part of sugar (as per sugar substitute package)	Reduced sugar, carbohydrate, and calories
Double the vanilla or almond extract	–	Increased flavor and sweetness
Add cinnamon	–	Increased flavor

CHOCOLATE CHIP, ALMOND CHIP COOKIES

These healthy cookie mounds are for people who love chocolate chips, chunky nuts, and a big handful of cookie! This treat is chockful of protein and fiber, too. In this "renewed" chocolate chip cookie recipe, you'll find whole-wheat flour (in place of traditional white flour), brown sugar baking blend (instead of all sugar for sweetness), and an extract to enhance sweetness. Enjoy a cookie as part of your carbohydrate foods.

THIS RECIPE CAN FIT IN THE FOLLOWING EATING PATTERNS: *vegetarian, **DASH***

NUMBER OF SERVINGS: 14 | **SERVING SIZE:** 1 cookie per serving
PREP TIME: 25 minutes | **COOK TIME:** 5 minutes

INGREDIENTS

- 2 cups whole-wheat flour
- 1/3 cup packed brown sugar substitute blend, such as Splenda brown sugar baking blend
- 1/2 tsp baking soda
- 3/4 tsp salt
- 6 Tbsp canola oil
- 2 large eggs
- 1 1/2 tsp cake batter extract or vanilla
- 3 oz slivered almonds
- 1/2 cup mini semi-sweet chocolate chip morsels

*An occasional sweet treat can be incorporated into most eating patterns, in moderation.

(Pointers on following page)

INSTRUCTIONS

1. Preheat oven to 375°F.
2. Whisk together the flour, brown sugar baking blend, baking soda, and salt in a medium bowl.
3. Place the oil, eggs, and extract in a medium bowl and beat with an electric mixer on high speed for 1 minute or until creamy. Reduce speed to medium and gradually add the flour mixture. Add the almonds and chips and beat until well blended.
4. Liberally coat a nonstick cookie sheet with nonstick cooking spray. Coat palms of hands with nonstick cooking spray and roll into 14 balls. Place about 2 inches apart. Using the palm of your hand or a fork, flatten each ball into a 2 1/2-inch diameter (about the size of a sausage patty). (You can coat your hand with a little bit of nonstick cooking spray to prevent sticking.)
5. Bake 5 minutes. The cookies will appear not to be done at this point. Remove from oven.
6. Coat both sides of a flat spatula with nonstick cooking spray, gently remove cookies, and place on cooling rack. Serve warm or room temperature.

CHOICES: 1 Starch, 1/2 Carbohydrate, 2 Fat

BASIC NUTRITIONAL VALUES: Calories 210 | Calories from Fat 110 | **Total Fat** 12.0 g | Saturated Fat 2.1 g | Trans Fat 0.0 g | **Cholesterol** 25 mg | **Sodium** 180 mg | **Potassium** 150 mg | **Total Carbohydrate** 22 g | Dietary Fiber 3 g | Sugars 6 g | Added Sugars 5 g | **Protein** 5 g | **Phosphorus** 110 mg

POINTERS

- Sugar does more in baked goods than just adding sweetness. It helps to create browning, crunch, and texture. That's why using a blend of sweetener and actual sugar is needed in this recipe.
- The cookies will not be fully cooked when removed from the oven but will continue to gently cook while on the cooling rack. This is known as "residual cooking" or "carryover cooking."
- Cake batter extract is relatively new on the market. It is sold next to the vanilla extract in your spice aisle.
- Whenever you see a recipe calling for "vanilla," "butter," and "nut flavoring," use cake batter extract as the ingredient.

Other Swaps to Reduce Carbohdyrate

While the discussion in this section has focused on sugar thus far, keep in mind that sugar is just one source of carbohydrate. Table 2.7 includes a number of other swaps for you to consider that can reduce carbohydrate in recipes.

PROTEIN

Protein is found in many foods. Protein supplies energy and helps ward off hunger. Protein also helps build, repair, and maintain body tissues. Everybody needs protein to power their bodies regardless of whether they have diabetes or not. Good sources of protein include the following:

- Meat, poultry, and fish
- Eggs
- Milk, cheese, and yogurt
- Soy, beans, and lentils
- Nuts and nut butters

TABLE 2.7   OTHER SWAPS TO REDUCE CARBOHYDRATE

Recipe Ingredient	Healthy Swap
Sugar	1/4 or 1/3 less sugar Sugar baking blend
Sugar added to coffee, tea, or other drinks	Sugar substitute Flavored extract
Bread crumb topping	Ground nuts

(continued)

TABLE 2.7   OTHER SWAPS TO REDUCE CARBOHYDRATE *(continued)*

Recipe Ingredient	Healthy Swap
Pasta/noodles	Spiralized zucchini, summer squash, or carrot
	Spaghetti squash
	Use half as much pasta and add nonstarchy vegetables like broccoli, cauliflower, spinach, mushrooms, tomatoes, and squash to add flavor and bulk
Cooked rice	Riced cauliflower
Potatoes	Cooked cauliflower (to replace half or more of the potatoes in casseroles or mashed potatoes)
Flour tortillas	Corn tortillas
Pizza crust	Thin crust; flatbread; cauliflower crust; low-carb, high-fiber, whole-wheat tortilla (see recipe for **Pizza Flats** on page 226), sweet bell pepper "crust" (see recipe for **Bell Pepper Pizza Poppers** on page 291)
Sandwich bread	Low-carbohydrate wrap
	Large lettuce leaf
Dairy milk	Unsweetened almond or soymilk
Jelly or syrup	Mashed fresh berries or thin apple/pear slices
Fruit canned in heavy syrup	Fruit canned in its own juice or water
	Fresh fruit
	Thawed unsweetened frozen fruit

Vegetables, cereals, and grain products also contain some protein but in much smaller amounts. A consideration with protein foods is that they may contain some fat—some sources much more than others. The box, "Breakfast Protein Power," contains 7 great ideas how to work protein into breakfast. For more, *the recipes on the following pages* are designed to help you fit protein in at breakfast, reduce carbohydrate, and feel satisfied.

Breakfast Protein Power

Find yourself getting hungry midmorning? Try adding a little protein to your breakfast to hold off hunger. Here are 7 ways to work protein into breakfast:

1. Have a boiled egg.
2. Scramble egg whites or egg substitutes (such as Egg Beaters).
3. Eat Greek or Icelandic yogurt (which is richer in protein than traditional yogurt).
4. Incorporate peanut butter, almond butter, or another nut butter (some people eat it out of the jar with a spoon, and others prefer spreading it on whole-grain toast or apple or pear slices).
5. Melt low-fat cheese on whole-grain toast.
6. Sprinkle almonds or walnuts on cereal or yogurt.
7. Add protein powder or powdered peanut butter to a smoothie.

FRESH SPINACH & TWO-CHEESE FRITTATA

A frittata is an egg-based dish that's a cross between an omelet and crustless quiche, including vegetables, cheese, and often meat. This protein-powered dish is packed with vegetables! It's a great way to add more vegetables to your breakfast or enjoy any time of day.

THIS RECIPE CAN FIT IN THE FOLLOWING EATING PATTERNS: vegetarian, low- or very-low-carbohydrate, DASH

NUMBER OF SERVINGS: 4 | **SERVING SIZE:** 1/4 frittata per serving
PREP TIME: 12 minutes | **COOK TIME:** 15 minutes | **STAND TIME:** 2 minutes

INGREDIENTS

- 1 cup chopped onions
- 1 (5-oz) package fresh baby spinach
- 2 oz reduced-fat cream cheese, cut into bitesize pieces
- 1 tsp dried Italian seasoning
- 1 cup egg substitute
- 1/4 tsp salt
- 1/8 tsp black pepper
- 3 oz grated reduced-fat sharp cheddar cheese
- 1/2 cup chopped tomato

INSTRUCTIONS

1. Heat a large nonstick skillet with nonstick cooking spray over medium heat. Cook onions 4 minutes or until golden. Add spinach and cook 1 minute or until just wilted, stirring constantly. Top with cream cheese and Italian seasoning. Pour the egg substitute over all.

2. Reduce to low heat, cover, and cook 10 minutes or until just set. Remove from heat, and sprinkle with the salt, pepper, cheddar cheese, and tomatoes. Let stand 2 minutes to allow cheese to melt and eggs to continue to cook without drying out.

Trick

- To stir the spinach easily, use two utensils as you would with a stir-fry. You have more control and the spinach will cook evenly.

COOK'S SWAP

- Substitute the egg substitute with 8 large egg whites, if desired.

CHOICES: 2 Nonstarchy Vegetable, 2 Lean Protein, 1 Fat
BASIC NUTRITIONAL VALUES: Calories 160 | Calories from Fat 70 | **Total Fat** 8.0 g | Saturated Fat 4.1 g | Trans Fat 0.0 g | **Cholesterol** 25 mg | **Sodium** 480 mg | **Potassium** 440 mg | **Total Carbohydrate** 9 g | Dietary Fiber 2 g | Sugars 4 g | Added Sugars 0 g | **Protein** 15 g | **Phosphorus** 185 mg

STRAWBERRY CHIA PUDDING

Looking for a make-ahead breakfast? Look no further! Prepare a batch of this on Sunday and you have a grab-and-go breakfast waiting for you every morning. Chia seeds get gelatinous when they sit in liquid for a period of time, creating a "pudding." They are also a great source of omega-3 fatty acids and fiber. This is a satisfying low-carbohydrate breakfast!

THIS RECIPE CAN FIT IN THE FOLLOWING EATING PATTERNS: vegetarian, low-fat, low- or very-low-carbohydrate, DASH

NUMBER OF SERVINGS: 4 | **SERVING SIZE:** 1/2 cup pudding plus 1/4 cup berries per serving
PREP TIME: 5 minutes | **CHILL TIME:** Overnight or at least 2 hours

INGREDIENTS

- 1/2 cup chia seeds
- 1 1/2 cups 2% milk
- 8 individual packets stevia
- 1 tsp vanilla
- Pinch of salt (about 1/16 tsp)
- 1 cup sliced strawberries

INSTRUCTIONS

1. Place all ingredients but the strawberries in a bowl and mix well. Let stand 3 minutes. Stir again until well blended.
2. Cover and refrigerate overnight or for at least 2 hours. Serve topped with the strawberries.

POINTER

- Make this even easier by pouring the chia mixture into four pint-size mason jars and then refrigerate overnight. Just top with berries and you have a "breakfast-on-the-go" ready when you are!

CHOICES: 1/2 Reduced-Fat Milk, 1 Carbohydrate, 1 1/2 Fat
BASIC NUTRITIONAL VALUES: Calories 190 | Calories from Fat 90 | **Total Fat** 10.0 g | Saturated Fat 2.0 g | Trans Fat 0.1 g | **Cholesterol** 5 mg | **Sodium** 85 mg | **Potassium** 300 mg | **Total Carbohydrate** 19 g | Dietary Fiber 10 g | Sugars 7 g | Added Sugars 0 g | **Protein** 8 g | **Phosphorus** 320 mg

DELICATE LEMON-ZESTED PANCAKES

Almond flour has been trending, and for good reason—it's low-carbohydrate, gluten-free, and rich in vitamin E and magnesium. These tender, tiny pancakes are delicate, so coating both sides of a flat spatula with nonstick cooking spray helps to slide the spatula under the pancakes without disturbing the shape. So light and so lemony!

THIS RECIPE CAN FIT IN THE FOLLOWING EATING PATTERNS: vegetarian, low- or very-low-carbohydrate, DASH

NUMBER OF SERVINGS: 4 | **SERVING SIZE:** 2 pancakes with 1/2 cup berries
PREP TIME: 10 minutes plus 15 minutes stand time | **COOK TIME:** 12 minutes

INGREDIENTS

- 1/2 cup almond flour
- 1 Tbsp sugar
- 1/2 tsp baking powder
- 1/8 tsp salt
- 1/2 cup 2% milk
- 1 large egg
- 1 1/2 tsp canola oil
- 1 1/2 tsp grated lemon zest
- 1 tsp vanilla
- 1 1/2 cups sliced strawberries
- 1/2 cup blueberries

INSTRUCTIONS

1. Whisk together the flour, sugar, baking powder, and salt in a medium bowl.
2. In a separate, whisk together the milk, egg, oil, lemon zest, and vanilla until well blended. Stir into the flour mixture until just blended. Let stand 15 minutes.
3. Meanwhile, preheat oven to 200°F. Combine berries in a medium bowl and set aside.
4. Heat a large nonstick skillet coated with nonstick cooking spray over low heat. Sprinkle a few drops of water on it. If the water evaporates quickly, the skillet is ready.
5. Stir the batter. Working in small batches, use a measuring spoon and spoon 2 Tbsp batter for each of 2 pancakes onto the skillet. Cook for 2 minutes, or until bubbles appear all over the surface and the bottoms are golden brown. Coat both sides of a spatula and gently turn the pancakes over. Cook for 1–2 minutes, or until golden brown on the bottoms.

(continued)

(Pointers on following page)

DELICATE LEMON-ZESTED PANCAKES (*continued*)

6. Place the pancakes in a single layer on a cooling rack, leaving space between. Don't cover the pancakes. Put in the oven to keep warm. Repeat process. You may want to coat skillet occasionally with nonstick cooking spray. Serve topped with equal amounts of the berries.

POINTERS

- If the berries are not in season and they need a little sweetness added, add 1–2 individual packets of stevia to the berries.
- Don't skip adding the 1 Tbsp sugar to the batter—it helps to give the proper texture and color to the pancakes.
- Because these pancakes are thin and delicate, small pancakes are easier to control while cooking.
- For another layer of flavor, top each serving with 2 Tbsp fat-free sour cream or Greek or Icelandic yogurt.

CHOICES: 1/2 Fruit, 1/2 Carbohydrate, 1 Lean Protein, 1 1/2 Fat

BASIC NUTRITIONAL VALUES: Calories 180 | Calories from Fat 100 | **Total Fat** 11.0 g | Saturated Fat 1.5 g | Trans Fat 0.0 g | **Cholesterol** 50 mg | **Sodium** 160 mg | **Potassium** 270 mg | **Total Carbohydrate** 15 g | Dietary Fiber 3 g | Sugars 10 g | Added Sugars 3 g | **Protein** 6 g | **Phosphorus** 195 mg

TURKEY BREAKFAST PATTIES WITH FRESH PEAR

Need a healthier option to traditional breakfast sausage patties? This dish is a welcome addition to your morning meal because these patties are slightly sweet (thanks to the addition of the ripe pears), and they're "bright" tasting (thanks to the addition of the fresh ginger). And they're great for dinner, too!

THIS RECIPE CAN FIT IN THE FOLLOWING EATING PATTERNS: low- or very-low-carbohydrate, DASH

NUMBER OF SERVINGS: 4 | **SERVING SIZE:** 2 patties per serving
PREP TIME: 13 minutes | **COOK TIME:** 6 minutes

INGREDIENTS

- 1 lb 93% lean ground turkey
- 1/2 cup diced *ripe* pear
- 1/2 cup chopped green onion (white and green portion)
- 1/2 cup finely chopped red bell pepper
- 1 Tbsp grated gingerroot
- 1/4 tsp salt
- 1/4 tsp crushed red pepper flakes
- 1 Tbsp canola oil

INSTRUCTIONS

1. Combine turkey, pear, onions, bell pepper, ginger-root, salt, and pepper flakes in a medium bowl. Shape into 8 small patties, about 2–2 1/2 inches in diameter.
2. Heat a large nonstick skillet over medium-low heat. Add the oil, and tilt skillet to coat bottom lightly. Cook the patties for 3 minutes on each side or until no longer pink in the center.

- This is great for entertaining, because they make great "sliders," too!

COOK'S SWAP

(Pointer, Tricks, and Box on following page)

CHOICES: 1/2 Carbohydrate, 3 Lean Protein, 1 Fat
BASIC NUTRITIONAL VALUES: Calories 230 | Calories from Fat 110 | **Total Fat** 12.0 g | Saturated Fat 2.7 g | Trans Fat 0.1 g | **Cholesterol** 85 mg | **Sodium** 230 mg | **Potassium** 360 mg | **Total Carbohydrate** 6 g | Dietary Fiber 1 g | Sugars 3 g | Added Sugars 0 g | **Protein** 22 g | **Phosphorus** 225 mg

POINTER

- Be sure to finely chop the vegetables, or it will be difficult to form the mixture into patties.

Tricks

- Adding a ripe pear provides a bit of sweetness to blend the flavors of the other ingredients.
- Adding the ginger provides an element of "freshness" and uniqueness to the traditional breakfast patties.

Why Fresh Ginger?

Fresh ginger adds so much more flavor than powdered ginger. Using fresh ginger is a little more effort, but it's totally worth it! Here are a few pointers for purchasing and preparing fresh ginger:

- When purchasing fresh ginger, there's no need to buy a large piece. If the ginger is in bulk bins at the grocery store, just break off a small piece (about the size of your thumb).
- To grate it, first peel off the papery skin using a vegetable peeler or a knife, or you can even use the edge of a spoon to scrape it off. Grate using the small side of a box grater or a microplane to get the most flavor and texture.
- Cover any unused portion of the ginger root tightly with plastic wrap and refrigerate up to 4 weeks.

Are You Getting a Mix of Protein Sources?

With the popularity of 10-oz steaks and three-egg omelets, there overall is generally no shortage of protein in the average American diet. Most Americans get plenty of protein but could benefit from more varied protein sources to improve nutrient and health benefits (such as lower-fat sources or sources with healthier fats). Take this fact into consideration if you choose to embrace a low- or very-low-carbohydrate (and thus higher-protein) eating pattern.

The amount of protein you need depends primarily on your age, sex, and level of physical activity. People with kidney disease may need differing amounts. Your RDN can confirm exactly how much protein is best for you.

Cook's Notes: 7 Protein Pointers

1. **Choose lean cuts of meat and poultry.** Lean meat and poultry are more heart-healthy because they have less fat and saturated fat than other meats (learn more about fats in the next section, beginning on page 53). Aim for 5 g fat or less per ounce of protein and trim away any visible fat. (See Table 2.8 for swaps for high-fat protein foods).

TABLE 2.8 SWAPS TO HEALTHIER OPTIONS FOR HIGHER-FAT AND HIGHER-CALORIE PROTEINS	
Recipe Ingredient	**Healthy Swap**
Ground beef	Extra-lean or lean ground beef
	Lean ground chicken (without the skin)
	Lean ground turkey (without the skin)
	Ground bison
	Lentils
	Mashed black beans
Beef prime rib	Beef tenderloin
Poultry with skin on	Poultry with skin removed
Meat in casserole	Replace part with vegetables (such as spinach, mushrooms, or eggplant in lasagna), beans, or lentils
Pork chop	Pork loin or tenderloin
Whole milk	2%, 1%, or fat-free milk
	Fat-free half-and-half
Whole-milk yogurt	Reduced-fat version (Greek or Icelandic yogurts are naturally richer in protein than traditional yogurt)
Regular cheese	Lower-fat version
	Use a lesser amount of a stronger-flavored cheese, since a little goes further in flavor (such as swapping in sharp cheddar for cheddar)
Ricotta cheese	Fat-free or light ricotta
	Low-fat cottage cheese

Words associated with lean cuts of meat include:

- 90% lean (or more)
- Chuck
- Flank
- Loin
- Round
- Tenderloin

2. **Fit in fish at least twice a week.** Many types of fish are rich in heart-healthy omega-3 fats, including halibut, herring, mackerel, salmon, sardines, trout, and tuna. Fried fish doesn't count though! One additional consideration when fitting in fish is that king mackerel, marlin, orange roughy, shark, swordfish, tilefish, ahi tuna, and bigeye tuna all contain high levels of mercury. Excessive amounts of mercury can cause serious health problems. Women who are pregnant or nursing or who plan to become pregnant within 1 year should avoid eating these fish. Find several *simple fish recipes* beginning on page 58.

3. **Use healthy cooking methods to cook proteins.** How you cook food matters. Table 2.9 shows better and best cooking methods in comparison to the least healthy cooking methods. Try to use and choose the "Better" and "Best" cooking methods more often. Changing the way you cook a food can significantly reduce fat and calories, making it a healthier option. For instance, switching from pan-fried pork loin chops to grilled pork loin chops takes you from one of the unhealthiest cooking methods to the healthiest.

TABLE 2.9   COOKING METHODS: LEAST HEALTHY, BETTER, AND BEST

Least Healthy	Better	Best
Pan-fried Deep-fried	Lightly stir-fry (with small amount of oil) Lightly sauté (with small amount of oil)	Air-fry Bake Broil Grill Microwave Nonstick skillet with nonstick cooking spray Poach Roast Steam

4. **Embrace plant-based proteins**. Make beans, lentils, or soy products the focus of your meals. While adding variety, this step will also save you money because these protein sources cost less than meat, poultry, and fish. Begin the week with "meatless Mondays" with a black bean soup for lunch or dinner, for instance. Or opt for a tofu stir-fry or red beans over brown rice.

5. **Nibble on nuts, seeds, and nut butters.** A small handful of almonds, pistachios, soy nuts, or walnuts provides crunch, protein, and heart-healthy fats. Sprinkle a few pine nuts or sunflower seeds on a salad or a few crushed pecans on oatmeal or yogurt. Lightly spread a slice of whole-wheat toast with peanut butter, almond nut butter, or soy nut butter.

6. **Mix in lean, soy-based proteins.** Try soy-based meat alternatives, such as soy-based "bacon," or meatless "beef" or "sausage" crumbles. Snack on soy nuts. Toss tofu or tempeh into soups, casseroles, or stir-fries. Substitute a veggie burger at lunch. Enjoy edamame as a side or snack.

7. **Don't forget eggs!** As a budget-friendly alternative to meat, switch in an egg. Eat egg yolks and whole eggs in moderation to manage dietary cholesterol intake. Egg whites and yolk-free liquid egg substitutes have no dietary cholesterol and little to no fat, so they are a heart-healthy alternative to whole eggs.

   - 1/4 cup of yolk-free liquid egg substitute = 1 whole egg

FAT: FRIEND OR FOE?

When referring to fat, it's important to differentiate between the role of fat in foods and uses of dietary fat in the body.

Fat in food . . .

- Carries flavor, fat-soluble vitamins, and other nutrients.
- Gives a smooth and creamy texture (such as in peanut butter, sauces, and dips).
- Adds moisture and shape to baked goods.
- Makes foods tender and moist or crispy and brown.

Dietary fat in the body . . .

- Carries fat-soluble vitamins so they can be used in your body.
- Supplies two fatty acids that your body needs but can't make. These fatty acids are linoleic acid and α-linolenic acid.
- Supplies energy in the form of calories.
- Helps satisfy hunger by making you feel full after you eat.

All Fats Are Not Created Equal

Although fat is often referred to in a general sense, there are actually three main types of fat. Each type has different effects, so it's important to know the healthy, high-quality fats from the unhealthy fats and how to swap the healthy fats for the unhealthy fats. Just as choosing high-quality foods is key to healthy eating, so is choosing high-quality fats.

Healthy fats: unsaturated fats

Unsaturated fats are the "heart-healthy," high-quality fats that come primarily from plant sources. These plant sources include avocado, canola oil, corn oil, olives, olive oil, and nuts. The Mediterranean eating style is rich in these heart-healthy, high-quality, plant-based fats. There are two types of unsaturated fats that are healthy, and you will see these listed on the Nutrition Facts label:

- Monounsaturated fats
- Polyunsaturated fats

Unhealthy fats: saturated fats and trans fats

Saturated fats and trans fats are not healthy for your heart. These two types of fats are broken down and listed on the Nutrition Facts label as well.

- **Saturated Fats** are solid fats that come primarily from animal sources. Examples are bacon or bacon grease, butter, cream cheese, and lard. Solid fats do to the blood vessels basically what pouring bacon grease down the kitchen sink does to the drain—they clog things up. Saturated fats also have been shown to worsen insulin resistance.

- **Trans Fats** found in foods come in two types: naturally occurring and artificial.
  - **Naturally occurring trans fats** are produced in the gut of some animals (cattle, sheep, goats, buffalo, deer, elk, and camels). Foods from these animals (such as milk, cheese, butter, and meat products) have naturally occurring trans fat, but they are present in very small amounts.
  - **Artificial trans fats,** created in food processing by transforming a liquid vegetable oil into a semi-solid fat (such as stick margarine or shortening), were phased out of the food supply 1 January 2020.

With type 2 diabetes, following an eating pattern that is lower in carbohydrate and higher in healthy fat may improve blood glucose, triglycerides, and HDL cholesterol. You can learn more about these eating patterns in Chapter 3. Eating more foods rich in unsaturated fat, in place of foods with saturated fat, may additionally improve LDL cholesterol (see Table 2.10 for healthy fat swaps and the lightly sweet bite recipe for *Toffee-Topped Chocolate Almonds* on page 56, which is packed with healthy fats). Hence, you can see that focusing on incorporating healthy fat sources is important. In general, replacing saturated and trans fat with unsaturated fats reduces total cholesterol and LDL cholesterol and benefits cardiovascular risk. Small changes really add up.

TABLE 2.10   TIPS FOR SWITCHING TO HEALTHY FATS

Choose these . . .		Rather than these . . .	
Monounsaturated Fats	**Polyunsaturated Fats**	**Saturated Fats**	**Trans Fats**
Avocado	Corn oil	Bacon	Vegetable shortening
Canola oil	English walnuts	Butter	Stick margarine
Nuts (almonds, Brazil, macadamia, peanuts, pecans, pistachios)	Flax seed	Coconut milk	
	Pine nuts	Coconut oil	
Nut butters (almond, cashew, peanut)	Pumpkin seeds	Cream	
	Safflower oil	Cream cheese	
Olives	Sesame seeds	Lard	
Olive oil	Soybean oil	Sour cream	
Peanut oil	Sunflower seeds and oil	Shortening	
	Tahini (sesame paste)		

6 Simple Switches to High-Quality Fat

1. Try unsweetened almond milk on your morning cereal rather than full-fat dairy milk.
2. Add avocado to a salad or drizzle avocado slices with a splash of balsamic vinegar and olive oil and a sprinkle of sunflower seeds.
3. Mash and spread avocado on a sandwich instead of mayonnaise.
4. Rather than adding butter or bacon drippings to vegetables, try a drizzle of olive oil.
5. Spread on a "buttery" spread containing plant stanols/sterols rather than butter. (Plant stanols and sterols are natural substances found in plant-based foods that may help lower cholesterol.)
6. Choose olives over cheese for an evening appetizer.

TOFFEE-TOPPED CHOCOLATE ALMONDS

Managing blood glucose doesn't mean you have to give up sweet treats! Many sweet treats, such as candy bars, are not only loaded with added sugars, they often have a dose of unhealthy fat. A healthier alternative to a candy bar, these lightly sweet bites feature heart-healthy fats from almonds and dark chocolate, topped with crushed sugar-free caramel candies.

THIS RECIPE CAN FIT IN THE FOLLOWING EATING PATTERNS*: vegetarian, low-carbohydrate, DASH

NUMBER OF SERVINGS: 9 | **SERVING SIZE:** 1 oz/about 4 pieces per serving
PREP TIME: 15 minutes | **COOK TIME:** 4 minutes

INGREDIENTS

- 1 (2.75-oz) package sugar-free caramel-flavored hard candies, such as Werther's, 25 pieces
- 7 oz whole almonds (about 1 3/4 cups)
- 2 oz 70% cacao chocolate bar, coarsely chopped
- 1/8 tsp salt

*An occasional sweet treat can be incorporated into most eating patterns, in moderation.

INSTRUCTIONS

1. Remove plastic wrappers from the candies. Place the candies in a small resealable plastic bag. Seal tightly and place on work surface. Using the smooth side of a meat mallet or bottom of a heavy bottle or can, crush the candies. Set aside.
2. Heat a large nonstick skillet over medium-high heat. Add almonds and cook 3 minutes or until fragrant, stirring frequently. Remove from heat and set aside.
3. Place chocolate bar in a medium microwave-safe bowl and microwave on high for 30 seconds. Stir and repeat two times or until chocolate has just melted. Add the almonds and stir until well coated.
4. Pour onto a foil-lined baking sheet coated with nonstick cooking spray and, working quickly, spread into a single layer (about 9 inches square). (Note: It does not have to be exactly square.) Immediately sprinkle evenly with the crushed candies and then the salt. Refrigerate 30–45 minutes or until chocolate is firm.
5. Break into bitesize pieces, about 1- to 1 1/4-inch pieces. Store in an airtight container in the refrigerator up to 2 weeks.

CHOICES: 4 Carbohydrate, 3 Fat

BASIC NUTRITIONAL VALUES: Calories 200 | Calories from Fat 140 | **Total Fat** 15.0 g | Saturated Fat 3.0 g | Trans Fat 0.0 g | **Cholesterol** 0 mg | **Sodium** 80 mg | **Potassium** 210 mg | **Total Carbohydrate** 15 g | Dietary Fiber 3 g | Sugars 3 g | Added Sugars 2 g | **Protein** 5 g | **Phosphorus** 125 mg

POINTERS

- Adding the salt on top brings out a delicious sweet/salty taste! This flavor would get lost otherwise.
- Be sure to buy 70% cacao or higher to get the benefits of the dark chocolate. You can certainly buy a higher percentage of cacao, but the higher you go, the less sweet it becomes.

Fatty fish rich in omega-3 fats:

- Halibut
- Herring
- Mackerel
- Salmon
- Sardines
- Trout
- Tuna

What about Omega-3 Fat?

While focusing on healthy fats, one notable type of polyunsaturated fat with heart-healthy benefits is known as omega-3 fat. Eating more omega-3 fat may help reduce risk for heart disease by decreasing total cholesterol and triglycerides and raising the HDL ("good") cholesterol. You may be familiar with omega-3 fat as the "fish fat." Many fish (especially fatty fish) are indeed rich in heart-healthy omega-3 fats. So it's recommended to eat fish at least twice a week. (Fried fish doesn't count though!) The recipes on pages 58-62 provide a number of options for healthy fish recipes. Even if you're not a huge fish fan, we hope you'll find at least one dish that works for you.

A Success Story of How to Fit in Fish Twice a Week

One client Tami worked with was not a huge fish fan, but she was willing to try eating more fish. She did not feel confident cooking fish at home, so here was her solution:

- Top a prepared "bag" salad with a foil pack of tuna or salmon at lunch on Monday and Wednesday.
- Make fish her "go to" order when dining out on the weekend. She would occasionally mix it up with tuna or salmon sushi.

Small changes, right? But as we've seen, small changes add up in the long run.

SKILLET TROUT FILLETS WITH RICH LEMON SAUCE

These delicate fillets cook quickly, so you'll definitely have time for this any day of the week. The fish is seasoned with an herb blend, cooked briefly, and then deglazed with wine and lemon, resulting in a smooth, "buttery" sauce. A healthy serving of omega-3s never tasted so good!

THIS RECIPE CAN FIT IN THE FOLLOWING EATING PATTERNS: low- or very-low-carbohydrate, DASH, Mediterranean

---

NUMBER OF SERVINGS: 4 | **SERVING SIZE:** 4 1/2 oz fillet and 1/4 cup topping per serving
PREP TIME: 13 minutes | **COOK TIME:** 10 minutes

INGREDIENTS

- 1 1/2 tsp dried Italian seasoning
- 1/2 tsp garlic powder
- 1 tsp paprika
- 4 (6-oz) trout fillets, rinsed and patted dry
- 1 Tbsp canola oil
- 1/4 cup dry white wine, such as Chardonnay
- 2 Tbsp fresh lemon juice
- 3 Tbsp light butter with canola oil
- 1/4 tsp salt
- 1/4 tsp black pepper
- 2 Tbsp finely chopped fresh parsley

INSTRUCTIONS

1. Combine Italian seasoning, garlic powder, and paprika in a small bowl. Sprinkle both sides of the fillets with the mixture.
2. Heat a large nonstick skillet over medium heat. Coat with nonstick cooking spray and add the oil and tilt skillet to coat bottom lightly. Cook fish, 3 minutes on each side or until fish flakes with a fork. Set aside on separate plate.
3. Add the wine to the pan residue. Bring to a boil over medium-high heat. Cook 30 seconds or until wine has almost evaporated, scraping bottom of pan to remove browned bits. Remove from heat and stir in the lemon juice and light butter. Stir until butter has melted. Spoon over fish, and sprinkle with salt, pepper, and parsley.

CHOICES: 5 Lean Protein, 2 1/2 Fat

BASIC NUTRITIONAL VALUES: Calories 330 | Calories from Fat 170 | **Total Fat** 19.0 g | Saturated Fat 3.8 g | Trans Fat 0.0 g | **Cholesterol** 105 mg | **Sodium** 310 mg | **Potassium** 670 mg | **Total Carbohydrate** 2 g | Dietary Fiber 1 g | Sugars 0 g | Added Sugars 0 g | **Protein** 36 g | **Phosphorus** 430 mg

POINTER

- Most of the alcohol from the white wine evaporates during cooking. If you'd prefer to leave out the alcohol entirely, omit the white wine and add another tablespoon lemon juice.

Trick

- Coating the nonstick skillet *and* adding a small amount of oil helps to keep the fish fillets moist and from sticking to the skillet, while keeping the overall fat down.

ROSEMARY ROASTED SALMON

Salmon is a superfood when it comes to delivering omega-3 fats. This recipe can help you meet the goal to fit in fish at least twice a week. Keeping a collection of your favorite salmon recipes is a great way to look forward to superfood dinners again and again.

THIS RECIPE CAN FIT IN THE FOLLOWING EATING PATTERNS: low- or very-low-carbohydrate, DASH, Mediterranean

NUMBER OF SERVINGS: 4 | **SERVING SIZE:** 4 1/2 oz fillet and 1/4 cup topping per serving
PREP TIME: 13 minutes | **COOK TIME:** 10 minutes

INGREDIENTS
Salmon:

- 4 (6-oz) salmon fillets, rinsed and patted dry
- 1 Tbsp extra-virgin olive oil
- 1 tsp dried rosemary
- 1/2 tsp black pepper

Topping:

- 3/4 cup chopped cucumber
- 1/4 cup finely chopped red onion
- 2 Tbsp fresh lime juice
- 2 Tbsp chopped fresh Italian parsley
- 1/4 tsp salt

INSTRUCTIONS

1. Preheat oven to 400°F.
2. Place salmon, skin side down, on a foil-lined baking sheet coated with nonstick cooking spray. Rub oil evenly over the tops of the fillets. Sprinkle evenly with the rosemary and black pepper.
3. Bake 10–12 minutes or until the fish flakes easily with a fork.
4. Meanwhile, combine the topping ingredients in a small bowl.
5. Serve salmon topped with the cucumber mixture.

CHOICES: 5 Lean Protein, 1 1/2 Fat

BASIC NUTRITIONAL VALUES: Calories 300 | Calories from Fat 140 | **Total Fat** 16.0 g | Saturated Fat 3.3 g | Trans Fat 0.0 g | **Cholesterol** 90 mg | **Sodium** 400 mg | **Potassium** 670 mg | **Total Carbohydrate** 3 g | Dietary Fiber 1 g | Sugars 1 g | Added Sugars 0 g | **Protein** 33 g | **Phosphorus** 450 mg

POINTERS

- For a bit of heat, add 1/8 tsp crushed pepper flakes or 1 jalapeno, seeded and finely chopped to the topping mixture.
- When buying salmon, make sure it's bright pink, not dull pink, for freshness. A quick sniff will let you know, too. If it smells "fishy," it's not fresh enough!

ALBACORE TUNA AND GREEN GRAPE SALAD

*Did you know that canned albacore tuna contains two times the amount of Omega-3 fats than that of light chunk tuna from a can? All canned tuna varieties are **not** the same! You might pay a bit more for the albacore variety, but you're getting a lot more flavor and nutritional benefits in return.*

THIS RECIPE CAN FIT IN THE FOLLOWING EATING PATTERNS: **low-carbohydrate, DASH, Mediterranean**

NUMBER OF SERVINGS: 4 | **SERVING SIZE:** 3 cups salad and 3 Tbsp dressing
PREP TIME: 12 minutes

INGREDIENTS
Dressing:
- 1/2 cup light mayonnaise
- 1/4 cup water
- 1 Tbsp curry powder
- 1 tsp cider vinegar
- 2 individual packages stevia

Salad:
- 8 oz baby kale mixture, such as Dole Power Up Greens
- 1/4 tsp black pepper
- 1 (8-oz) can sliced water chestnuts, drained and cut in half
- 2 cups green grapes, halved
- 2 oz slivered almonds
- 4 (5-oz) cans low-sodium solid white albacore tuna in water, rinsed and drained
- 1/2 cup finely chopped red onion

INSTRUCTIONS

1. Whisk together the dressing ingredients in a small bowl.
2. Arrange equal amounts of the kale mixture in four bowls. Top with dressing and then sprinkle pepper over all. Top with the water chestnuts, grapes, and almonds (arranged in sections). Sprinkle evenly with the tuna and onion.

CHOICES: 5 Fruit, 1/2 Carbohydrate, 2 Nonstarchy Vegetable, 3 Lean Protein, 2 Fat
BASIC NUTRITIONAL VALUES: Calories 360 | Calories from Fat 150 | **Total Fat** 17.0 g | Saturated Fat 1.8 g | Trans Fat 0.0 g | **Cholesterol** 25 mg | **Sodium** 350 mg | **Potassium** 930 mg | **Total Carbohydrate** 30 g | Dietary Fiber 6 g | Sugars 16 g | Added Sugars 1 g | **Protein** 28 g | **Phosphorus** 415 mg

POINTERS

- For an additional layer of flavor, sprinkle 1 Tbsp chopped fresh cilantro over each serving.
- Be sure to look for low-sodium albacore in water—there are a lot of choices on the market.
- For additional sweetness, add 1–2 more individual packets of stevia to the dressing before topping the greens.

Tricks

- The addition of vinegar to the dressing brightens the dressing without overpowering it with a vinegary flavor.
- Rinsing and draining the tuna removes some of the "fishy" taste from the tuna, but be sure to drain well.

Did You Know?

1 oz walnuts (about seven whole nuts) meets daily omega-3 needs.

It's not just fish!

Omega-3 fat is not just found in fish, which is good news for vegetarians and vegans. If you are following a plant-based eating pattern, plant sources of omega-3 fat include:

- Chia seeds
- Walnuts
- Flax (ground/milled)
- Soy
- Canola oil

Here are 10 easy ways to work in more heart-healthy omega-3 fats

1. Top a mini whole-wheat breakfast bagel with fat-free cream cheese and smoked salmon.
2. Add protein to a green salad with foil-packed tuna or salmon.
3. Use dining out as an opportunity to order fish if you don't want to cook fish at home.
4. Opt for a tuna or salmon "burger" instead of a beef burger.
5. Munch on a small handful of walnuts for a snack or sprinkle chopped walnuts over a high-fiber cold cereal or yogurt.
6. Switch in chia pudding for breakfast. (Find a recipe for *Strawberry Chia Pudding* on page 46.)
7. Sprinkle ground flaxseed or chia seeds on oatmeal.

8. Stir ground flaxseed into moist, dark dishes such as chili, stew, or meatloaf. A good rule of thumb is 1 Tbsp flaxseed per serving. It's likely that no one will even notice.
9. Grab a handful of soy nuts for a snack.
10. When oil is called for in baking, use canola oil.

While eating foods rich in omega-3 fat can be beneficial, evidence at the time of publication does not support a beneficial role for the routine use of omega-3 dietary supplements.

How Much Fat Is Enough? Moderation Is the Mantra

While there is a definite consensus that high-quality fat should be priority, there is no conclusive "ideal" recommended daily amount of fat. A generally acceptable range for fat intake is 20–35% of total daily calories. So, doing the math, that would mean 45–78 g fat per day for an average 2,000 calories. This example gives you some numbers to put things into perspective.

Given that fat, regardless if it's healthy or unhealthy, is a significant source of calories (more than double that of carbohydrate or protein), moderation is really the mantra. Small changes really add up. Consider the following two examples, which are healthy, but add up quick.

Avocado

Eating avocado is a healthier fat option and is in line with the plant-based and Mediterranean-style eating patterns (learn more about these eating patterns in Chapter 3), but calories can add up quickly. An average avocado runs 250–300 calories.

Peanut butter

Spreading peanut butter on apple slices can be a delicious snack, but, again, calories can add up quickly. Spread peanut butter a little lighter using 1 Tbsp instead of 2 Tbsp and you save 100 calories. Or switch to a rehydrated powdered peanut butter (such as PB2) and get 70% fewer calories.

Recipe Renewal: How to Fix the Fat

Many recipes won't do well in a totally fat-free world because fat carries out important functions in food as we discussed earlier. Consider what role fat plays in foods when you're thinking about making changes in a recipe to reduce fat. To recap, here are the roles of fat in foods:

- Carries flavor, fat-soluble vitamins, and other nutrients
- Gives a smooth and creamy texture (such as in peanut butter, sauces, and dips)
- Adds moisture and shape to baked goods
- Makes foods tender and moist or crispy and brown

5 Tips to Trim Calories from Fat

1. Choose lean cuts of meat and poultry and trim off visible fat. (Refer to the Protein Pointers earlier on page 51 for more protein tips.)
2. Order sauces and dressings on the side when dining out so you can control the amount that goes on your food.
3. Choose tomato-based sauces instead of creamy ones.
4. Skip extra cheese. If a casserole calls for a sprinkle of cheese on top, try leaving it off. Or if eating out and extra cheese is an option, skip it and see how your food tastes. Even a single slice of cheese on a sandwich or burger can add around 100 calories.
5. Manage portions, since the amount of fat that you eat depends not only on what you eat, but also on how much you eat.

Cook's Notes: 5 Strategies to Cut Fat in Recipes

1. **Use reduced-fat or fat-free ingredients whenever possible.** For example, swap in low-fat or fat-free Greek or Icelandic yogurt or reduced-fat or fat-free sour cream in place of regular sour cream in dips. Or swap in low-fat milk or fat-free milk for full-fat whole milk in pudding.
2. **Skim the fat.** After you make a soup or stew, add ice cubes to congeal the fat on top of the soup for easy skimming. While the ice will cool the soup, you can quickly rewarm it. Alternately, refrigerate the soup and skim the fat off the top before reheating. Each tablespoon of fat you skim will save more than 130 calories.
3. **Opt out of or reduce by half the high-fat, high-calorie extras or toppings in your recipe.** For instance, you may decide to reduce nuts or coconut by half or forego altogether a whipped cream topping, a dollop of sour cream, or a sprinkle of cheese.
4. **Switch up the cooking method.** Choose baked and grilled foods over fried foods when possible. For example, pick grilled shrimp or roasted chicken over fried varieties.
5. **Swap out the basting liquid.** If the recipe directions call for basting the meat or vegetables in oil or drippings, use a small amount of fat-free vegetable broth or dry wine.

Fat Replacers: At a Glance

You may have heard of fat replacers. As the name implies, they are used to replace part or all of the fat in some foods and thus can reduce fat and calorie intake. Fat replacers can be carbohydrate-based, protein-based, or chemically altered fat-based. If using a "fat-free" or "low-fat" product, be sure to take a look at Total Carbohydrate on the Nutrition Facts label, because while lower in fat, these products may be higher in carbohydrate if the fat replacer is carbohydrate (meaning they can raise your blood glucose).

- Products made using commercial fat replacers may have less fat and fewer calories, but if you eat a larger portion of a reduced-fat food, you lose any potential calorie savings.
- Be mindful of portion sizes and the calorie and carbohydrate content of these products.

Your RDN or diabetes healthcare team can help you decide if including products with fat replacers in your meal plan is the right choice for you.

Remember, fats are the most concentrated source of calories. So, cutting fat also cuts calories. Although the end product is likely not exactly the same once fat has been replaced, many fat substitutions produce delicious and moist end products. Table 2.11 shows you tips for swapping out unhealthy fats and including higher-quality fats (such as those that are part of the Mediterranean eating pattern).

Now let's put some swaps into action to fix the fat in some traditional high-fat recipes. If you are a fried chicken fan, Table 2.12 gives a few swaps to give fried chicken a healthy makeover to reduce fat, calories, and sodium, while adding flavor and fiber. Make only one swap at a time so you can note the effect. The recipe *Downhome Fried Chicken Tenders* on page 70 then puts these tips into action.

TABLE 2.11   TIPS TO SWAP OUT UNHEALTHY FATS AND LOWER CALORIES

Recipe Ingredient	Healthy Swap
Butter or oil to sauté	Canola oil, olive oil, nonstick cooking spray and nonstick pan, or sodium-free broth
Butter or shortening in baking	Replace half with applesauce, mashed bananas, puréed prunes, or puréed pumpkin Add 3 Tbsp ground flax seed plus 1 Tbsp water in place of each tablespoon of fat or oil
Butter or mayonnaise for spreads	Nonfat or reduced-fat versions Mashed avocado
Whole egg	1/4 cup liquid egg substitute (such as Egg Beaters) 2 egg whites
Mayonnaise	Light or low-fat mayonnaise Mashed avocado Hummus
Heavy cream	Evaporated skim milk Fat-free half-and-half Replace half with fat-free plain yogurt
Cream cheese	Reduced-fat or light American Neufchatel Fat-free ricotta cheese Low-fat cottage cheese puréed until smooth
Cream sauce (like alfredo sauce)	Tomato or marinara sauce
Whole milk	2%, 1%, or fat-free milk Fat-free half-and-half

(continued)

TABLE 2.11   TIPS TO SWAP OUT UNHEALTHY FATS AND LOWER CALORIES *(continued)*

Recipe Ingredient	Healthy Swap
Sour cream	Reduced-fat or fat-free sour cream, Greek yogurt, or Icelandic yogurt
Regular cheese	Lower-fat version Use a lesser amount of a stronger-flavored cheese, since a little goes further in flavor (such as swapping sharp cheddar for mild cheddar)
Bacon	Turkey bacon Canadian bacon Smoked turkey Vegetarian bacon or bacon bits
Ground beef	Extra-lean or lean ground beef Lean ground chicken (without the skin) Lean ground turkey (without the skin) Lentils Mashed black beans
Meat in a casserole	Replace part with vegetables (such as spinach, mushrooms, or eggplant in lasagna), beans, or lentils
Oil in oil-based marinade	Balsamic or other flavored vinegar Citrus juice Fat-free broth

TABLE 2.12   SWAPS TO MAKE FRIED CHICKEN HEALTHIER

Use this . . .	Instead of this . . .	And you get . . .
Skinless chicken	Chicken pieces with skin on	Reduced fat and calories
Nonfat buttermilk to marinate	Whole buttermilk to marinate	Reduced fat and calories
1/4 cup liquid egg substitute or 2 egg whites	Each whole egg	Reduced fat and calories
Crushed high-fiber cereal (such as Fiber One)	White flour	Increased fiber
Cayenne pepper, paprika, sage	Salt	Reduced salt/sodium and increased flavor
Air-frying or baking with non-stick cooking spray	Frying	Reduced fat and calories

DOWNHOME FRIED CHICKEN TENDERS

In this "renewed recipe" you'll find 2% milk and egg whites used to reduce fat in the egg wash (instead of whole milk and whole eggs), lean chicken tenderloins to reduce fat and to allow for quick and even pan cooking (instead of larger pieces of chicken with skin), a nonstick skillet with a small amount of healthy oil (instead of deep fried), and paprika to enhance color.

THIS RECIPE CAN FIT IN THE FOLLOWING EATING PATTERNS: **low-carbohydrate, DASH**

NUMBER OF SERVINGS: 4 | **SERVING SIZE:** 2 chicken tenders per serving
PREP TIME: 15 minutes | **COOK TIME:** 10 minutes

INGREDIENTS

- 1/3 cup 2% milk
- 2 egg whites
- 8 chicken tenderloins, about 1 1/4 lb total
- 1 1/4 cups panko bread crumbs
- 1 1/2 tsp paprika
- 1 tsp dried thyme
- 1 tsp garlic powder
- 1/2 tsp dried dill
- 1/4 tsp black pepper
- 2 Tbsp canola oil
- 1/2 tsp salt, divided use

INSTRUCTIONS

1. Whisk together the milk and egg whites in a medium bowl, add the chicken, and toss until well coated. Combine the bread crumbs, paprika, thyme, garlic powder, dill, and black pepper in a shallow dish, such as a pie pan.
2. Coat the chicken pieces one at a time with the bread crumb mixture, pressing down lightly to allow the crumbs to adhere, and place on a dinner plate. Repeat coating of chicken pieces with bread crumb mixture.
3. Heat oil in large nonstick skillet over medium-high heat until hot. Place chicken in skillet. Immediately reduce heat to medium, sprinkle chicken evenly with 1/4 tsp salt, and cook 5 minutes. Turn pieces over, sprinkle evenly with remaining 1/4 tsp salt, and cook 5 minutes or until no longer pink in center.
4. Serve chicken warm or cold.

CHOICES: 1 Starch, 4 Lean Protein, 1 Fat
BASIC NUTRITIONAL VALUES: **Calories 290** | Calories from Fat 100 | **Total Fat** 11.0 g | Saturated Fat 1.7 g | Trans Fat 0.0 g | **Cholesterol** 80 mg | **Sodium** 410 mg | **Potassium** 340 mg | **Total Carbohydrate** 13 g | Dietary Fiber 1 g | Sugars 2 g | Added Sugars 0 g | **Protein** 33 g | **Phosphorus** 260 mg

POINTERS

- Be sure to use a large skillet. You don't want to "crowd" the chicken pieces to allow even cooking and crisping.
- Some of the egg mixture and panko bread crumbs will be discarded, but you need that much to coat the chicken easily and to allow bread crumbs to remain flaky and not soggy.
- Leftovers are best reheated in an oven, toaster oven, or air fryer to maintain crispness, instead of a microwave.

Trick

- If you need a food to have more color or browning, incorporate paprika into the dish. It acts as a blender for color and flavor and works well with other ingredients. Paprika doesn't overpower or interfere with the flavor profile of the dish.

Macaroni and cheese is a classic comfort food that's laden with fat and calories. To spark your thinking, Table 2.13 introduces several swaps that can improve the health of the recipe without losing the wonderful cheesy flavor. Make one swap at a time so you can note the effect. The recipe *Sneaky Two-Cheese Mac & Cheese* on page 73 then shows you how these swaps can be used to best effect.

TABLE 2.13 SWAPS TO MAKEOVER MACARONI AND CHEESE		
Use this . . .	**Instead of this . . .**	**And you get . . .**
A smaller amount of sharp or extra-sharp cheddar or pepper jack	Mild cheddar	Reduced fat and calories
Reduced-fat cheese	Full-fat "regular" cheese	Reduced fat and calories
Low-fat cottage cheese or part-skim ricotta cheese	Some of the full-fat cheese	Reduced fat and calories
Light trans fat–free margarine/buttery spread	Butter	Reduced fat and calories
Fat-free milk	Whole milk or cream	Reduced fat and calories
Part-skim ricotta or reduced-fat sour cream	Whole milk, cream, butter	Reduced fat and calories
Whole-wheat or high-fiber pasta	Refined white pasta	Increased fiber
Crushed high-fiber cereal topping	Dry white bread crumb topping	Increased fiber
Pepper, paprika, or nutmeg	Salt	Reduced salt/sodium and increased flavor
Broccoli, cauliflower, spinach, mushrooms, tomatoes, and squash	Some pasta	Reduced calories, increased fiber and flavor

SNEAKY TWO-CHEESE MAC & CHEESE

This "renewed recipe" incorporates some cauliflower to bulk up the macaroni component and reduce carbohydrate in each serving. And the use of whole-grain rotini rather than traditional rotini bumps up the fiber. While this mac and cheese incorporates reduced-fat cheeses, it remains creamy because of the reduced-fat cream cheese. Plus, you get up to 35% of your day's requirement of calcium and 20% vitamin C in every single serving of this transformed and creamy pasta dish.

THIS RECIPE CAN FIT IN THE FOLLOWING EATING PATTERNS: vegetarian, low-carbohydrate, DASH

NUMBER OF SERVINGS: 4 | **SERVING SIZE:** 1 cup per serving
PREP TIME: 10 minutes | **COOK TIME:** 12 minutes

INGREDIENTS

- 6 oz whole-grain rotini, such as Barilla
- 1 cup frozen or fresh cauliflower, cut or smashed into small florets
- 1/4 cup reserved pasta water
- 1/4 cup 2% milk
- 1 Tbsp canola oil
- 1/2 tsp salt
- 1/8 tsp cayenne pepper
- 3 oz shredded reduced-fat sharp cheddar cheese
- 1 1/2 oz reduced-fat cream cheese, cut into small pieces

INSTRUCTIONS

1. Cook pasta according to package directions, adding the cauliflower 5 minutes before cooking time has ended. Remove from heat and drain pasta mixture, reserving 1/4 cup of the pasta water.
2. Return drained pasta mixture to pot, and place over low heat. Add the 1/4 cup pasta water, milk, oil, salt, and cayenne pepper. Stir until well blended. Gradually add the cheddar cheese and the cream cheese. Stir until cheeses have melted.

POINTER

- Be sure to use small cauliflower florets so they can "hide" easily in the pasta mixture. If using frozen cauliflower, you can smash the florets while they are still in the bag with a rolling pin or a skillet to break them up.

CHOICES: 2 Starch, 1 Medium-Fat Protein, 1 Fat
BASIC NUTRITIONAL VALUES: Calories 270 | Calories from Fat 110 | **Total Fat** 12.0 g | Saturated Fat 4.7 g | Trans Fat 0.0 g | **Cholesterol** 25 mg | **Sodium** 520 mg | **Potassium** 330 mg | **Total Carbohydrate** 33 g | Dietary Fiber 6 g | Sugars 3 g | Added Sugars 0 g | **Protein** 13 g | **Phosphorus** 310 mg

DIETARY FIBER

Dietary fiber is another notable nutrient because it plays an important role in promoting good health. Sometimes referred to as "roughage," dietary fiber is the indigestible portion of plant foods. Fiber is what gives plants shape. Some plant foods have more fiber than others. For instance, oats, dried beans, and pulses have a significant amount of fiber, while refined white rice or refined white wheat flour have a minimal amount. Just as fiber provides shape and bulk to plants, fiber bulks up the contents of your intestinal tract and helps promote feeling full. Your body cannot digest or absorb fiber, so instead of being used for energy, fiber passes through your body, providing a number of positive health benefits along the way, including the following:

- Aids digestion
- Promotes bowel movement regularity and colon health
- Lowers the risk of some diseases, including heart disease and cancer
- Helps lower cholesterol (specifically the "soluble" type that's found in oats, dried beans, and psyllium)
- Helps prevent blood glucose spikes

Because of these health benefits, fiber-rich eating is encouraged for people with diabetes (as for the general public). The Mediterranean, vegetarian and vegan, and DASH eating patterns in particular (all reviewed in Chapter 3) can help you achieve a fiber-rich diet.

How Much Dietary Fiber Do You Need?

Most Americans fall short on the amount of fiber and whole grains (which are richer in fiber than refined grains) in their eating patterns. The average American gets around 15 g fiber per day, whereas the recommended healthy amount is 14 g for every 1,000 calories consumed, which means *about 25 g daily for adult women and 38 g daily for adult men.*

Your RDN can recommend ways to increase the amount of high-fiber foods in your eating plan or help you decide if including fiber-fortified foods in your plan is the right choice for you.

Whole grains: another way to get more fiber

Because of the general health benefits of fiber and whole grains, *the recommendation for those with or at risk for type 2 diabetes is to aim for at least half of their grains being whole grains.*

Most Americans are close to the target amounts for total grains, but not enough are **whole** grains, with too many being refined grains. Whole grains are foods containing the entire grain kernel (which means the bran, germ, and endosperm). These foods have more fiber and nutrients. Choosing whole-grain products in place of refined-grain products is one way to reduce intake of refined grains, while conversely increasing intake of whole grains.

There are many whole grain foods from which to choose. *Familiar examples* of whole grains include brown rice, oatmeal, popcorn, quinoa, and wild rice. *Less familiar examples* include buckwheat, bulgur, farro, freekeh, millet, and spelt. Check out the Oldways Whole Grains Council website to learn much more about these whole grains and easy ways to enjoy them: https://wholegrainscouncil.org.

Quick Tips to Increase Your Fiber Intake

Make at least half of your grains whole grains.

Here's an illustration how:

- **Breakfast:** Enjoy steel-cut oats (see *Cinnamon Steel-Cut Oats* recipe on page 265).
- **Lunch:** Choose 100% whole-wheat bread over white or "wheat" bread.
- **Dinner:** Use brown rice or quinoa instead of white rice, or enjoy a whole-grain salad like tabbouleh.
- **Snack:** Munch on popcorn for a snack.

Eat 3–5 cups of fruit and vegetables each day.

- If you fall short on fruits and vegetables, think 25% more. That means if you're eating 2 cups total each day for instance, try adding

How to Get Your Daily Fiber

You don't have to eat huge portions of plant foods to get the recommended 25–38 g of fiber daily. Here is an example of how you can fit that fiber in through three intentional food choices:

Food	Fiber
1/2 cup raspberries at breakfast	4 g
1 medium pear at lunch	5 g
1 cup navy beans at dinner	19 g
Total	**28 g**

1/2 cup more (25%), working toward the goal of 3–5 cups per day.

- Vary your fruit and vegetable choices. Choose these foods in different colors so you get a good mix of vitamins and minerals.
- Drink 4 oz (1/2 cup) of low-sodium tomato or vegetable juice for a quick and low-carbohydrate vegetable serving.
- Add fresh berries to your morning yogurt or oatmeal.
- Grill vegetable kabobs as part of a barbecue meal. Favorite grilled vegetables include cherry tomatoes, mushrooms, bell peppers, zucchini, squash, and onion chunks.

Eat fruits and vegetables with the edible skins on.

- A potato with the skin on has twice the fiber of a peeled potato.
- A 4-oz apple with skin on has double the fiber of a 1/2-cup portion of unsweetened applesauce, even though they both contain about 15 g carbohydrate.

Eat more legumes (dried beans, peas, and lentils).

- Add garbanzo beans (also known as chickpeas) or kidney beans to a salad.
- Have a cup of black bean, split pea, lentil, or navy bean soup at lunch.

3 Tips to Tolerate Fiber

1. Increase fiber intake slowly, to allow your body time to adapt.
2. Drink more water and liquids, because fiber soaks up liquids.
3. Try an enzyme-based dietary supplement designed to reduce gas and bloating (such as Beano).

- Spread mashed pinto beans on a whole-wheat tortilla, sprinkle lightly with low-fat cheese or diced avocado, and roll up.

Stick close to nature—the less processed the plant food, the more fiber it contains.

- A whole orange is more filling and has nearly three times more fiber than orange juice.
- Blend fruits and vegetables in a blender rather than "juicing" them. When you "juice," you don't get the fiber in whole fruits and vegetables.

Recipe Renewal: How to Fit in More Fiber

Fiber is loaded with health benefits! And for most, fitting more fiber into recipes is a good strategy for better health.

With even one intentional swap, you can fit more fiber into a variety of recipes from breakfast to lunch or dinner. Table 2.14 shows you a few swaps to get you on the way to filling up with more fiber, and the recipe *Banana Oat Muffins* on page 79 gives you a concrete example.

Switching out a few ingredients in a muffin recipe or "quick bread," such as banana bread, can increase fiber and reduce sugar, calories, and fat. Make one swap at a time and note the effect (see Table 2.15 for more).

Is It True You Need to Subtract Fiber from the Total Carbohydrate Count?

Have you heard talk about subtracting fiber off the total carbohydrate count to get what some call "net carbs"? Actually, for most people who count carbohydrate, figuring out net carbs is not routinely necessary. And it's one more calculation to have to do. Individuals who take mealtime insulin and adjust the dose based on their carbohydrate count may choose to do so when eating foods that contain a lot of fiber.

Cook's Notes: 3 Strategies to Fit in More Fiber

1. **Look for opportunities to fit in more vegetables (especially nonstarchy vegetables).** An example of fitting in more vegetables could be simply increasing the amount the recipe calls for (such as extra tomatoes or beans in chili, maybe in place of part of the beef). You could also top thin-crust pizza with peppers, onions, mushrooms, tomatoes, and hot peppers in place of meat toppings. Or you could fit in vegetables in unique ways (such as adding grated carrot to meatloaf, grated zucchini in a casserole, chopped broccoli or spinach to scrambled eggs, or kale to a smoothie).
2. **Bring on the beans.** Both cooked dried beans and canned beans are an excellent source of fiber. Drain and rinse canned beans to remove around 40% of the sodium.
3. **Experiment with a variety of whole grains**. Barley, buckwheat, bulgur, millet, quinoa, sorghum, and whole rye are all whole grains that can lend fiber and a different flavor profile to recipes, in place of white rice for instance. To save time, cook extra and freeze in portions to use later as a quick side dish.

TABLE 2.14 SWAPS TO FIT IN MORE FIBER

Recipe Ingredient	Healthy Swap
All-purpose flour	Whole-wheat flour replacing 1/4–1/2 of all-purpose flour
White rice	Barley, brown rice, farro, or quinoa
White pasta	Whole-wheat or fiber-enriched pasta
Bread crumbs (as a binder)	Rolled oats, instant barley, or almond meal
White bread or bread crumbs	Whole-wheat or whole-grain bread or bread crumbs
Ground beef	Replace half with brown lentils or cooked beans such as pinto beans, black beans, kidney beans, or Great Northern beans (if canned, drain and rinse to remove nearly half the sodium)
Fresh fruit, peeled	Fresh fruit with edible peels left on (such as apples, pears, peaches, and plums)

TABLE 2.15 SWAPS TO MAKE OVER MUFFINS OR BANANA BREAD

Use this . . .	Instead of this . . .	And you get . . .
Whole-wheat flour	All-purpose flour (swap for up to 1/2)	Increased fiber
1/4–1/2 cup mashed banana	1/4–1/2 cup oil	Increased flavor, reduced fat and calories
1/4–1/2 cup unsweetened applesauce	1/4–1/2 the oil	Reduced fat and calories
1/4 cup liquid egg substitute	One whole egg	Reduced fat and calories
Two egg whites	One whole egg	Reduced fat and calories
Double the vanilla extract	NA	Increased flavor
Almond extract (start with 1/4–1/2 tsp)	NA	Increased flavor
1/2 finely cup grated carrot	NA	Increased fiber, flavor, and moisture
1/4–1/3 less sugar Sugar baking blend	Full amount of sugar	Reduced sugar, carbohydrate, and calories

BANANA-OAT MUFFINS

Bananas get softer and sweeter as they ripen. "Overripe" bananas may be too mushy to eat raw, but they are perfect for adding to baked goods—they can replace some of the sugar and oil in baked goods while adding extra fiber and nutrients. In this "renewed recipe," you'll find fiber-rich oats and whole-wheat flour replacing white flour; mashed banana adding flavor and replacing some sugar and oil; and sweetness from the brown sugar substitute baking blend, cinnamon, and extract in place of some sugar.

THIS RECIPE CAN FIT IN THE FOLLOWING EATING PATTERNS: vegetarian, low-fat, low-carbohydrate, DASH

NUMBER OF SERVINGS: 15 | **SERVING SIZE:** 1 muffin per serving
PREP TIME: 15 minutes | **COOK TIME:** 20 minutes

INGREDIENTS

- 1 1/2 cups quick-cooking oats
- 1 cup whole-wheat flour
- 1 tsp baking powder
- 1 1/2 tsp ground cinnamon
- 1/2 tsp salt
- 3/4 cup 2% milk
- 1/3 cup brown sugar substitute blend, such as Splenda brown sugar baking blend
- 2 large eggs
- 3 Tbsp canola oil
- 1 1/2 tsp cake batter extract or vanilla
- 4 very ripe bananas, mashed (1 1/2 cups total)
- 3 oz chopped pecans

INSTRUCTIONS

1. Preheat oven to 350°F.
2. Spray two nonstick muffin pans with nonstick cooking spray.
3. Whisk together the oats, flour, baking powder, cinnamon, and salt in a large bowl until well blended.
4. Whisk together the milk, brown sugar substitute blend, eggs, oil, and extract in a medium bowl until well blended. Stir the bananas into the milk mixture until well blended.
5. Add to the flour mixture with the nuts and stir until *just* blended. Do not overmix.
6. Spoon into muffin cups, filling each about 3/4 full.
7. Bake 20 minutes or until wooden pick inserted comes out clean. Cool in pan 5 minutes. Remove from pan; serve warm or let cool to room temperature.

(Pointers on following page)

CHOICES: 1 Starch, 1/2 Carbohydrate, 1 1/2 Fat

BASIC NUTRITIONAL VALUES: Calories 180 | Calories from Fat 80 | **Total Fat** 9.0 g | Saturated Fat 1.1 g | Trans Fat 0.0 g | **Cholesterol** 25 mg | **Sodium** 120 mg | **Potassium** 200 mg | **Total Carbohydrate** 22 g | Dietary Fiber 3 g | Sugars 6 g | Added Sugars 2 g | **Protein** 4 g | **Phosphorus** 140 mg

▼ **POINTERS**

- Store leftovers in an airtight container up to 48 hours. If planning on storing longer, refrigerate or freeze for peak flavors.
- Store overripe bananas unpeeled in the freezer to use later in baking.
- To bring out the rich flavors, microwave on high setting 15–20 seconds or until warm.
- Add 2 tsp grated orange rind or grated ginger to batter for another layer of flavor.

Another breakfast favorite is French toast. Take a look at a simple recipe for this classic; think about some easy changes you can make to reduce the fat, sugar, and salt while increasing the fiber and flavor. Table 2.16 gives a list of common French toast ingredients and swaps you can make to the recipe. Make one swap at a time and note the effect. Then check out our "renewed recipe" *Creamy Yogurt and Berry–Topped French Toast* on page 81 to see how we used these tips to make our own healthier version.

TABLE 2.16   SWAPS TO TURNAROUND FRENCH TOAST

Use this . . .	Instead of this . . .	And you get . . .
100% whole-wheat bread	White bread	Increased fiber
Low-fat or fat-free milk	Whole milk	Reduced fat and calories
1/4 cup liquid egg substitute OR Two egg whites	One whole egg	Reduced fat and calories
1/2 tsp salt	1 tsp salt	Reduced salt/sodium
1 tsp extract (vanilla, almond, maple, raspberry, strawberry)	Sugar	Reduced sugar, carbohydrate, and calories; increased flavor
Cinnamon	NA	Increased flavor
Fresh berries or unsweetened frozen berries, thawed	Regular syrup	Increased fiber; decreased sugar
Sugar-free syrup	Regular syrup	Reduced sugar and calories

CREAMY YOGURT AND BERRY–TOPPED FRENCH TOAST

This "renewed recipe" uses 100% whole-wheat bread instead of white bread, which adds fiber; 2 egg whites in place of 1 whole egg to reduce fat and cholesterol; and reduced-fat milk and Greek yogurt in place of full-fat varieties. The sweetness comes from stevia, cinnamon, and fresh strawberries instead of added sugar or syrup.

THIS RECIPE CAN FIT IN THE FOLLOWING EATING PATTERNS: vegetarian, low-carbohydrate, DASH

NUMBER OF SERVINGS: 4 | **SERVING SIZE:** 2 slices French toast, 1/4 cup yogurt mixture, and 1/2 cup strawberries per serving

PREP TIME: 15 minutes | **COOK TIME:** 10 minutes

INGREDIENTS

- 1 cup plain 2% Greek yogurt
- 2 tsp vanilla extract, divided use
- 4 individual packets stevia
- 1/8 tsp salt
- 8 slices 100% whole-wheat bread, divided use
- 4 large eggs
- 2 egg whites
- 3/4 cup 2% milk
- 1 tsp ground cinnamon
- 2 Tbsp canola oil, divided use
- 2 cups sliced strawberries

(Pointers on following page)

INSTRUCTIONS

1. Whisk together the yogurt, 1 tsp of the vanilla, stevia, and salt in a small bowl and set aside.
2. Place 4 bread slices on the bottom of a 9 × 13-inch baking pan.
3. Whisk together the eggs, egg whites, milk, remaining 1 tsp vanilla, and cinnamon in a medium bowl or 2-cup measuring cup until well blended.
4. Pour half of the egg mixture over the bread slices and gently turn bread slices over several times to coat.
5. Heat a large nonstick skillet over medium-low heat. Add 1 Tbsp of the oil, tilt to coat bottom lightly. Add the 4 egg-soaked bread slices and cook 2 minutes on each side or until lightly golden.
6. Set cooked bread slices aside on separate plate and cover to keep warm. Repeat steps 2–5 with the rest of the egg mixture, bread slices, and remaining 1 Tbsp oil.
7. Serve topped with equal amounts of the yogurt mixture and berries.

CHOICES: 1 1/2 Starch, 1/2 Fruit, 1/2 Reduced-Fat Milk, 2 Medium-Fat Protein, 1/2 Fat

BASIC NUTRITIONAL VALUES: Calories 380 | Calories from Fat 140 | **Total Fat** 16.0 g | Saturated Fat 3.7 g | Trans Fat 0.1 g | **Cholesterol** 195 mg | **Sodium** 470 mg | **Potassium** 510 mg | **Total Carbohydrate** 36 g | Dietary Fiber 5 g | Sugars 12 g | Added Sugars 0 g | **Protein** 23 g | **Phosphorus** 360 mg

POINTERS

- Placing the bread slices in a shallow casserole dish makes for easier coverage of the bread slices, and doing it in batches helps keep the bread intact rather than falling apart.
- Salt may seem like a surprising addition to vanilla, but adding a small amount of salt will provide a richer, creamier taste to the yogurt without adding more fat.

6 Pointers if your blood pressure is high (>120/80 mmHg)

1. Decrease sodium toward 2,300 mg/day.
2. If overweight, work on weight loss (even a 5- to 10-lb loss can make an impact).
3. Embrace a DASH-style eating pattern (reviewed in Chapter 3).
4. Moderate alcohol intake (if you choose to drink alcohol). *Moderate is defined as no more than one alcoholic drink per day for women and no more than two drinks per day for men.*
5. Move more; sit less.
6. Increase potassium intake (unless your health-care team advises against it because of other health conditions).

SODIUM

Why the Concern about Sodium?

Too much sodium can lead to significant health problems. One big concern is high blood pressure, which is common among many people with type 2 diabetes. High blood pressure, in turn, may increase your risk for heart disease, stroke, kidney disease, and damage to vision. There is wide agreement in the health-care world that the average American's sodium intake of 3,500 mg/day is excessive and should be reduced, especially to manage blood pressure. For people with diabetes, as for the general public, the goal is to scale sodium back and *hold your overall daily sodium intake to 2,300 mg or less.* (Significantly lower sodium goals may be considered on an individual basis. However, preference, palatability, availability, and cost of low-sodium foods are factors that must be considered.)

To put that 2,300-mg goal in perspective, *1 tsp salt contains about 2,300 mg sodium.* Sodium is found in most food categories. Most sodium consumed in the U.S. comes from salt added during commercial food processing and preparation. Table 2.17 shows how the sodium in processed, canned foods compares to the sodium in fresh version.

Finding Sodium

On food packages, the Nutrition Facts label is the best place to find information about sodium. (Learn more about the Nutrition Facts label in Chapter 5). This information can guide you in making lower-sodium choices.

TABLE 2.17	HOW THE SODIUM IN PROCESSED, CANNED FOODS COMPARES TO THE SODIUM IN FRESH AND FROZEN VERSIONS
Food	**Sodium**
1/2 cup canned corn, plain	175 mg
1/2 cup frozen corn, plain	1 mg
1/2 cup canned diced tomatoes	130 mg
1/2 cup fresh diced tomatoes	5 mg

So what's the takeaway? Sticking close to nature saves sodium.

Although labels may grab your attention with a claim that a food is "low sodium" or "reduced sodium," check the exact sodium content on the Nutrition Facts label to see how it measures up against your sodium goals. *Generally, aim for single servings of a food with <400 mg sodium and meals with <800 mg sodium.*

If you see the following claims on labels, here's what they mean:

- **Salt/sodium-free:** <5 mg sodium per serving
- **Very-low-sodium:** 35 mg sodium or less per serving
- **Low-sodium:** 140 mg sodium or less per serving
- **Reduced-sodium:** At least 25% less sodium than in the original product
- **Light-in-sodium or lightly salted:** At least 50% less sodium than the regular product

- **No-salt-added or unsalted:** No salt added during processing, but the product is not necessarily sodium-free

Foods that are high in sodium may not necessarily taste salty. Check out the sodium content of the foods in Table 2.18, remembering that <2,300 mg per day is the goal.

7 Simple Steps to Shake Down Sodium

1. **Stick close to nature.** The easiest way to limit sodium is to choose fresh, whole foods that are as close to their natural state as possible. Although small amounts of sodium are naturally present in whole foods, the content is minimal compared with that in processed foods.

2. **Rinse and drain canned vegetables and beans** to remove up to 40% of the sodium.

TABLE 2.18   SURPRISING SODIUM LEVELS IN SOME FOODS

We all seem to know that things like potato chips and frozen foods can be high in sodium. But sodium is sometimes found in surprising places, as this table shows.

Food	Sodium
1/4 cup salsa from a jar	389 mg
3 oz turkey lunchmeat	660 mg
2 slices of 14-inch thin-crust cheese pizza	760 mg
1 cup canned chunky chicken noodle soup (that's not even half the can!)	850 mg
1 cup low-fat cottage cheese	918 mg
1 Tbsp soy sauce	1,005 mg

4 Swaps to make over condiments

Condiments often add a significant amount of sodium. Here are four condiment swaps that lower sodium. These ideas may get you thinking about other swaps you could make.

1.   Swap in sliced cucumbers for pickles on a sandwich.
2.   Swap in cherry tomatoes for olives at happy hour.
3.   Swap in whole-grain mustard for yellow mustard (many of the whole-grain or stoneground mustards are lower in sodium per serving).
4.   Swap in mashed avocado for mayonnaise on a sandwich or burger.

3.   **Go for fresh meat when you can.** Fresh foods are generally lower in sodium. Meats and poultry may be brined, so check the Nutrition Facts label closely for sodium content. Go for fresh or frozen (not processed) poultry, pork, and lean meat rather than canned, smoked, or processed meats like luncheon meats, sausages, and corned beef.
4.   **Consider your condiments.** Sodium in barbecue sauce, ketchup, salad dressing, soy sauce, and many other condiments adds up quickly. Choose "lite" or reduced-sodium soy sauce and no-salt-added ketchup. Add oil and vinegar to a salad rather than bottled salad dressings, and brush meats lightly with barbecue sauce rather than slathering on the barbecue sauce.

5. **Choose no-salt-added** canned goods or plain frozen or steam-in-the-bag vegetables without added sauces.
6. **Omit salt** from the water when cooking pasta and rice.
7. **Use a salt grinder to help manage added salt.** Grinding salt is an easy way to add small, controlled amounts. You can even measure with a measuring spoon what each grind yields. Disposable prefilled salt (and pepper) grinders are inexpensive and usually found in the spice section.

Do You Savor the Flavor of Salt? Reset Your Salt Preference

The taste for salt is an acquired one. Just as you can become used to the taste of salty foods, you can "unlearn" that taste preference—in as little as a week—as Tami has seen in many clients. Over time, the less salt- and sodium-rich foods you eat, the lower your salt threshold or preference will become. You'll be able to taste the salt at lower amounts. For instance, a regular salted-top cracker may taste too salty once you are used to lightly salted crackers.

While working toward "resetting" your salt preference or threshold, focus on adding in other flavorful ingredients and begin to appreciate the natural flavor of your food. Tami will never forget hearing a client proclaim, "Wow, I never realized how flavorful green beans are. Now that I've gotten used to less salt, I am appreciating their natural flavor."

Salt Substitutes: At a Glance

Salt substitutes typically come in a shaker and resemble salt. Familiar brands include Morton Salt Substitute and NoSalt. The key difference is that salt substitutes contain potassium chloride instead of sodium chloride. Potassium chloride tastes somewhat like sodium chloride (salt), although some people complain of a metallic taste. Be cautious about salt substitutes with potassium chloride. Excess potassium can be a problem for people with certain heart conditions, kidney problems, or people who take certain blood pressure medications. Your RDN or diabetes health-care team can help you decide if including a salt substitute is the right choice for you.

The taste for salt is an acquired one, and you can "unlearn" that preference.

Flavor Boosters to Help Reset Salt Preference

- **Herbs,** such as green onion, basil, cilantro, parsley, or red pepper flakes
- **Aromatics,** such as ginger or garlic

> **Tip**
>
> You can swap fresh and dried herbs in many recipes.
>
> **1 Tbsp fresh herbs** = 1 tsp dried herbs.

- **Vinegars,** such as balsamic, red wine, white wine, or rice
- **Citrus juices,** such as lemon or lime
- **Strong veggies,** such as spinach or kale
- **Mushrooms,** which boost the savory umami flavor
- **Salt-free seasoning blends,** such as Mrs. Dash or McCormick Perfect Pinch

10 Ways to Cut Back Sodium Without Sacrificing Taste

1. Whisk 1/8 tsp dried thyme or oregano instead of salt into eggs or liquid egg substitute before scrambling.
2. Season mashed potatoes with dried, crushed rosemary, garlic powder, and black pepper in place of salt and butter.
3. Use crushed red pepper flakes to turn up the flavor in everything from soups, to meats, to salads, or even pizza.
4. Forgo the butter, sour cream, and salt on your baked potato and instead drizzle with 1 tsp olive oil mixed with a sprinkle of fresh chives.
5. Dress up your favorite oil and vinegar dressing with 1/4–1/2 tsp dried thyme.
6. Add a splash of flavor, instead of a shake of salt, with balsamic vinegar, white wine vinegar, red wine vinegar, or other flavored vinegar.
7. Finish off asparagus, broccoli, a green salad, or fish with a squeeze of fresh lemon or lime juice and fresh ground pepper.
8. Add a dash of chili powder or smoked paprika to corn instead of salt.
9. Add aromatic ingredients, like onion, green onion, garlic, and ginger, to your dishes.
10. Sample a salt-free herb seasoning blend in place of salt. For examples, check out our *Mediterranean Herb Blend* and *Taco/Chili Seasoning Mix* on pages 87–88.

MEDITERRANEAN HERB BLEND

Salt-free blends can all taste the same after a while and can be costly. But this aromatic Mediterranean-style salt-free herb blend will have you reaching for it while saving some cash! The secret is in the "kick" from the fragrant rosemary, the heat from the pepper flakes, and the color from dried mustard, and the end result is beautiful. Use it on chicken, pork, seafood, and steamed veggies.

THIS RECIPE CAN FIT IN THE FOLLOWING EATING PATTERNS: All

MAKES ABOUT 1/4 cup total
PREP TIME: 3 minutes

INGREDIENTS

- 2 Tbsp dried basil
- 1 Tbsp dried oregano
- 2 tsp dried rosemary
- 1 1/2 tsp onion powder
- 1 tsp garlic powder
- 1/2 tsp dried mustard
- 1/4 tsp crushed pepper flakes

INSTRUCTIONS

1. Combine all ingredients in a small jar. Secure with lid. Shake until well blended.
2. Store at room temperature.

POINTER

- Use this herb blend to season lean fish, chicken, or pork. Sprinkle over both sides of the meat, and then cook in the oven, on the stove, or on the grill. Finish with a splash of lemon juice at time of serving.

CHOICES: Free Food
BASIC NUTRITIONAL VALUES: This recipe does not contain significant nutritional content.

TACO/CHILI SEASONING MIX

Seasoning packets, such as chili seasoning, can be loaded with sodium (even the lower-sodium varieties) and taste relatively bland. In this salt-free mix, instant coffee granules add "meatiness" along with smoked paprika.

THIS RECIPE CAN FIT IN THE FOLLOWING EATING PATTERNS: All

MAKES ABOUT 1/3 cup total
PREP TIME: 3 minutes

INGREDIENTS

- 2 Tbsp chili powder
- 1 Tbsp smoked paprika
- 1 1/2 Tbsp ground cumin
- 1 Tbsp dried oregano
- 2 tsp instant coffee granules
- 2 tsp coarsely ground black pepper

INSTRUCTIONS

1. Combine all ingredients in a small jar. Secure with lid. Shake until well blended.
2. Store at room temperature.

POINTERS

- Using homemade spice and herb blends without salt allows you to control how much salt ends up in your dish. Start by seasoning your dish with the spice blend. Taste while cooking, and then add salt a little bit at a time if needed.
- While this seasoning mix is designed for tacos and chili, it's also great for a single cut of meat like a chicken breast, pork chop, or sirloin, or other dishes, such as soups, stews, kabobs, or grain bowls. Or, stir some into plain fat-free Greek yogurt to serve on top of tacos or chili.

CHOICES: Free Food
BASIC NUTRITIONAL VALUES: This recipe does not contain significant nutritional content.

Recipe Renewal: How to Shake off Salt

When considering how to shake off some salt to renew a favorite recipe, keep in mind salt's function in foods. Salt generally has one of these functions:

- Adds flavor
- Helps preserve food
- Aids in the rising of yeast breads

With salt adding so much to the flavor of foods, it can be tricky to cut sodium without feeling everything will be bland and tasteless. Fortunately, that's not the case. See Table 2.19 for more ideas on how to lower sodium in foods.

For example, consider chili. Chili is an ultimate cold-weather comfort food and one-pot meal. It's also an easy slow-cooker meal and

Cook's Notes: 7 Strategies to Reduce Salt

1. **Add salt at the end of cooking or on the surface of a food (instead of mixing it in).** You'll use less and taste it more.
2. **Taste your food before adding salt.** That may seem logical, but shaking on salt before ever tasting the food can become a habit for some. Removing the saltshaker from the table is a simple way to slash salt intake.
3. **Swap in herbs and spices as a replacement for part or all of the salt in recipes.** Herbs such as basil, bay leaves, dill, parsley, sage, tarragon, and thyme are versatile. Spices such as cayenne, cinnamon, garlic, ginger, black pepper, and lemon pepper are flavorful in a variety of foods. Or switch in one of the many salt-free seasoning blends.
4. **Pump up freshly ground pepper.** Freshly ground black pepper from a grinder has a striking flavor difference as opposed to fine ground black pepper. You'll see that many of the recipes in this book incorporating black pepper call for fresh or course ground pepper for that reason.
5. **Trim the salt in recipes.** In many recipes, the amount of salt can be cut in half without much change in taste or texture, and in some cases, salt can be completely eliminated.
6. **Substitute lower-sodium versions.** A few ideas include using no-salt-added canned vegetables, unsalted stock or broth, reduced-sodium soy sauce, and reduced-sodium seasoning blends.
7. **Cut back on high-sodium foods in your recipes.** You may find you can eliminate, or cut by half, salty recipe ingredients such as ham, pickles, olives, salted nuts, mustard, ketchup, and barbecue sauce.

one that freezes well to grab and go on busy days and have in the freezer for backup meals. It's great. It is also often packed with salt and sodium. Table 2.20 gives you a few swaps to keep chili hearty and satisfying but healthier. Make one swap at a time so you can note the effect, and than check out our *Hearty Turkey Chili with Beans* on page 92.

TABLE 2.19 INGREDIENT SWAPS TO REDUCE SODIUM/SALT	
Recipe Ingredient	**Healthy Swap**
Salt	Reduce amount by half or eliminate (unless yeast baked good, which requires salt for leavening)
	Fresh or dried herbs and spices, salt-free seasoning, black pepper, or lemon pepper
	Aromatic ingredients like onion, green onion, garlic, and ginger
Salt on vegetables	Squeeze of fresh lemon or lime juice
	Splash of flavored vinegar (such as red wine, white wine, balsamic, or rice wine)
Salt in cooking water	Omit the salt when boiling potatoes or when cooking pasta, rice, or other grains
Seasoned salts (such as garlic salt or onion salt)	Salt-free herb and spice seasonings such as garlic powder, onion powder, onion flakes, or celery seed
Soy sauce	Reduced-sodium soy sauce
Broth or stock	Low-sodium or unsalted broth or stock
Canned vegetables	No-salt-added canned vegetables and tomato products (rinse and drain canned vegetables to remove close to half of the sodium)
	Plain frozen vegetables

TABLE 2.20　SWAPS TO GIVE YOUR CHILI A MAKEOVER

Use this . . .	Instead of this . . .	And you get . . .
Chili powder, cumin, and cayenne pepper	Premixed chili seasoning	Reduced sodium; increased flavor
Splash of fresh lime juice or cider vinegar	NA	Brightened flavor
Lean ground turkey	Ground beef (or reduce the ground beef and mix together)	Reduced fat and calories
One or more beans (pinto, kidney, Great Northern, navy, black beans), rinsed and drained to reduce sodium	Ground beef (or reduce the ground beef and mix together)	Increased fiber; reduced fat and calories
Whole grains (such as farro, barley, bulgur, or wheat berries)	Part of meat	Increased fiber and flavor; reduced fat and calories
Cubed zucchini, peppers, and carrots in addition to tomatoes	Part or all of meat	Increased fiber and flavor
No-salt-added canned tomatoes	Regular canned tomatoes	Reduced sodium
Fresh toppings such as chopped avocado, cilantro, and diced red onion	Shredded cheese	Reduced fat and calories
Fat-free Greek yogurt or fat-free sour cream for topping	Sour cream	Reduced fat and calories

HEARTY TURKEY CHILI WITH BEANS

Chili is satisfying right off the stove and is one of those recipes that just keeps getting better, whether you serve it the next day or the day after, freeze it, or reheat it. This "renewed recipe" holds down the salt while it pumps up the flavor with oregano; the heady, smoky aroma of cumin; and a little help from smoked paprika! Lean ground turkey is swapped in place of ground beef to reduce fat, with peppers and kidney beans adding bulk, fiber, and flavor to the chili.

THIS RECIPE CAN FIT IN THE FOLLOWING EATING PATTERNS: low-fat, low- or very-low-carbohydrate, DASH

NUMBER OF SERVINGS: 6 | **SERVING SIZE:** About 1 1/4 cups per serving

PREP TIME: 10 minutes | **COOK TIME:** 30 minutes

INGREDIENTS

- 1 Tbsp canola oil
- 1 lb 93% lean ground turkey
- 1 (15-oz) can no-salt-added kidney beans, rinsed and drained
- 1 (14-oz) package frozen pepper stir-fry
- 1 (14.5-oz) can no-salt-added stewed tomatoes
- 12 oz light beer, such as Miller Lite, or 1 1/2 cups unsalted beef stock
- 1/4 cup chili powder
- 2 tsp smoked paprika
- 2 tsp dried oregano
- 1/2 tsp salt
- 5 tsp ground cumin, divided use

INSTRUCTIONS

1. Heat oil in a Dutch oven or large saucepan over medium-high heat. Add the turkey and cook 3 minutes or until no longer pink, stirring occasionally. Add the remaining chili ingredients, except 2 tsp of the cumin.

2. Bring to a boil, reduce heat, and simmer, uncovered, for 25 minutes or until peppers are very tender and mixture has thickened. Stir in remaining 2 tsp cumin. Serve immediately with optional toppings (see Pointers), or cool and refrigerate or freeze for later.

CHOICES: 1/2 Starch, 3 Nonstarchy Vegetable, 2 Lean Protein, 1 Fat

BASIC NUTRITIONAL VALUES: Calories 270 | Calories from Fat 90 | **Total Fat** 10.0 g | Saturated Fat 2.0 g | Trans Fat 0.1 g | **Cholesterol** 55 mg | **Sodium** 320 mg | **Potassium** 710 mg | **Total Carbohydrate** 24 g | Dietary Fiber 7 g | Sugars 7 g | Added Sugars 0 g | **Protein** 21 g | **Phosphorus** 265 mg

COOK'S SWAPS

- If no-salt-added stewed tomatoes are unavailable, use the regular variety, but reduce added salt to 1/4 tsp instead of 1/2 tsp.
- For a vegetarian or vegan dish, substitute the ground turkey with a 15-oz can no-salt-added black beans, rinsed and drained. Use beer or vegetable broth instead of beef broth.

POINTERS

- Flavors improve overnight in the refrigerator.
- Be sure to use smoked paprika rather than plain paprika for the flavor.
- Top each serving with 2 Tbsp 2% plain Greek yogurt and diced onion, if desired.
- This dish freezes well. Freeze in portion-size amounts to eliminate the guesswork. For best results when reheating, thaw in the refrigerator first, and then microwave until heated through. Or, reheat in a saucepan on the stove.

Trick

- Adding a small amount of the cumin at the end of the cooking time brings out the flavor of the cumin without giving a "musky" taste to the dish, which happens when too much cumin is added during the cooking process.

Besides chili, consider green bean casserole. For over 50 years, green bean casserole has been a favorite dish found on many tables, especially during the holiday season. This casserole is traditionally made with canned green beans, canned cream soup, milk, sour cream, and canned fried onions. That is a lot of canned foods with a lot of sodium. Table 2.21 shows a few swaps to reduce sodium, saturated fat, and calories. Make one swap at a time and note the effect.

POTASSIUM

Most of the nutrients we've covered in this chapter are the big hitters—carbohydrate, fat, protein, fiber, and sodium—so why devote an entire section to potassium? Because potassium helps to lower or control blood pressure, and that's incredibly important for people with diabetes. While the goal is to eat less sodium, the opposite is generally true for potassium. It is important to note that excess potassium can be a problem for people with certain heart conditions or kidney problems or people who take

TABLE 2.21 SWAPS TO MAKE OVER OLD-FASHIONED GREEN BEAN CASSEROLE

Use this . . .	Instead of this . . .	And you get . . .
Steam-in-the-bag green beans or no-salt-added canned green beans	Regular canned green beans	Reduced sodium
Reduced-sodium, reduced-fat cream of mushroom soup (such as Campbell's Healthy Request)	Regular cream of mushroom soup	Reduced saturated fat and sodium
Fat-free milk or unsweetened almond milk	Whole milk	Reduced fat and calories
Light sour cream	Regular sour cream	Reduced fat and calories
Chow mein noodles	Canned fried onions	Reduced fat and calories
1/2 the amount fried onions, crushed (crushed onions covers casserole to impart flavor with less)	Regular amount of canned fried onions	Reduced fat and calories
Fresh onions lightly sautéed or roasted/caramelized with a splash of olive oil	Regular canned fried onions	Reduced fat and calories
Toasted sliced almonds	1/2 or all of regular canned fried onions	Reduced saturated fat

certain medications. Your RDN or diabetes health-care team can help you decide if including more potassium is the right choice for you.

Eating foods high in potassium can help lower blood pressure by reducing the adverse effects of sodium on blood pressure. In general, adults need around 4,700 mg daily (unless you have a health reason to consume less). Potassium is often under-consumed. An easy way to bump up potassium is to eat more fruits, vegetables, and legumes. The DASH-style eating pattern reviewed in Chapter 3 emphasizes potassium-rich foods.

Choose Potassium-Rich Foods More Often

Bananas are one familiar source of potassium, but there are many more potassium-rich foods. Examples include:

- Apricots
- Beet greens

- Citrus fruits
- Juices (such as carrot, orange, pomegranate, and prune)
- Leafy greens
- Lentils
- Milk
- Nuts
- Potatoes
- Some fish (cod, halibut, salmon, trout, tuna)
- Soybeans
- Spinach
- Sweet potatoes
- Tomatoes and tomato products
- White beans
- Yogurt (fat-free and low-fat)

Food manufacturers now list potassium content and the % Daily Value (% DV) of potassium per serving on the Nutrition Facts label. Learn more about the Nutrition Facts food label in Chapter 5.

With even one intentional swap, you can fit more potassium into a variety of recipes from breakfast to lunch or supper. Table 2.22 includes a few swaps to get you on the way to getting enough potassium in your day.

One Way to Get Half of Your Daily Potassium in One Meal

Would you like to get 2,351 mg in one meal? Then try this!

- 3 oz cooked salmon (534 mg)
- 1 medium sweet potato with skin (542 mg)
- 1/2 medium sliced avocado with 1 cup diced tomato drizzled with olive oil vinaigrette (893 mg)
- 1 cup skim milk (382 mg)

Recipe Renewal: How to Fortify Flavor

No matter how healthy the recipe, good taste and flavor are the most important ingredients. Consumer research shows that taste is actually the top reason Americans favor one food over another. With that said, it stands to reason that if you're reducing some ingredients in a recipe to cut back on fat, sugar, and salt, you may need to fortify flavor in other ways. Check out our *Chili'd Buttery Shrimp* on page 98 to see how we were able to boost flavor but keep things healthy.

TABLE 2.22   TIPS TO SWAP IN MORE POTASSIUM

Use this . . .	Instead of this . . .	And you get . . .
Spinach, raw (167 mg/cup)	Iceberg lettuce, chopped (78 mg/cup)	Increased potassium
Plain low-fat yogurt (573 mg/cup)	Sour cream (331 mg/cup)	Increased potassium; decreased fat and calories
Shelled edamame, cooked (676 mg/cup)	Green peas (195 mg/cup)	Increased potassium and protein
Cooked beet greens (1,310 mg/cup)	Cooked collard greens (222 mg/cup)	Increased potassium
Mashed avocado as a sandwich spread (140 mg/2 Tbsp)	Mayonnaise as a sandwich spread (5 mg/2 Tbsp)	Increased potassium and healthy fats; decreased calories
Sliced banana in a fruit salad (537 mg/cup)	Sliced apple in a fruit salad (118 mg/cup)	Increased potassium

Cook's Notes: 5 Tips to Enrich and Enhance Flavor

1. **Start with the freshest ingredients.** While fresh fruits and vegetables are ideal, frozen versions are generally frozen immediately after picking, so they retain flavor better than the canned, processed versions. Also, they're lower in sodium. You may consider a patio or backyard garden, frequenting the local farmer's market, or joining a community-supported agriculture (CSA) with a local farm to access the freshest and locally grown produce.
2. **Experiment with herbs.** For easy access, you may choose to have a windowsill herb garden or try an indoor gardening kit, such as the popular AeroGarden. These are fool-proof, dirt-free, indoor gardens where you can grow a variety of herbs, vegetables, and other plants. Either way, you can have fresh herbs to snip. *Here are three tips on how to incorporate herbs:*
    o Keep in mind that dried herbs are stronger flavored than fresh herbs. So if using dried herbs, swap 1 tsp of a dried herb in place of 1 Tbsp of the fresh variety.

(continued)

Cook's Notes: 5 Tips to Enrich and Enhance Flavor *(continued)*

- For chilled foods, such as salad dressings and dips, add herbs several hours before serving to allow time for their flavors to blend.
- For hot dishes, such as soups or sauces, add fresh herbs toward the end of the cooking time, so the flavor doesn't cook away.

3. **Pep up flavor with peppers.** Try fresh green, red, yellow, and orange peppers of all types, from sweet to heat. Use fresh or dried peppers. Or, add a dash of hot pepper sauce or red chili paste.

4. **Add tang with grated lemon, lime, or orange peel or juice.** The acidic ingredients help elevate and balance flavor with minimal calories.

5. **Add a burst of flavor with an intensely flavored condiment.** Fresh fruit or vegetable salsa, horseradish, and wasabi are three ways to add flavor without lots of sodium, fat, or calories.

Practice fortifying flavor with the following recipes. These recipes are packed with herbs, spices, and other flavorful ingredients, so they are bursting with flavor without lots of added salt.

CHILI'D BUTTERY SHRIMP

Flavor pops in this recipe from the herbs, spices, aromatic onion, and fresh lemon without added salt. Many people aren't aware that shrimp and chili powder already have some salt, so no need to add more. While the light butter does contain a little salt as well, adding it at the end helps keep the sodium "up front" instead of getting lost or absorbed into the ingredients while cooking. You taste it more! This is a great tip you can consider putting into practice with other recipes.

THIS RECIPE CAN FIT IN THE FOLLOWING EATING PATTERNS: low-fat, low- or very-low-carbohydrate, DASH

NUMBER OF SERVINGS: 4 | **SERVING SIZE:** 1/2 cup per serving
PREP TIME: 7 minutes | **COOK TIME:** 7 minutes

INGREDIENTS

- 1 cup chopped onion
- 1 lb peeled raw shrimp
- 1 Tbsp chili powder
- 1/2 tsp dried oregano
- 1/2 tsp garlic powder
- 1/8 tsp cayenne pepper
- 1 lemon
- 1/4 cup light butter with canola oil

INSTRUCTIONS

1. Heat a large nonstick skillet over medium heat. Coat skillet with nonstick cooking spray, add onions, and cook 3 minutes or until golden. Add the shrimp, chili powder, oregano, garlic powder, and cayenne pepper. Cook 4 minutes or until shrimp is opaque in the center.
2. Remove from heat. Cut lemon in half and squeeze the juice of a lemon half over the dish, and stir in the light butter until melted. Serve in shallow bowls. Cut remaining lemon half into four wedges and serve alongside the shrimp.

CHOICES: 1/2 Carbohydrate, 3 Lean Protein
BASIC NUTRITIONAL VALUES: Calories 170 | Calories from Fat 60 | **Total Fat** 7.0 g | Saturated Fat 2.1 g | Trans Fat 0.0 g | **Cholesterol** 180 mg | **Sodium** 210 mg | **Potassium** 360 mg | **Total Carbohydrate** 6 g | Dietary Fiber 1 g | Sugars 2 g | Added Sugars 0 g | **Protein** 23 g | **Phosphorus** 240 mg

COOK'S SWAP

- For a Mediterranean-style twist, substitute light butter with 2 Tbsp extra-virgin olive oil.
- Serve over a mixture of 1 (8.8-oz) package prepared brown rice, such as Uncle Ben's Ready Rice and/or 1 cup no-salt-added black beans for a quick high-fiber, one-dish meal.
- For a low-carb meal, serve over salad greens with avocado and a light creamy ranch-style dressing.

TIKKA MASALA–STYLE CHICKEN AND VEGETABLES

"Tikka masala" is simply an Indian-style dish of small pieces of meat (in this case, chicken) in a creamy mildly spiced sauce. Creaminess in this dish comes from the light coconut milk. To minimize sodium, flavor is boosted by aromatic onion, sweet raisins, spicy curry powder, ginger, cilantro, and a surprise ingredient—hot sauce! A dash of hot sauce is a great way to use less sodium but still get plenty of flavor. So instead of reaching for the saltshaker, try a dash of hot sauce on foods. Choose a hot sauce that's on the mild side, such as Frank's or Crystal, if you shy away from really hot flavors.

THIS RECIPE CAN FIT IN THE FOLLOWING EATING PATTERNS: low-fat, low-carbohydrate, DASH

NUMBER OF SERVINGS: 4 | **SERVING SIZE:** 1 cup per serving
PREP TIME: 15 minutes | **COOK TIME:** 36 minutes | Stand time: 30 minutes

INGREDIENTS

- 12 oz boneless, skinless chicken thigh meat, cut into bite-size pieces (about 1-inch pieces)
- 1 cup chopped onion
- 1 1/2 cups frozen sliced carrots
- 1 (8-oz) can no-salt-added tomato sauce
- 3/4 cup water
- 1/4 cup raisins
- 2 tsp curry powder
- 1 cup plus 2 Tbsp light coconut milk
- 3/4 cup frozen, thawed green peas
- 2 tsp grated ginger
- 2 tsp hot sauce, such as Frank's
- 1/4 tsp salt
- 1/2 cup chopped fresh cilantro
- 1 (8.8-oz) package prepared brown rice, such as Uncle Ben's Ready Rice

INSTRUCTIONS

1. Heat a large nonstick skillet coated with nonstick cooking spray over medium-high heat. Add chicken and onion, and cook 6 minutes or until beginning to lightly brown on edges, stirring occasionally. Add carrots, tomato sauce, water, raisins, and curry powder. Bring to a boil over medium-high heat, reduce heat to low, cover, and cook 25 minutes or until carrots are very tender.

2. Stir the coconut milk, peas, ginger, hot sauce, and salt into the chicken mixture and cook 5 minutes.

3. Remove from heat, stir in the cilantro, cover, and let stand 30 minutes to blend flavors and bring out the sweetness.

4. At time of serving, prepare rice according to package directions, spoon equal amounts into each of four shallow bowls, and spoon chicken mixture over rice.

COOK'S SWAPS

- For a vegetarian and a vegan dish, substitute chicken with firm tofu cut into cubes or 1 (15-oz) can of no-salt-added chickpeas, rinsed and drained.
- For a low-carb dish, serve over riced cauliflower instead of brown rice.

Tricks

- Adding raisins is the "sweet" secret to this recipe. The sweetness of the dried fruit is released slowly while providing a bit of texture and fiber to the dish.
- Adding grated fresh ginger to a dish helps to bring out the sweetness of the dish while providing a kick of heat.

POINTERS

- Don't skip the 30-minute stand time . . . it's crucial to the overall flavor of the dish.
- This is a great make-ahead dish because the flavors blend and intensify with time in the refrigerator, so it's even better the next day. To reheat, place in a medium saucepan and cook, covered, over medium heat until heated through.
- There's a wide variety of coconut milk on the shelves. For this recipe, you want the kind of coconut milk that is sold in cans, not the nondairy milk substitute varieties sold in cartons. Standard coconut milk contains coconut cream as well as coconut milk, which makes it high in fat. Be sure to buy the "lite" or "light" coconut milk variety, which has the lowest fat content.

CHOICES: 1 1/2 Starch, 1/2 Fruit, 2 Nonstarchy Vegetable, 2 Lean Protein, 1 Fat

BASIC NUTRITIONAL VALUES: Calories 330 | Calories from Fat 100 | **Total Fat** 11.0 g | Saturated Fat 5.0 g | Trans Fat 0.0 g | **Cholesterol** 75 mg | **Sodium** 380 mg | **Potassium** 850 mg | **Total Carbohydrate** 41 g | Dietary Fiber 6 g | Sugars 14 g | Added Sugars 0 g | **Protein** 21 g | **Phosphorus** 320 mg

ALCOHOL AND DIABETES: HOW DO THEY MIX?

We will close out this chapter with a few words about alcohol, how to incorporate it in a safe manner if you choose to drink, and share a "mocktail" recipe as a nonalcoholic option to cocktails, as well as a wonderful, soothing hot drink.

. . . .

The American Diabetes Association recommends no more than one alcoholic drink per day for women and no more than two drinks per day for men.

. . . .

Whether it's a beer with friends after work, a glass of wine at a dinner party, or a champagne toast on New Year's Eve, alcoholic beverages are frequently part of today's social life. So, you may be wondering how alcohol and diabetes mix. Ultimately, alcohol intake is an individual choice, taking into account any potential medication interactions. If you like to enjoy an occasional alcoholic beverage, the good news is that you most likely can continue to do so (unless some of your medications or other health conditions prevent it). Moderation is the key. As noted earlier in this chapter, the American Diabetes Association recommends no more than one alcoholic drink per day for women and no more than two drinks per day for men. This consumption is moderate and sensible and generally has minimal short- or long-term negative effects on blood glucose in adults with type 2 diabetes. In fact, some data show improved blood glucose and insulin sensitivity with moderate intake. (However, evidence does *not* suggest to start consuming alcohol if you don't already.) That said, more than three drinks a day for men (or 21 drinks a week) and more than two drinks a day for women (or 14 drinks a week) on a consistent basis may contribute to elevated blood glucose.

What Counts as One Drink?

One alcoholic drink has about 100 calories and is equal to:

- 12 oz beer
- 5 oz dry red or white wine
- 5 oz champagne
- 1 1/2 oz distilled spirits
- 3 1/2 oz dessert wine

3 Considerations If You Choose to Sip an Occasional Alcoholic Beverage

1. **Calories.** Alcohol has no real nutritional value, but you do need to factor in the calories, especially if you are trying to lose weight. Consider as well that alcohol consumption reduces inhibitions and

self-control, which may lead to munching down more calories and carbohydrate than planned.

2. **Carbohydrate.** When it comes to carbohydrate, **straight distilled spirits** (including gin, rum, tequila, vodka, and whiskey) do not have any carbohydrate and thus do not directly raise blood glucose levels. However, the carbohydrate in **mixed drinks *can* raise your blood glucose.** For instance, a 4-oz mojito made with rum contains 16 g carbohydrate. **Dry wines and champagne** have minimal carbohydrate, although **sweet dessert wines** are a different story. For sweet dessert wines, you'll need to count the equivalent of 1 carbohydrate choice (15 g carbohydrate) for a 5-oz glass. **Light beers** (<4.5% alcohol by volume) and low-carbohydrate beers are lower in carbohydrate than regular or dark beers. For a 12-oz serving, light beers are equivalent to 1/2 carbohydrate choice (about 7.5 g carbohydrate), whereas **regular beer** is 1 carbohydrate choice (15 g carbohydrate) and **dark beers** are 1–1 1/2 carbohydrate choices. If you take insulin and adjust the dose based on how much carbohydrate you consume,

talk with your health-care team about how to factor in carbohydrate-containing alcoholic beverages.

3. **Risk for low blood glucose with alcohol.** Moderate alcohol consumption generally has a minimal effect on blood glucose in people with type 2 diabetes (with the exception of carbohydrate-rich beverages). However, it's important to be aware of the potential increased risk for hypoglycemia (including during the night or fasting the next morning) when consuming alcohol, especially if taking diabetes medications for which hypoglycemia is a side effect, or if using insulin. Why? Very simply put, one of your liver's jobs is to put out glucose to help maintain your blood glucose levels, but when you drink alcohol, the liver switches priority to processing the alcohol, and thus glucose output is decreased. As a result, blood glucose levels may drop—sometimes too low. **Consuming alcohol with food and more frequent blood glucose monitoring can minimize risk of hypoglycemia consequent to alcohol while sleeping.** Talk with your healthcare team if you are unsure if this may be a risk for you.

Alcohol Alternatives

Looking for a lower-alcohol alternative?

- Try a wine spritzer. Mix two parts wine with one part club soda.
- Choose beer with a lower alcohol content.
- Dilute mixed drinks with club soda, seltzer, or extra ice.

Looking for nonalcoholic alternatives?

- Choose club soda, sparkling water, or water with a twist of lemon, lime, or orange.
- Drink diet tonic water with a twist of lime.
- Enjoy diet soda with a twist of lemon, lime, or orange.
- Try nonalcoholic beer.
- Make "virgin" cocktails, also known as "mocktails."

APPLE-CITRUS TWIST

One word . . . refreshing! Don't skip the splash of vanilla—it helps blend all of the flavors together. Once you've tried it, you'll understand! This is great as a virgin "mocktail," or you can add vodka or rum for a special adult beverage.

THIS RECIPE CAN FIT IN THE FOLLOWING EATING PATTERNS: vegetarian, vegan, low- or very-low-fat, low-carbohydrate, DASH

NUMBER OF SERVINGS: 1 | **SERVING SIZE:** About 2/3 cup juice mixture plus 1/2 cup ice per serving
PREP TIME: 5 minutes

INGREDIENTS

- 1/3 cup apple juice
- 1 orange slice, halved
- 1/8 tsp vanilla extract
- 1/3 cup diet gingerale
- 1/2 cup crushed ice

INSTRUCTIONS

1. Combine the juice, halved orange slices, and the vanilla in a glass. Gently stir in the gingerale. Then add the ice. Serve immediately.

POINTERS

- Make several servings at a time: combine the juice, orange slices, and vanilla in a pitcher. Cover and refrigerate up to 48 hours in advance. At time of serving, gently stir in gingerale and pour over ice.
- Add 1 Tbsp vodka or rum, if desired.

CHOICES: 1 Fruit
BASIC NUTRITIONAL VALUES: Calories 45 | Calories from Fat 0 | **Total Fat** 0.0 g | Saturated Fat 0.0 g | Trans Fat 0.0 g | **Cholesterol** 0 mg | **Sodium** 10 mg | **Potassium** 115 mg | **Total Carbohydrate** 11 g | Dietary Fiber 1 g | Sugars 10 g | Added Sugars 0 g | **Protein** 0 g | **Phosphorus** 10 mg

HOT & FRESH MINTED "TEA"

Sometimes the simplest is best! This pure, natural "tea" is a soothing hot beverage, or add a splash of rum for a warm, sugar-free "mojito."

THIS RECIPE CAN FIT IN THE FOLLOWING EATING PATTERNS: All

NUMBER OF SERVINGS: 2 | **SERVING SIZE:** 1 cup per serving
PREP TIME: 5 minutes | **STAND TIME** 2 minutes

INGREDIENTS

- 2 cups water
- 1 (0.75-oz) package fresh mint leaves, rinsed and stems removed (about 1 cup lightly packed)

INSTRUCTIONS

1. Bring water to a full boil in a small saucepan.
2. Meanwhile, place the mint in two mugs (pressing down into mugs, if necessary). Pour boiling water over mint (making sure mint is totally immersed). Cover and let stand 2 minutes. Stir to release mint flavors.

Trick

- Cover your cup while the mint is steeping with a saucer or a square of foil to hold in the heat.

COOK'S SWAP

- For a light alcoholic drink, add 1 Tbsp light rum per cup.

CHOICES: None

BASIC NUTRITIONAL VALUES: Calories 5 | Calories from Fat 0 | **Total Fat** 0.0 g | Saturated Fat 0.0 g | Trans Fat 0.0 g | **Cholesterol** 0 mg | **Sodium** 15 mg | **Potassium** 55 mg | **Total Carbohydrate** 1 g | Dietary Fiber 1 g | Sugars 0 g | Added Sugars 0 g | **Protein** 0 g | **Phosphorus** 5 mg

Eating Patterns To Fill A Healthy Plate

Everything that you eat and drink over time matters. The right mix can help you be healthier now and in the future. It's important to find what works for you and your family within your food preferences, health goals, and budget. Small changes can lead to healthier choices you can enjoy. This chapter focuses on the seven different eating patterns demonstrated to benefit blood glucose and heart health (plus one popular but controversial eating pattern—paleo—that's shown mixed results) and how to portion your plate accordingly using the Diabetes Plate Method as a guide.

EATING PATTERNS

What Is an Eating Pattern?

An eating *pattern* is basically a combination of different foods, food groups, and beverages consumed. Evidence shows that there are a variety of different eating patterns acknowledged to be beneficial in managing type 2 diabetes:

- Vegetarian or vegan
- Low-fat
- Very-low-fat (such as Ornish or Pritikin)
- Low-carbohydrate
- Very-low-carbohydrate
- DASH (Dietary Approach to Stop Hypertension)
- Mediterranean-style

107

No one pattern has emerged as being superior to the others. The first six in particular are beneficial for weight loss. The low-carbohydrate and very-low-carbohydrate patterns have been shown to help lower blood glucose and may reduce the need for certain diabetes medications. These benefits are most pronounced in the first 3–6 months, but longer-term results are mixed because low-carb eating patterns can be hard to stick to long term. That said, reducing overall carbohydrate intake from what you are currently eating can be applied to most of the eating patterns. If you have blood glucose above target or want to try to reduce diabetes medications, reducing carbohydrate can help.

Mediterranean is the main eating pattern that has reported reduced risk of major cardiovascular events. Vegetarian or vegan, low-fat, low-carbohydrate/very-low-carbohydrate, and DASH eating patterns have demonstrated cardiovascular-protective benefits. Your registered dietitian nutritionist can provide much more in-depth information on the specific cardio-protective benefits of each.

It's worth noting that the paleo eating pattern has also been reviewed and showed mixed results from a few small studies, although many people choose to follow a paleo eating pattern and may see success on a personal level.

VEGETARIAN OR VEGAN (PLANT-BASED) EATING PATTERN

Focused around plant foods, the plant-based eating pattern often results in weight loss and lower blood glucose and LDL cholesterol (the "bad" cholesterol). Plant-based eating means eating more fruits, vegetables, whole grains, nuts, legumes, and soy products (Table 3.1). This eating pattern is rich in the "healthy stuff"—fiber, vitamins, minerals, phytochemicals (healthy plant compounds), and healthy fats. It is low in the "unhealthy stuff"—saturated fat and cholesterol.

Key Factors Common Among the Eating Patterns

Each eating pattern is unique in what foods it includes and excludes and how calories are distributed among macronutrients, but there are also three key factors that each pattern has in common:

1. It emphasizes nonstarchy vegetables.
2. It minimizes added sugar and refined grains.
3. It emphasizes choosing whole foods over highly processed foods to the extent possible.

Embrace a More Plant-Based Eating Pattern 1 Meal, 1 Day, 1 Week at a Time

- Make beans, lentils, or soy products the focus of your meals. While adding variety, this will also save money because these protein sources cost less than meat, poultry, and fish.
- Begin the week with "meatless Mondays"—eat only plant-based meals and snacks for 1 whole day each week. If you're looking for inspiration, try the ***Antipasto Romaine Wraps*** on page 112, which make a great lunch option.
- Add in a vegetarian breakfast with whole-grain cereal, almond milk, and half of a banana.
- Give a favorite recipe a plant-based makeover.

3 Simple swaps to live a little more plant-based

1. Try plant-based, unsweetened "dairy" products such as almond milk or soymilk. They are an easy swap in most recipes.
2. Swap cooked lentils in place of ground beef in tacos, sloppy joes, or Shepherd's pie.
3. Swap black beans in place of pork, chicken, or ground beef in burritos or enchiladas.

Plant-based items to stock up on

- **Fresh vegetables:** Carrots, celery, beets, bell peppers, and onions have a longer shelf-life than some other vegetables and can be used in a variety of recipes. Fresh greens are good for a quick salad, sautéing, steaming, or tossing in scrambles, soups, or stews.
- **Fresh fruits:** Apples, clementines, grapes, oranges, and pears last a long time in the fridge and make quick snacks.
- **Nuts and seeds:** Almonds, cashews, peanuts, pistachios, and walnuts are a few ideas. If you buy in bulk, store extras in the freezer in resealable plastic bags to keep them from spoiling, and pull them out as you need them.
- **Unsweetened, plant-based milk:** Almond, rice, or soy are options to keep on hand.
- **Condiments:** Use salsa and/or hot sauce to spice up the flavor.
- **Hummus:** Dunk vegetables in hummus or spread on a sandwich.
- **Nut butters or tahini:** Spread on toast or sandwiches, or use in dressings.
- **Freezer staples:** These staples can include frozen plain vegetables, frozen unsweetened fruit, cooked whole grains, cooked beans, and whole-wheat or corn tortillas. Freeze cooked extra beans and grains in 1-cup containers and pull out and incorporate into meals later.

TABLE 3.1   FACTS AND FOODS FOR A VEGETARIAN OR VEGAN EATING PATTERN

Vegetarian or Vegan Eating Pattern
Revolves around plant-based foods

Description	Sample Meal Ideas
• Focused around plant-based foods (such as vegetables, beans, lentils, nuts and seeds, fruit, whole grains, soy, and other plant-based products) • Rich in fiber and phyto-chemicals (healthy plant compounds) • **Vegetarian approach** (also known as lacto-ovo vegetarian) excludes animal flesh foods, but includes eggs (ovo) and/or dairy (lacto) products • **Vegan approach** excludes any animal products or flesh foods	*Vegetarian* **BREAKFAST:** Egg scrambled with onion, red pepper, and spinach; slice of toasted whole-grain bread spread with mashed avocado or hummus; tomato or vegetable juice **LUNCH:** Kale salad with quinoa, pomegranate seeds, mandarin orange sections, mukimame (shelled edamame/soybeans), walnuts, vinaigrette **DINNER:** Black bean burger with lettuce, tomato, onion, on 100% whole-wheat bun; sautéed zucchini, mushrooms, tomatoes, and artichokes; milk **SNACKS:** Smoothie made with Greek yogurt, unsweetened frozen fruit and almond or soymilk *Vegan* **BREAKFAST:** 100% whole-grain seeded bread toasted and topped with almond butter, sliced strawberries, blueberries, and unsalted sunflower seeds; almond or soymilk **LUNCH:** Vegan tomato basil soup topped with pan-cooked tempeh; small plum **DINNER:** Tofu stir-fried with broccoli, snow peas, water chestnuts, mushrooms, and baby corn over farro **SNACKS:** Pumpkin seeds, soy nuts, dried cherries

Plant Power Formula

If your goal is to eat more plant-based foods, try using the plant power "formula," a method for pulling together a plant-based meal. Using this formula, you can pull together a multitude of delicious, wholesome options. Here's how it works:

1. Choose a whole grain.
2. Add a plant protein (such as beans, lentils, tofu, or nuts).
3. Add a fruit or vegetable.

Applying the plant power formula at breakfast:
1. Choose a whole grain: steel-cut oats.
2. Add a plant protein: toasted almonds.
3. Add a fruit or vegetable: blueberries and raspberries.

Applying the plant power formula at lunch:
1. Choose a whole grain: quinoa.
2. Add a plant protein: chickpeas or lentils.
3. Add a fruit or vegetable: kale, tomatoes, or broccoli; then drizzle with olive oil vinaigrette.

Applying the plant power formula at dinner:
1. Choose a whole grain: brown rice.
2. Add a plant protein: veggie chili with beans over the rice.
3. Add a fruit or vegetable: fresh strawberries.

ANTIPASTO ROMAINE WRAPS

Wrap this savory antipasto salad in a lettuce leaf for a low-carb, vegetarian lunch option.

THIS RECIPE CAN FIT IN THE FOLLOWING EATING PATTERNS: vegetarian, low-fat, low- or very-low-carbohydrate, DASH, Mediterranean

NUMBER OF SERVINGS: 4 | **SERVING SIZE:** 1 cup tomato mixture plus 3 lettuce leaves per serving
PREP TIME: 12 minutes

INGREDIENTS

- 3 Roma tomatoes, chopped (about 1 1/2 cups total)
- 1 1/2 cups sliced mushrooms
- 3/4 cup no-salt-added navy beans, rinsed and drained
- 1 1/2 oz sliced pepperoncini peppers
- 3 oz crumbled feta cheese
- 1 1/2 Tbsp dried oregano
- 2 Tbsp cider vinegar
- 2 Tbsp extra-virgin olive oil
- 1/8 tsp salt
- 12 large romaine lettuce leaves

INSTRUCTIONS

1. Combine all ingredients, except lettuce leaves, in a medium bowl. Gently stir until well blended.
2. Spoon 1/3 cup of the tomato mixture in each lettuce leaf, and fold edges over as you would a hot dog in a bun.

POINTER

- This is a great make-ahead dish. Store the salad in the refrigerator up to 48 hours, and spoon into the lettuce leaves just before serving.
- Freeze the remaining navy beans in a small resealable plastic bag for later use. Thaw frozen beans by placing in a colander and running cold water over them for 30 seconds. Drain well.

CHOICES: 1/2 Starch, 1 Nonstarchy Vegetable, 1 Medium-Fat Protein, 1 1/2 Fat
BASIC NUTRITIONAL VALUES: Calories 200 | Calories from Fat 110 | **Total Fat** 12.0 g | Saturated Fat 3.7 g | Trans Fat 0.2 g | **Cholesterol** 15 mg | **Sodium** 330 mg | **Potassium** 510 mg | **Total Carbohydrate** 17 g | Dietary Fiber 6 g | Sugars 5 g | Added Sugars 0 g | **Protein** 9 g | **Phosphorus** 180 mg

RUSTIC SWEET POTATO POBLANO SOUP

When you hear the term "plant-based," you may initially think of light in substance and green. This soup will make you rethink "plant-based"! Packed with peppers, onions, sweet potato, beans, and tomatoes, this soup is so filling you won't even miss the meat if you're trying to embrace a more plant-based approach to eating.

THIS RECIPE CAN FIT IN THE FOLLOWING EATING PATTERNS: vegetarian, vegan, low-fat, DASH

NUMBER OF SERVINGS: 4 | **SERVING SIZE:** 1 1/2 cups per serving
PREP TIME: 15 minutes | **COOK TIME:** 28 minutes

INGREDIENTS

- 2 Tbsp extra-virgin olive oil, divided use
- 2 poblano chili peppers, seeded and chopped
- 1 cup chopped onion
- 1 (10-oz) sweet potato, unpeeled and chopped
- 1 (15-oz) can no-salt-added black beans, rinsed and drained
- 1 (14.5-oz) can no-salt-added diced tomatoes
- 1 (14-oz) can low-sodium vegetable broth
- 1 1/2 tsp smoked paprika
- 1 tsp ground cumin
- 1/2 tsp salt
- 1 1/2 tsp hot sauce, such as Frank's

INSTRUCTIONS

1. Heat 1 Tbsp oil in a large saucepan over medium-high heat. Cook peppers and onions 8 minutes or until beginning to richly brown on edges, stirring occasionally. Add the sweet potato, beans, tomatoes, broth, paprika, and cumin.

2. Bring to a boil over high heat, reduce heat, and cover and simmer 18–20 minutes or until potatoes are very tender. Remove from heat and stir in the remaining 1 Tbsp oil, salt, and hot sauce.

POINTERS

- This freezes well. Freeze in portion-size containers so you won't have to measure later on.
- No need to peel the potatoes; the skin adds a bit more fiber to every bite.

CHOICES: 2 Starch, 2 Nonstarchy Vegetable, 1 Fat

BASIC NUTRITIONAL VALUES: Calories 260 | Calories from Fat 60 | **Total Fat** 7.0 g | Saturated Fat 1.1 g | Trans Fat 0.0 g | **Cholesterol** 0 mg | **Sodium** 510 mg | **Potassium** 950 mg | **Total Carbohydrate** 41 g | Dietary Fiber 8 g | Sugars 10 g | Added Sugars 0 g | **Protein** 10 g | **Phosphorus** 205 mg

CREAMY BUTTERNUT SQUASH SOUP WITH GINGER

Adding the smallest amount of "powerhouse" beans adds to the creaminess in this soup while boosting the fiber and protein. And adding the fresh ginger and fresh cilantro makes this recipe "pop"!

THIS RECIPE CAN FIT IN THE FOLLOWING EATING PATTERNS: vegetarian, low-fat, DASH

NUMBER OF SERVINGS: 4 | **SERVING SIZE:** 1 1/4 cups soup plus 3 Tbsp yogurt per serving
PREP TIME: 17 minutes | **COOK TIME:** 23 minutes

INGREDIENTS

- 12 oz pre-chopped fresh butternut squash
- 1/2 (15-oz) can no-salt-added navy beans, rinsed and drained
- 1 cup chopped red bell pepper
- 1/2 cup chopped onion
- 1/2 cup fresh or frozen sliced carrots
- 1/2 tsp dried thyme
- 1 1/2 cups water
- 1 cup light coconut milk
- 1 Tbsp grated ginger (see tips for using fresh ginger on page 50)
- 3/4 tsp salt
- 1/4 tsp black pepper
- 1/2 cup chopped fresh cilantro
- 3/4 cup plain fat-free Greek yogurt

INSTRUCTIONS

1. Combine squash, beans, bell pepper, onion, carrots, thyme, and water in a large saucepan. Bring to a boil over high heat. Reduce heat, cover, and simmer 20 minutes or until carrots are very tender.
2. Working in batches, purée the squash mixture in a blender.
3. Return to the saucepan, add the coconut milk, ginger, salt, and pepper. Place over medium heat and cook until heated through, about 2 minutes. Stir in half of the cilantro. Top with remaining cilantro and yogurt.

CHOICES: 1 1/2 Starch, 1 Nonstarchy Vegetable, 1 Lean Protein

BASIC NUTRITIONAL VALUES: Calories 180 | Calories from Fat 35 | **Total Fat** 4.0 g | Saturated Fat 3.2 g | Trans Fat 0.0 g | **Cholesterol** 4 mg | **Sodium** 490 mg | **Potassium** 760 mg | **Total Carbohydrate** 28 g | Dietary Fiber 7 g | Sugars 7 g | Added Sugars 0 g | **Protein** 11 g | **Phosphorus** 215 mg

COOK'S SWAPS

- Not a cilantro fan? Just replace it with fresh parsley instead.
- For a vegan dish, sub the Greek yogurt for a nondairy yogurt, or omit and serve with a lime wedge instead.

POINTERS

- Freezes well. Store in portion-size amounts for a "grab and go" lunch.
- To make store-bought cilantro (or fresh parsley) last longer, remove the band that's often tied around the bunch when purchased. Then cut 1/2 inch off the bottom of the stems and place in a glass of water. It should last in the refrigerator at least 2 weeks. Be sure to use a wide-bottom glass or jar and store near the back of the refrigerator to keep it from tipping over.

LOW-FAT AND VERY-LOW-FAT EATING PATTERNS

While there are plenty of "low-fat" and "fat-free" packaged foods at the grocery store, the best way to follow a low-fat eating pattern is to focus on *real* whole foods that are naturally low in fat. For example, choose very lean proteins prepared in ways that keep them low-fat (such as a whitefish fillet that's grilled) and low-fat or fat-free dairy foods. Reducing fat means that you will likely be eating more carbohydrate foods. This change might confuse you given that carbohydrate raises blood glucose. What's important is the **type** of carbohydrate foods you choose (see Table 3.2 for examples of healthy choices). By going mainly for foods that are plant-based sources (filled with fiber), you can satisfy hunger without raising blood glucose too much. Foods like oats, beans, lentils, and berries fill the bill. Fiber will fill you up without raising blood glucose.

4 Swaps to Make Through the Day to Swap Out Fat and Swap in Fiber to Fill You Up

1. At breakfast, swap in oats in place of granola cereal.
2. At lunch, swap in hummus on a whole-grain sandwich rather than mayonnaise.
3. At dinner, swap in beans for meat. (Or smother your meat in nonstarchy vegetables, like we've done in our *Skillet Sirloin and Broccoli* on page 119.)
4. At snacks, swap in roasted chickpeas or edamame in place of chips.

4 Tips to Make the Move from Low-Fat to Very-Low-Fat

1. Instead of light mayonnaise, reach for mustard for your sandwich or wrap.
2. Instead of light microwave popcorn for a whole-grain snack, go for do-it-yourself air-popped microwave popcorn. No air popper needed!
   How to: Place popcorn kernels in a brown lunch-size paper bag. Fold over the top of the bag a couple of times. Microwave on high until the popping has a one-second gap. This usually takes around 1 1/2 to 2 1/2 minutes. The popping time may vary. Sprinkle in red pepper flakes, black pepper, ground cinnamon, or cocoa powder and shake the bag to coat.
3. Swap out 2% or 1% milk for skim milk.
   How to: To transition your taste buds, try mixing 2% with 1% until you're used to that, and then mix 1% with skim and transition on to skim milk.
4. Swap out light sour cream for fat-free sour cream or fat-free Greek yogurt.

TABLE 3.2　FACTS AND FOODS FOR A LOW-FAT OR VERY-LOW-FAT EATING PATTERN

Low-Fat and Very-Low-Fat Eating Patterns
Low-fat:
≤30% of total calories coming from fat
≤10% of total calories coming from saturated fat

Very-low-fat:
Further reduction of fat to 10% of total calories coming from fat. (For an average 1,800 calories, that means less than 20 g fat each day.)

Description	Sample Meal Ideas
<ul><li>Emphasizes fiber-rich vegetables (both nonstarchy and starchy), beans, fruits, whole grains, fat-free dairy</li><li>Lean proteins, including beans, fish, and egg whites</li><li>Low-fat dairy products</li><li>Carbohydrate-rich foods, with focus on unprocessed, high-fiber foods.</li><li>Very-low-fat pattern includes 30–60 g fiber daily.</li></ul>	*Low-fat:* **BREAKFAST:** Egg white scramble with tomato and basil in a whole-wheat tortilla; small banana; fat-free milk **LUNCH:** Vegetable soup; turkey on whole-grain seeded bread with mustard, lettuce, tomato, cucumber; cherries **DINNER:** Shrimp and vegetable stir-fry over riced cauliflower; fresh pineapple **SNACKS:** Low-fat popcorn; kiwi *Very-low-fat:* **BREAKFAST:** Steel-cut oats with cinnamon and raisins; fat-free milk **LUNCH:** Navy bean soup; arugula or spinach with vinaigrette; fresh raspberries **DINNER:** Grilled chicken over black beans and brown rice topped with fresh cilantro and fresh salsa **SNACKS:** Pear; edamame

Let's Do the Math for Fat Grams for an Average 1,800-Calorie Diet

To eat **30%** of calories from fat, eat no more than 60 g total fat each day.

$$1{,}800 \text{ calories} \times 0.30 = 540 \text{ calories}$$

$$540 \text{ divided by 9 calories per gram of fat} = \textbf{60 g} \text{ total fat}$$

To eat **10%** of calories from saturated fat (or total fat for very-low-fat eating pattern), eat no more than 20 grams each day.

$$1{,}800 \text{ calories} \times 0.10 = 180 \text{ calories}$$

$$180 \text{ calories divided by 9 calories per gram of fat} = 20 \text{ g saturated fat}$$

SKILLET SIRLOIN & BROCCOLI

It's said that we eat with our eyes . . . well, you'll really want to bite into this! This dish has brilliant green broccoli, bright red peppers, and richly browned beef drizzled with a dark glossy reduction.

THIS RECIPE CAN FIT IN THE FOLLOWING EATING PATTERNS: low-fat, low-carbohydrate, DASH

NUMBER OF SERVINGS: 4 | **SERVING SIZE:** 1/2 cup beef, 1 cup vegetables, 1/2 cup pasta, and 1 Tbsp sauce per serving
PREP TIME: 15 minutes | **COOK TIME:** 15 minutes

INGREDIENTS

- 4 oz multi-grain rotini, such as Barilla Plus
- 4 tsp canola oil, divided use
- 8 oz red bell pepper, cut into 1-inch chunks (about 1 1/2 cups total)
- 1 cup chopped onion
- 2 cups fresh broccoli florets
- 1 tsp garlic powder
- 1/2 tsp salt, divided use
- 1/4 tsp black pepper, divided use
- 12 oz boneless top sirloin steak, trimmed of fat and cut into bitesize pieces
- 1/2 cup dry red wine
- 1 Tbsp balsamic vinegar
- 1 Tbsp reduced-sodium soy sauce

INSTRUCTIONS

1. Cook pasta according to package directions, drain well.
2. Meanwhile, heat a large nonstick skillet over medium-high heat. Add 2 tsp of the oil, tilt skillet to coat bottom lightly, cook the bell pepper and onions for 6 minutes, and add the broccoli and garlic powder; cover and cook 2 minutes. Stir in 1/4 tsp of the salt and 1/8 tsp of the pepper. Set aside on a serving platter. Cover to keep warm.
3. Add the remaining 2 tsp oil, and tilt skillet to coat bottom lightly. Add beef in a single layer in the skillet and do not stir for 2 minutes. Stir and cook 1 minute. Place on top of the vegetables. Cover to keep warm.
4. Add the wine, vinegar, soy sauce, remaining 1/4 tsp salt, and remaining 1/8 tsp pepper to pan residue in skillet. Bring to a boil over medium-high heat, and cook 3 minutes or until reduced to 1/4 cup.
5. Divide pasta between four shallow bowls and top with vegetables and beef. Drizzle sauce over all.

(Cook's Swap and Pointer on following page)

CHOICES: 1 1/2 Starch, 2 Nonstarchy Vegetable, 2 Lean Protein, 1 Fat
BASIC NUTRITIONAL VALUES: Calories 290 | Calories from Fat 70 | **Total Fat** 8.0 g | Saturated Fat 1.6 g | Trans Fat 0.0 g | **Cholesterol** 45 mg | **Sodium** 480 mg | **Potassium** 770 mg | **Total Carbohydrate** 30 g | Dietary Fiber 5 g | Sugars 6 g | Added Sugars 0 g | **Protein** 24 g | **Phosphorus** 315 mg

COOK'S SWAP

- For a very-low-carb dish, add another 8 oz green bell pepper and another 1 cup onion when stir-frying the vegetables and omit the pasta.
- For a very-low-fat dish, use skinless chicken breast instead of beef.

POINTER

- For a slightly sweeter dish, remove the reduced sauce from heat and stir in one individual packet of stevia before spooning over the beef and vegetables.

LOW-CARBOHYDRATE AND VERY-LOW-CARBOHYDRATE EATING PATTERNS

Individuals have different "tolerances" for carbohydrate. Because sustaining a very-low-carbohydrate approach can be challenging for some, assess what is doable for you and individualize to suit your needs. Table 3.3 has several examples of healthy food selections when eating a low-carbohydrate diet.

4 Tips to Make the Move from Low-Carbohydrate to Very-Low-Carbohydrate

- At breakfast, swap in chia pudding in place of oats (see recipe for *Strawberry Chia Pudding* on page 46).
- At lunch, go for a lettuce leaf wrap over a low-carb tortilla wrap (see the *Antipasto Romaine Wraps* on page 112).
- At dinner, opt for cauliflower crust pizza over thin-crust pizza.
- At a snack, switch from fat-free yogurt to fat-free cottage cheese.

Flip back to Chapter 2 for more practical tips on reducing carbohydrate (see page 17).

TABLE 3.3 FACTS AND FOODS FOR A LOW-CARBOHYDRATE OR VERY-LOW-CARBOHYDRATE EATING PATTERN

Low Carbohydrate and Very-Low-Carbohydrate Eating Patterns

Low-Carbohydrate:
There's not a consistent definition of "low carbohydrate," but the amount of carbohydrate eaten is moderately low (26–45% of total daily calories).

Very-Low-Carbohydrate:
Further limits carbohydrate-containing foods. Typically contains only 20–50 g nonfiber carbohydrate each day.

Description	Sample meal ideas
<ul><li>Emphasizes nonstarchy vegetables</li><li>Emphasizes protein from meat, poultry, fish, shellfish, eggs, cheese, nuts, and seeds</li><li>Fats from animal foods, oils, butter, avocado</li><li>Some choose to include fruit</li><li>Avoids starchy and sugary foods (such as pasta, rice, potatoes, bread, and sweets)</li><li>Very-low-carbohydrate meals are typically high in fat with more than half of the calories coming from fat (to learn more about healthy fat sources, see Chapter 2)</li></ul>	*Low-carbohydrate:* **BREAKFAST:** Steel-cut oats with almond or peanut butter stirred in; *Lean Green Pineapple Smoothie* (recipe on page 309) **LUNCH:** Turkey caprese wrap: small whole-wheat tortilla filled with smoked turkey, sliced tomato, slice of fresh mozzarella, fresh basil leaves (or pesto); grapes **DINNER:** Grilled chicken breast, roasted Brussels sprouts, small baked sweet potato topped with trans fat–free margarine, cinnamon, and toasted pecans **SNACKS:** Apple slices spread with low-fat cottage cheese and sprinkled with cinnamon; unsalted or lightly salted almonds *Very-low-carbohydrate:* **BREAKFAST:** Veggie omelet or scramble with low-fat cheese and topped with diced avocado; fresh blackberries and raspberries with a dollop of Greek yogurt **LUNCH:** Green salad with tuna or salmon (foil pack for ease), sliced almonds, vinaigrette dressing without added sugars **DINNER:** Turkey meatballs and marinara over zucchini spirals sprinkled with Parmesan cheese; chopped romaine with light Caesar dressing **SNACKS:** String cheese; peanuts; cucumber slices with salsa for dipping

Let's Do the Math for Carbohydrate for an Average 1,800-Calorie Diet

For an average 1,800 calories, 26–45% of total daily calories from carbohydrate is 117–203 g carbohydrate a day (or 34–63 grams per meal if split evenly between meals with one 15-g carbohydrate snack).

$$1,800 \text{ calories} \times 0.26 = 468 \text{ calories}$$

$$468 \text{ calories divided by 4 calories per gram of carbohydrate} = 117 \text{ g carbohydrate}$$

$$1,800 \text{ calories} \times 0.45 = 810 \text{ calories}$$

$$810 \text{ calories divided by 4 calories per gram of carbohydrate} = 203 \text{ g carbohydrate}$$

SKILLET-SEARED GREEN PEPPER CHICKEN

Using generous amounts of peppers, onions, and especially almonds pumps up the fiber in this low-carb recipe while adding tons of hearty texture and rich flavor!

THIS RECIPE CAN FIT IN THE FOLLOWING EATING PATTERNS: **low- or very-low-carbohydrate, DASH**

NUMBER OF SERVINGS: 4 | **SERVING SIZE:** 1 1/2 cups
PREP TIME: 15 minutes | **COOK TIME:** 14 minutes

INGREDIENTS

- 8 boneless skinless chicken tenderloins, about 1 lb total
- 1 Tbsp salt-free grilling seasoning blend, such as Mrs. Dash
- 1 Tbsp canola oil, divided use
- 2 tsp Worcestershire sauce
- 2 large green bell peppers, seeded and thinly sliced (about 12 oz total)
- 1 large onion, thinly sliced vertically (about 6 oz total)
- 2 garlic cloves, minced (1 tsp)
- 1/2 tsp salt
- 3 oz slivered almonds
- 1 avocado, chopped
- 1 lime, cut into 4 wedges

INSTRUCTIONS

1. Sprinkle both sides of the chicken pieces with seasoning blend.
2. Heat a large nonstick skillet over medium-high heat. Add 1 tsp of the oil, and tilt skillet to coat bottom. Add the chicken and cook 3 minutes or until no longer pink in center, turning occasionally. Stir in the Worcestershire sauce. Set aside on separate plate.
3. Heat the remaining 2 tsp oil in the skillet. Add the peppers and onions and cook 8 minutes or until vegetables are richly browned. Stir in the garlic and cook 30 seconds, stirring constantly. Add the chicken with any accumulated juices, almonds, and salt. Cook 1 minute or until chicken is heated through. Serve topped with the avocado and lime wedges.

CHOICES: 1/2 Carbohydrate, 1 Nonstarchy Vegetable, 4 Lean Protein, 3 Fat
BASIC NUTRITIONAL VALUES: Calories 380 | Calories from Fat 210 | **Total Fat** 23.0 g | Saturated Fat 2.8 g | Trans Fat 0.0 g | **Cholesterol** 65 mg | **Sodium** 380 mg | **Potassium** 750 mg | **Total Carbohydrate** 17 g | Dietary Fiber 7 g | Sugars 5 g | Added Sugars 0 g | **Protein** 30 g | **Phosphorus** 325 mg

COOK'S SWAPS

- You could try this recipe with other lean meats instead of chicken—boneless pork loin chops also work well.
- Any color of bell pepper works in this recipe—use multiple colors for a more colorful dish.

DIETARY APPROACHES TO STOP HYPERTENSION (DASH) EATING PATTERN

DASH stands for Dietary Approaches to Stop Hypertension. This eating pattern has helped individuals improve blood pressure and lower diabetes risk, as well as lose weight. Table 3.4 has tips on how to incorporate DASH-friendly foods into your eating plan.

5 Tips to Transition to a DASH-Style Eating Pattern

Specific examples of the foods mentioned below follow later in the chapter.

1. **Begin to work in more nonstarchy vegetables.** Add one nonstarchy vegetable at lunch one day and at dinner the next.
2. **Add a fresh fruit at one meal or as a snack.**
3. **Add in a fat-free or low-fat dairy until you're up to three a day.** Examples of these foods could be low-fat milk at breakfast, a Greek yogurt for lunch, and kefir or drinkable yogurt for a snack. If you do not tolerate lactose (milk sugar), try lactose-free varieties.
4. **Limit meat to a portion the size of a deck of cards twice a day.** If you eat more than that, gradually reduce portion sizes by one-third or one-half at each meal. The *Pineapple Pork Stir-Fry* recipe on page 126 is designed to serve up the perfect portion of meat per serving.
5. **Incorporate a meatless meal twice a week.** This meal could be something like a nut butter sandwich on whole-grain bread, a pasta primavera with whole-grain pasta, or a vegetarian chili.

4 Tips to Eat Less Sodium

1. **Keep salt out of view and off the kitchen counter and table.** If you feel the need to shake a seasoning onto foods, use a salt-free herb blend (such as Mrs. Dash). Recipes for two *salt-free seasoning blends* can be found on pages 87–88.
2. **Cut back on salt a little at a time.** Your taste or preference for salt will lessen over time (for many, in as little as a week).
3. **Be careful with condiments.** Foods like ketchup, pickles, soy sauce, and many salad dressings are high in sodium.
4. **Go for fresh.** Most of the sodium eaten is in processed foods. Fresh, close-to-nature foods are generally lower in sodium.

TABLE 3.4   FACTS AND FOODS FOR A DASH EATING PATTERN

DASH Eating Pattern
The DASH eating pattern is designed to help lower blood pressure by emphasizing plant foods and by reducing fat and sodium intake.

Description	Sample Meal Ideas
• Emphasizes vegetables, fruits, and low-fat or fat-free dairy products • Includes whole grains • Includes lean proteins such as poultry, fish, and nuts • Reduced in saturated fat, red meat, sweets, and sugar-containing beverages	**BREAKFAST:** Whole-grain cereal with low-fat milk, blueberries, and sliced almonds **LUNCH:** Salad greens topped with grilled chicken, cucumber, tomato, no-salt- added canned white beans, avocado, walnuts, and vinaigrette; clementine **DINNER:** Lemon garlic shrimp over quinoa; sautéed spinach or kale; small whole-grain roll with trans fat–free margarine; sliced strawberries with a dollop of low-fat vanilla Greek yogurt **SNACKS:** Unsalted pistachios; sliced pear sprinkled with cinnamon

PINEAPPLE PORK STIR-FRY

When trying to reduce your sodium intake, skip the saltshaker and go a different direction by adding a little natural sweetness, such as fresh or canned fruits, or even a small amount of dried fruits. In this dish, you've got sweetness, a bit of heat, and a pop of fresh ginger to pull out the flavors!

THIS RECIPE CAN FIT IN THE FOLLOWING EATING PATTERNS: low-fat, low-carbohydrate, DASH

NUMBER OF SERVINGS: 4 | **SERVING SIZE:** 1 1/2 cups pork mixture
PREP TIME: 20 minutes | **COOK TIME:** 22 minutes

INGREDIENTS

- 1 1/2 Tbsp canola oil, divided use
- 1 lb pork tenderloin, cut in thin strips
- 3 cups broccoli florets
- 2 cups matchstick carrots
- 2 (8-oz) cans pineapple tidbits, in own juice
- 2 1/2 Tbsp reduced-sodium soy sauce
- 2 Tbsp cider vinegar
- 1/8 tsp salt
- 1 cup chopped green onion (green and white parts total), divided use
- 1 Tbsp grated ginger (find tips for preparing fresh ginger on page 50)
- 3 individual packets stevia

INSTRUCTIONS

1. Heat 1 1/2 tsp of the oil in a large nonstick skillet over medium-high heat. Tilt skillet to coat bottom lightly. Add the pork and cook 7 minutes or until beginning to brown on edges, stirring occasionally. Set aside on separate plate.
2. Heat remaining 1 Tbsp oil. Add the broccoli and carrots and cook 3 minutes or until broccoli is tender-crisp. Add to the pork.
3. Add pineapple and its juices, soy sauce, vinegar, and salt. Bring to a boil over medium-high heat. Boil 8 minutes or until thickened. Add the pork, vegetables, and any accumulated juices, 3/4 cup green onions, and ginger. Return to a boil and boil 1 minute or until heated through. Remove from heat, stir in stevia, and serve topped with remaining 1/4 cup green onions.

(Pointer and Trick on following page)

CHOICES: 1 Fruit, 2 Nonstarchy Vegetable, 3 Lean Protein, 1 Fat
BASIC NUTRITIONAL VALUES: Calories 290 | Calories from Fat 80 | **Total Fat** 9.0 g | Saturated Fat 1.5 g | Trans Fat 0.0 g | **Cholesterol** 60 mg | **Sodium** 510 mg | **Potassium** 1190 mg | **Total Carbohydrate** 29 g | Dietary Fiber 5 g | Sugars 21 g | Added Sugars 0 g | **Protein** 25 g | **Phosphorus** 275 mg

POINTER

- Be sure the broccoli florets are the same size; if not, they will cook unevenly. One-inch florets are generally the ideal size for a stir-fry.

Trick

- Slicing the pork can be quick and easy, if you cut the raw pork into 1/4-inch-thick slices and then cut each slice into 1/4-inch-thick strips.

Mediterranean-Style Eating Pattern

The Mediterranean-style eating pattern has been linked to a lower risk of type 2 diabetes, along with improved blood glucose and weight and reduced risk of heart attack and stroke. This eating plan is not low-fat but is rich in monounsaturated fat (heart-healthy fat) from plant sources such as olives and nuts. There is no one "right" way to follow the Mediterranean-style eating pattern, since there are many countries around the Mediterranean Sea, and people in the different areas eat different foods. Rather, consider the information in Table 3.5 as general guidelines.

10 Ways to Eat "More Mediterranean"

1. Replace butter and margarine with healthful oils such as olive or canola oil. Use these oils for cooking, dip bread in flavored olive oil, or lightly spread olive oil on whole-grain breads.

2. Choose protein foods such as skinless chicken and turkey, fish, beans, lentils, nuts, and other plant-based protein sources. Substitute fish and poultry for red meat (see the *Mediterranean Shrimp and Greek Olive Stir-Fry* on page 131 for a flavorful seafood take on stir-fry). When red meats are eaten, choose lean cuts and keep portions small (about the size of a deck of cards).

3. Eat fish at least twice each week. Fresh or water-packed tuna, salmon, trout, mackerel, and herring are good choices.

4. Aim for three to five servings of vegetables each day.

5. Choose whole-grain breads and cereals, as well as whole-grain pasta and rice products.

6. Season meals with herbs and spices rather than salt.

7. Snack on nuts or seeds instead of snack foods like chips and crackers. Keep almonds, cashews, pistachios, and walnuts on hand for quick snacks. Try tahini (sesame seed paste) as a dip or spread for bread.

8. Enjoy fruit to satisfy a sweet tooth.

9. Go for small portions of cheese or yogurt.

TABLE 3.5   FACTS AND FOODS FOR A MEDITERRANEAN-STYLE EATING PATTERN

Mediterranean-Style Eating Pattern
Traditional Mediterranean meals feature foods grown all around the Mediterranean Sea. This eating style is easily adaptable to today's busy lifestyle.

Description	Sample Meal Ideas
• Emphasis on plant-based foods (such as vegetables, beans, lentils, nuts and seeds, fruit, and whole grains) • Fish and other seafood • Olive oil as the main dietary fat • Dairy products (mainly yogurt and cheese) in low to moderate amounts • Fewer than four eggs per week • Red meat in small amounts and limited frequency • Fresh herbs and spices for flavor • Wine in low to moderate amounts • Water is the go-to beverage • Concentrated sugars or honey are infrequently used	**BREAKFAST:** Greek yogurt topped with chopped figs and unsalted pistachios **LUNCH:** Whole-wheat pita stuffed with hummus, salad greens, tuna, dressed with olive oil and fresh lemon juice; date stuffed with almond butter **DINNER:** Grilled fish; tomato, cucumber, olive, and feta salad; lentils; watermelon; glass of red wine (if you choose to drink wine) **SNACKS:** Nectarine or peach; walnuts or almonds

10. If you drink alcohol, consume a moderate amount with a meal (no more than one glass for women or two glasses for men is recommended).

6 Simple Swaps to Healthy Mediterranean-Style Fats

1. Top whole-grain toast with almond butter or peanut butter rather than butter.

Natural nut butter is best (rather than the kind with added fat or sugar). If you have trouble with the natural nut butter separating, screw on the lid tightly and store the jar upside down. When you turn it right-side-up to open it, the oil will be in the bottom rather than on the top.

2. Try almond milk on your morning cereal rather than dairy milk.

3. Mash and spread avocado on a sandwich rather than mayonnaise.
4. Add crunch to a salad with almonds, pecans, pistachios, pumpkin seeds, toasted sesame seeds, or sunflower seeds instead of bacon or croutons.
5. Lightly dip crusty bread in olive oil rather than slathering with butter.
6. Choose olives over cheese for a snack or happy hour.

4 Mediterranean-Style Whole Grains

1. **Barley.** Barley can be used in salads, as a breakfast cereal with fruit and nuts, as a side with onions and garlic, and in soups.
2. **Bulgur.** Bulgur cooks quickly and can be enjoyed in salads. Tabbouleh salad made with tomatoes, cucumbers, garlic, fresh parsley, mint, lemon juice, and olive oil is flavorful!
3. **Whole-wheat couscous.** Couscous has a neutral flavor, a fine texture, cooks quickly, and becomes fluffy when cooked. Enjoy it as a side dish in place of rice. Serve stews or roasted vegetables over it.
4. **Farro.** Farro is rich in fiber and protein and makes a great side dish, or addition to soups and salads.

Vegetables Common to the Mediterranean-Style Eating Pattern

Vegetables are a staple of the Mediterranean eating pattern. Cooked vegetables are often drizzled with olive oil and sometimes a squeeze of lemon. Mediterranean-style vegetables include the following:

artichokes	cucumbers	peppers
arugula	eggplant	potatoes
beets	fennel	radishes
broccoli	greens	rutabaga
Brussels sprouts	leeks	scallions
cabbage	mushrooms	shallots
carrots	nettles	sweet potatoes
celeriac	okra	tomatoes
celery	onions	turnip
chicory	peas	zucchini

Fruits Common to the Mediterranean Eating Pattern

Whole fresh fruit is the ever-present "sweet treat." Mediterranean-style fruits include the following:

apples	figs	peaches
apricots	grapefruit	pears
avocado	grapes	pomegranates
cherries	melons	strawberries
clementines	nectarines	tangerines
dates	oranges	

4 Tips on How to Eat "More Mediterranean-Style" When Dining Out

Of course, dining at a Greek or Mediterranean restaurant is the easy answer. If that's not an option, here are 4 tips to make most restaurant meals work:

1. Choose fish or seafood as your main dish.
2. Order a side of nonstarchy vegetables, beans, or lentils.
3. Ask that olive oil be used for any fat required in the dish.
4. Choose whole-grain bread from the bread basket if you opt for bread, and then dip the bread in olive oil instead of spreading with butter.

MEDITERRANEAN SHRIMP AND GREEK OLIVE STIR-FRY

The Mediterranean eating pattern bursts with fresh flavors. In this recipe, there's concentrated sweet sun-dried tomatoes, briny Greek olives, and a generous amount of oregano and garlic tossed with spicy shrimp and pasta.

THIS RECIPE CAN FIT IN THE FOLLOWING EATING PATTERNS: low-carbohydrate, DASH, Mediterranean

---

NUMBER OF SERVINGS: 4 | **SERVING SIZE:** 3/4 cup shrimp mixture and 1/2 cup pasta
PREP TIME: 15 minutes | **COOK TIME:** 12 minutes

INGREDIENTS

- 4 oz dried multigrain spaghetti noodles, broken in half, such as Barilla Plus
- 2 Tbsp extra-virgin olive oil, divided use
- 1 lb raw peeled shrimp, rinsed and patted dry
- 1 large red bell pepper, seeded and cut into thin strips
- 1 1/2 oz sun-dried tomato pieces (about 1/3 cup)
- 16 pitted Kalamata olives (about 2 oz), chopped
- 2 garlic cloves, minced
- 1 Tbsp dried oregano
- 1/4 tsp crushed pepper flakes
- 4 tsp grated Parmesan cheese

INSTRUCTIONS

1. Cook pasta according to package directions. Drain well.
2. Meanwhile, heat 1 Tbsp oil in a large nonstick skillet over medium-high heat. Add the shrimp, bell peppers, and sun-dried tomatoes. Cook 4 minutes or until shrimp are opaque in center, stirring frequently. Stir in the olives, garlic, oregano, and pepper flakes. Cook 30 seconds, stirring constantly.
3. Remove from heat and stir in the remaining 1 Tbsp oil.
4. Serve over drained pasta. Top with Parmesan cheese.

CHOICES: 1 1/2 Starch, 2 Nonstarchy Vegetable, 3 Lean Protein, 1 Fat
BASIC NUTRITIONAL VALUES: Calories 340 | Calories from Fat 110 | **Total Fat** 12.0 g | Saturated Fat 1.3 g | Trans Fat 0.0 g | **Cholesterol** 175 mg | **Sodium** 380 mg | **Potassium** 850 mg | **Total Carbohydrate** 31 g | Dietary Fiber 5 g | Sugars 7 g | Added Sugars 0 g | **Protein** 30 g | **Phosphorus** 405 mg

COOK'S SWAP

- For a very-low-carbohydrate dish, substitute pasta with 2 (12-oz) packages frozen zucchini spirals, cooked according to package directions.

POINTER

- When purchasing raw shrimp with shells and heads on, allow 1/3 of the weight to be shells and heads discarded, so buy 1 1/3 lbs. If possible, use fresh (never-frozen) shrimp or shrimp that are free of preservatives (for example, shrimp that have not been treated with salt or STPP [sodium tripolyphosphate]).

PALEO EATING PATTERN

As mentioned earlier in this chapter, the paleo eating pattern has also been reviewed and showed mixed results from a few small studies. Many people choose to follow a paleo eating pattern and may feel they see success on a personal level. This eating pattern focuses on foods that would have been eaten by the hunter-gatherer cavemen. There is no "one way" to eat paleo. This eating pattern is based largely on eating close-to-nature "real" food. See Table 3.6 for an idea of what paleo-style meals may look like if you have interest in this eating approach.

5 Paleo-Style Swaps

1. Swap in riced cauliflower in place of rice or brown rice (which is a grain).
2. Instead of noodles, try spiralized zucchini or yellow squash or spaghetti squash (many grocery stores sell spiralized vegetables, or you can purchase an inexpensive spiralizer for home use).
3. Instead of peanut butter (a legume), swap in almond butter.
4. Swap in finely chopped vegetables (such as carrots, bell peppers, onions, and mushrooms) in place of beans.
5. Swap in crunchy fresh vegetables (such as carrot or celery sticks) in place of crackers.

HOW TO BEGIN ADOPTING AN EATING PATTERN

Based on what current research shows, here's when you might choose one eating pattern over another:

- **If you have prediabetes:** Mediterranean, vegetarian or vegan, low-fat, or DASH may work.

TABLE 3.6 FACTS AND FOODS FOR A PALEO EATING PATTERN

Paleo Eating Pattern
Emphasizes foods presumed to have been the only foods available to or consumed by humans during the Paleolithic era (hence the name "paleo")

Description	Sample Meal Ideas
• Emphasizes lean meat, fish, shellfish, vegetables, eggs, nuts, and berries • Avoids grains, legumes (beans, lentils, and peanuts), dairy, salt, refined fats, and sugar • Fats are largely healthy fats.	**BREAKFAST:** Stir-fried broccoli slaw topped with fried egg cooked in nonstick skillet; diced mango and strawberries sprinkled with chia seed **LUNCH:** Salad with rotisserie chicken, dried cranberries, pecans, apple slices, and vinaigrette **DINNER:** Grilled or baked salmon, sautéed zucchini with red and yellow peppers; roasted butternut squash **SNACKS:** Blueberry banana chia smoothie made with unsweetened almond milk; roasted chickpeas

- **If you are trying to lose weight:** Vegetarian or vegan, low-fat or very-low-fat, low-carbohydrate or very-low-carbohydrate, or DASH may be beneficial.

- **If you are trying to improve lipids:** Choose Mediterranean, vegetarian or vegan, low-carbohydrate, or very-low-carbohydrate.

- **If you are trying to lower blood pressure:** Opt for very-low-fat, low-carbohydrate or very-low-carbohydrate, or DASH.

- **If you are struggling with lowering blood glucose/A1C:** Mediterranean, vegetarian or vegan, or low-carbohydrate or very-low-carbohydrate can be helpful.

- **If you want to reduce the risk of major cardiovascular event:** Choose Mediterranean.

As always, talk with your registered dietitian nutritionist or diabetes care team to choose what eating pattern is best for you and is one that you can stick to long term. Be sure to consider your personal food preferences, budget, and other personal factors when adapting healthier eating behaviors.

Tip

In adopting a new-to-you eating pattern, start with one meal, 1 day, each week. You don't have to overhaul everything at one time. Making a major change all at once can feel overwhelming. Small changes add up and make a difference.

How to spread out your eating

Most people worry about *what* to eat, but it's also important to think about *when* you eat. Skipping meals or having some meals that are much larger than others can cause swings in your blood glucose levels. It's generally best to spread your carbs and calories throughout the day as three meals that are about the same size (and one or two snacks if that's part of your meal plan). Spreading out your eating will help to satisfy hunger and keep blood glucose levels steady.

PUTTING A HEALTHY EATING PATTERN INTO PRACTICE WITH THE DIABETES PLATE METHOD

Making healthy food choices begins with how you portion or fill your plate. Are you familiar with the Diabetes Plate Method? It is a helpful and practical approach to embrace an eating pattern and manage portions.

. . . .

The Diabetes Plate Method is a helpful and practical approach to embrace an eating pattern and manage portions.

. . . .

Planning Your Portions and Creating a Healthy Plate in 4 Easy Steps

A 9-inch plate is about the right size to use for the Diabetes Plate Method. While many think first about the meat or protein, vegetables (the nonstarchy kind) become the focus with the Diabetes Plate Method. Nonstarchy vegetables are low in calories and carbohydrate and don't have much effect on blood glucose. Imagine a line down the middle of the plate. Then on one side, cut it again, so you will have three sections on your plate.

- **Step 1: Fill half of your plate with nonstarchy vegetables.** These vegetables include foods like salad greens, broccoli, green beans, carrots, and tomatoes. Try to vary your vegetables. There is an extensive list in this chapter on page 136.
- **Step 2: Fill one-quarter of your plate with protein.** Protein foods include fish,

chicken, turkey, lean beef or pork, or tofu. Try to vary your protein routine.

- **Step 3: Fill a quarter of your plate with carbohydrate foods such as grains, starchy vegetables, beans, legumes, fruit, and milk/yogurt.** If your meal plan allows, you can add a glass of milk or a serving of another carbohydrate food, such as fruit, outside of your plate as well. Focus on whole fruits instead of juice or processed fruit. Try to include whole grains as much as possible, such as brown rice, quinoa, barley, or bulgur. Make the move to low-fat and fat-free milk and yogurt.
- **Step 4: Choose water or other zero-calorie drinks** (such as unsweetened tea, sparkling water, or an occasional diet lemonade or diet soda).

Figure 3.1 shows just what the Diabetes Plate Method plate looks like.

The Diabetes Plate Method is an easy way to plan meals. This method doesn't require any counting or too much thinking. You can create a balanced meal using the Diabetes Plate Method at home, at work, and when you eat out. One of the questions Tami has received frequently over the years is, "How high can you pile your plate?" A great question! The answer is no higher than a deck of cards is thick. That will help keep portions in check.

You see that sweet treats are not part of the Diabetes Plate Method. Sweets are not off

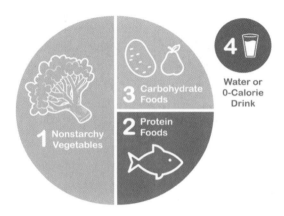

FIGURE 3.1   THE DIABETES PLATE METHOD

1 Nonstarchy Vegetables

2 Protein Foods

3 Carbohydrate Foods

4 Water or 0-Calorie Drink

limits. But fewer added sugars are best for anyone, whether they have diabetes or not.

BREAKING DOWN THE PLATE: IDEAS ON HOW TO FILL EACH SECTION

Vegetables: Nonstarchy and Starchy

There are both nonstarchy vegetables and starchy vegetables. It's important to know the difference. You will want to fill half of your plate with nonstarchy vegetables. They only have about 25 calories (and 5 grams carbohydrate) for a 1/2-cup serving if cooked, or a 1-cup serving if raw, and they are high in fiber, vitamins, and minerals. In our experience, people are often looking for easy ways to up their vegetable intake, particularly when it comes to nonstarchy vegetables. You'll find lots of practical tips in this section on how to fit in vegetables in flavorful ways.

Starchy vegetables on the other hand have three times more calories and carbohydrate for the same serving size, which is why you want to eat smaller portions, fitting them into one-quarter of your plate along with other carbohydrate foods like whole grains, legumes, lentils, fruit, and dairy. Plants are the star of the plate instead of protein!

There are well over 70 different nonstarchy vegetables! Here are some examples:

- Asparagus
- Broccoli
- Cabbage
- Carrots
- Cauliflower
- Cucumber
- Eggplant
- Green beans
- Greens
- Lettuce
- Mushrooms
- Okra
- Onion
- Peppers
- Spinach
- Tomatoes
- Vegetable juice

Starchy vegetables include:

- Acorn squash
- Butternut squash
- Corn
- Green peas
- Hominy
- Parsnips
- Plantain
- Potato
- Pumpkin
- Sweet potato

Here are 4 things to know about vegetables

1. **Vary your vegetables.** Eat a variety from all five subgroups: dark green, red and orange, legumes (beans and peas), starchy, and other. Each subgroup contributes a different combination of nutrients, which is why it is important to get a variety.

How does a "combination food" fit into the Diabetes Plate Method?

Let's use a thin-crust vegetable pizza as an example. Say you ate two slices of a medium pizza. Let's break it down and figure out how it follows the Diabetes Plate Method.

- **What kinds of foods go into it?**
  Flour (grain) in the crust, peppers, onions, tomatoes, tomato sauce, olives, mushrooms, and cheese
- **What parts of the plate would they go on?**
  - Peppers, onions , tomatoes, tomato sauce, olives, mushrooms: Nonstarchy vegetable half of the plate
  - Cheese: Protein quarter of the plate
  - Flour (grain) in the crust: Carbohydrate foods quarter of the plate
- **How much of the plate would they take up?** They'd all be pretty close to filling the plate following the Diabetes Plate Method, except for the nonstarchy vegetables, which may fall a little short of filling half the plate.
- **What are a few foods you could add to fill in the nonstarchy vegetable section when eating pizza?** A couple of ideas are adding a green side salad or extra veggie toppings.

2. **Enjoy them raw, cooked, fresh, frozen, or canned without added sodium, fat, or sugar.** If you can't find a no-salt-added version of canned vegetables, then rinse and drain them to wash away about 40% of the sodium.

3. **Keep vegetables healthy by preparing them in healthful ways**: raw, roasted, grilled, microwaved, stir-fried, sautéed, or steamed. You'll learn how to roast vegetables later in this chapter and find several recipes.

4. **If you currently eat more starchy vegetables than nonstarchy vegetables, try mixing starchy and nonstarchy vegetable(s) together.** It will reduce the carbohydrate if you eat the same portion. For instance, mix sautéed chopped kale with sweet potatoes or mix tenderly cooked cauliflower with potatoes when making mashed potatoes.

Here are 8 ways to simplify fitting in more vegetables

1. **Savor some vegetable soup.** Beyond garden vegetable soup, try tomato soup, pumpkin soup, or roasted caramelized carrot soup. Look for reduced- or low-sodium options. Or make a batch and freeze in portioned microwavable containers. Check out recipes for *Rustic Sweet Potato-Poblano Soup* on page 113 and *Creamy Butternut Squash Soup with Ginger* on page 114.

2. **When dining out, ask for an extra side of vegetables or a side green salad** in place of a potato, rice, or fried side.

3. **Get ahead of the game.** Buy pre-prepped fresh vegetables (many markets sell them packaged, cut up, and ready to cook) or cut-up broccoli, cauliflower, and carrots to have on hand to roast, microwave, or mix with a vinaigrette dressing for a salad.

4. **Explore fast ways to cook.** You can't beat the ease of steam-in-the-bag fresh and frozen vegetables. Or steam vegetables like asparagus spears, fresh green beans, or bok choy in the microwave. Place in a microwave-safe dish with a small amount of water, cover, and cook. Find two quick prep recipes for *Cheddar-y Squash Halves* on page 139 and *Quick-Fix Asparagus* on page 140.

5. **Roast vegetables while the rest of the meal is cooking.** Enjoy some now and eat the rest chilled or reheated for meals later in the week. This preparation of vegetables is one of our favorites! See our tried-and-true "formula" to *roast vegetables* page 151, along with several recipes. It also works on the grill. We place the veggies in a disposable aluminum pan and cook on a hot grill, stirring periodically. It's delicious!

6. **Create a DIY (do-it-yourself) superfoods salad bar.** Creating your own *salad bar* right in your refrigerator is a simple and tasty way to fit in more vegetables. See the instructions on page 145.

7. **Pile a variety of vegetables on sandwiches.** Whether it is a sandwich or wrap, pile on cucumber slices, tomato slices, spinach leaves and/or other greens, onion, bell pepper, or fresh banana pepper or jalapeno pepper slices for a little heat.

8. **Pair raw vegetables with a yogurt-based dip or hummus.** This combination is a quick and tasty way to fit in a vegetable serving, particularly if you buy ready-to-eat veggies like baby carrots. Three *dip recipes* follow on pages 142–144.

CHEDDAR-Y SQUASH HALVES

Need a quick, nonstarchy vegetable side to complement your plate? Simply cut tender summer squash in half, cook briefly, and then top with pre-chopped chilies and cheese. This dish is an effortless side that looks great, and tastes even better.

THIS RECIPE CAN FIT IN THE FOLLOWING EATING PATTERNS: vegetarian, low- or very-low-fat, low- or very-low-carbohydrate, DASH

NUMBER OF SERVINGS: 4 | **SERVING SIZE:** 1 squash half per serving
PREP TIME: 6 minutes | **COOK TIME:** 10 minutes | **STAND TIME:** 1 minute

INGREDIENTS

- 2 yellow squash (about 7 oz each), halved lengthwise
- 1/2 tsp ground cumin
- 1/8 tsp black pepper
- 1/4 cup canned diced mild green chilies
- 2 oz shredded reduced-fat sharp cheddar cheese

INSTRUCTIONS

1. Heat a large nonstick skillet over medium-high heat. Coat both sides of squash halves with nonstick cooking spray. Place cut side down in skillet and cook 3 minutes. Turn and sprinkle with cumin, black pepper, and green chilies. Reduce heat to medium-low, cover, and cook 7 minutes or until squash are tender-crisp.
2. Remove from heat, sprinkle with cheese, cover, and let stand 1 minute to allow cheese to melt.

COOK'S SWAPS

- For a vegan dish, substitute the cheese with 1 Tbsp extra-virgin olive oil drizzled over all at the end of the cooking time.

Trick

- For a bit more "zing" to your cheese, omit 1 oz cheddar cheese and add 1/2 oz reduced-fat blue cheese.

CHOICES: 1 Nonstarchy Vegetable, 1 Fat
BASIC NUTRITIONAL VALUES: Calories 70 | Calories from Fat 30 | **Total Fat** 3.5 g | Saturated Fat 1.8 g | Trans Fat 0.0 g | **Cholesterol** 10 mg | **Sodium** 180 mg | **Potassium** 290 mg | **Total Carbohydrate** 5 g | Dietary Fiber 1 g | Sugars 3 g | Added Sugars 0 g | **Protein** 5 g | **Phosphorus** 120 mg

QUICK-FIX ASPARAGUS

Asparagus can easily overcook, but not if you try this cooking technique. Just wrap, zap, and it's done to perfection!

THIS RECIPE CAN FIT IN THE FOLLOWING EATING PATTERNS: All

NUMBER OF SERVINGS: 4 | **SERVING SIZE:** about 6 spears
PREP TIME: 4 minutes | **COOK TIME:** 3 minutes

INGREDIENTS

- 1 lb asparagus spears, ends trimmed
- 1 lemon, halved
- 1 Tbsp extra-virgin olive oil
- 1/2 tsp dried rosemary
- 1/4 tsp salt
- 1/8 tsp black pepper

INSTRUCTIONS

1. Wrap asparagus in several sheets of wet paper towels. Place on a microwave-safe plate and cook on high setting for 3 minutes.
2. Carefully remove paper towels. Place asparagus on plate, squeeze lemon halves evenly over all, drizzle with oil, and sprinkle evenly with the rosemary, salt, and pepper.

Trick

- No need to break off each end of the asparagus one at a time. Often the asparagus is sold with a rubber band wrapped around it—leave the band on, hold the bunch of asparagus firmly in place, and cut off the ends all at once on a cutting board with a sharp knife.

CHOICES: 1 Nonstarchy Vegetable, 1/2 Fat
BASIC NUTRITIONAL VALUES: Calories 50 | Calories from Fat 30 | **Total Fat** 3.5 g | Saturated Fat 0.5 g | Trans Fat 0.0 g | **Cholesterol** 0 mg | **Sodium** 150 mg | **Potassium** 180 mg | **Total Carbohydrate** 4 g | Dietary Fiber 2 g | Sugars 2 g | Added Sugars 0 g | **Protein** 2 g | **Phosphorus** 45 mg

Share a colorful vegetable platter

One colorful healthy option to take to the next social gathering is a vegetable platter. It can help ensure that you have a low-carbohydrate option and meet the goal of covering half of your plate with nonstarchy vegetables. Sure, you can purchase a premade vegetable platter. However, you can also quickly put one together including both familiar vegetables, as well as a variety of others for a taste twist. For convenience, you may choose to purchase some of the vegetables already prepped and cut up.

Rather than compartmentalizing each type of vegetable, jam everything possible onto a colorful plate or platter, using a bit of care to make sure that colors are spaced out and that all the vegetables are showing their best side. Scatter two or three small bowls of flavored hummus, guacamole, or olive tapenade throughout for dunking the vegetables. You may even choose to add small bowls of olives or nuts. Here are some vegetable options you may wish to include:

For a taste twist	Familiar standbys
Asparagus of different colors (lightly steamed and chilled)	Broccoli florets
	Cauliflower florets
Baby corn	Celery sticks

For a taste twist	Familiar standbys
Broccoli rabe or broccolini (lightly steamed)	Baby carrots
Cherry or grape tomatoes (of different colors if available)	Cucumber sticks or slices
Edamame (soybeans in the pod)	
Jicama sticks	
Red, green, yellow, and orange bell pepper strips	
Sugar snap peas	
Zucchini or summer squash strips	

Get creative with your dips! There are so many different flavors and styles of dips that go great with raw vegetables. If buying a store-bought dip, check the Nutrition Facts label (learn more about the label in Chapter 5) and choose one lower in fat, saturated fat, and sodium. Also check the added sugars—choose a dip with little or no added sugar. Or, make your own! The ***Garlic Yogurt Dip, Cannellini Bean Hummus,*** and ***Peanut Lime Dipping Sauce*** recipes on pages 142–144 are quick and easy dips to pair with raw vegetables.

GARLIC YOGURT DIP WITH CAPERS

Add this Mediterranean-inspired dip to your next veggie tray. Fresh lemon, dill, garlic, and capers blend with creamy Greek yogurt for a refreshing and flavorful dip. It's delicious with veggies, such as cucumber slices, grape tomatoes, celery, yellow squash spears, broccoli, and whole petite peppers!

THIS RECIPE CAN FIT IN THE FOLLOWING EATING PATTERNS: vegetarian, low- or very-low-fat, low- or very-low-carbohydrate, DASH, Mediterranean

NUMBER OF SERVINGS: 5 | **SERVING SIZE:** 2 Tbsp per serving
PREP TIME: 5 minutes

INGREDIENTS

- 1 Tbsp capers, drained
- 1 garlic clove, minced
- 2 tsp extra-virgin olive oil, divided use
- 1/8 tsp salt
- 1/2 cup 2% plain Greek yogurt
- 1 Tbsp fresh lemon juice
- 2 Tbsp chopped fresh dill, divided use

INSTRUCTIONS

1. Place the capers, garlic, 1 tsp of the oil, and salt in a small bowl. Using the back of a spoon or fork, mash the capers. Add the yogurt, lemon juice, and 1 Tbsp of the dill. Stir until well blended.
2. Drizzle the remaining 1 tsp oil over the yogurt mixture and sprinkle the remaining 1 Tbsp dill over all.

POINTERS

- This dish may be made a day ahead. Cover with plastic wrap and refrigerate until time of serving.
- May substitute dill with mint, if desired.

Trick

- Mashing the capers helps to release the salty flavorful juices and helps to blend with the other ingredients. The capers would be too salty and too intense if left intact.

CHOICES: 1/2 Fat

BASIC NUTRITIONAL VALUES: Calories 35 | Calories from Fat 20 | **Total Fat** 2.5 g | Saturated Fat 0.5 g | Trans Fat 0.0 g | **Cholesterol** 0 mg | **Sodium** 110 mg | **Potassium** 40 mg | **Total Carbohydrate** 2 g | Dietary Fiber 0 g | Sugars 1 g | Added Sugars 0 g | **Protein** 2 g | **Phosphorus** 35 mg

CANNELLINI BEAN HUMMUS

Take a break from the store-bought variety and cut the cost while you're at it with this flavorful, super-easy-to-make hummus. Toss all the ingredients in a blender, whirl, and serve (or store for later). Dunk your favorite raw vegetables in it, or use as a spread on veggie and cheese sandwiches or wraps!

THIS RECIPE CAN FIT IN THE FOLLOWING EATING PATTERNS: All

NUMBER OF SERVINGS: 10 | **SERVING SIZE:** 2 Tbsp per serving
PREP TIME: 5 minutes

INGREDIENTS

- 1 (15.5-oz) can no-salt-added cannellini beans, rinsed and drained
- 1 garlic clove, peeled
- 3 Tbsp water
- 1 Tbsp cider vinegar
- 1 tsp onion powder
- 2 Tbsp extra-virgin olive oil
- 1/2 tsp salt
- 2 Tbsp chopped fresh basil

INSTRUCTIONS

1. Combine beans, garlic, water, vinegar, and onion powder in a blender. Secure lid and purée until smooth.
2. Place in a bowl, stir in the oil and salt and serve topped with basil.

POINTERS

- This dish may be made up to a week in advance. Cover with plastic wrap and refrigerate. Wait to chop and add basil until serving time.
- Store in small containers for easy portion control.

CHOICES: 1/2 Starch, 1/2 Fat
BASIC NUTRITIONAL VALUES: Calories 60 | Calories from Fat 25 | **Total Fat** 3.0 g | Saturated Fat 0.4 g | Trans Fat 0.0 g | **Cholesterol** 0 mg | **Sodium** 115 mg | **Potassium** 125 mg | **Total Carbohydrate** 7 g | Dietary Fiber 2 g | Sugars 1 g | Added Sugars 0 g | **Protein** 3 g | **Phosphorus** 45 mg

PEANUT LIME DIPPING SAUCE

Not only kids can be finicky when it comes to healthy snacking and eating enough nonstarchy veggies. But all ages will enjoy this flavorful peanut dipping sauce. The creaminess from the peanut butter coupled with the salty sweetness from the soy sauce and sweetener is a scrumptious treat to switch up the taste of veggies. Serve with veggies, such as broccoli, baby carrots, cauliflower, red pepper strips, sugar snap peas, blanched asparagus spears, zucchini spears, or blanched green beans.

THIS RECIPE CAN FIT IN THE FOLLOWING EATING PATTERNS: vegetarian, vegan, low-fat, low- or very-low-carbohydrate, DASH

NUMBER OF SERVINGS: 4 | **SERVING SIZE:** 2 Tbsp per serving
PREP TIME: 5 minutes

INGREDIENTS

- 1/4 cup plus 1 Tbsp peanut butter
- 2 Tbsp water
- 1 Tbsp fresh lime juice
- 1 tsp reduced-sodium soy sauce
- 1–2 individual packets stevia

INSTRUCTIONS

1. Combine all ingredients in a small microwave-safe bowl. Microwave on high setting for 10–15 seconds or until peanut butter is very soft. Stir until well blended.

POINTERS

- Cover any leftovers and refrigerate up to 2 weeks.
- For a thinner dipping consistency (after refrigerated), microwave on a high setting for 10–15 seconds. The warmed dip could also be used as a drizzle over other dishes like grilled chicken or vegetables.

COOK'S SWAP

- Substitute peanut butter with almond butter, if desired.

CHOICES: 1 High-Fat Protein, 1/2 Fat

BASIC NUTRITIONAL VALUES: Calories 120 | Calories from Fat 90 | **Total Fat** 10.0 g | Saturated Fat 2.1 g | Trans Fat 0.0 g | **Cholesterol** 0 mg | **Sodium** 140 mg | **Potassium** 170 mg | **Total Carbohydrate** 4 g | Dietary Fiber 1 g | Sugars 2 g | Added Sugars 1 g | **Protein** 5 g | **Phosphorus** 75 mg

How to Make a DIY Superfoods Salad Bar

Would you be more likely to eat a salad if everything was prepped and you had options?

By creating a do-it-yourself (DIY) "salad bar" of superfoods right in your own refrigerator, you can pull together a fast superfoods salad. Superfoods are nutrient-rich foods that can power-pack meals and snacks to enhance your eating pattern and positively affect health. Keep in mind that there is no single food that holds the key to good health—it's the combination of foods that you portion out on your plate.

Here's the how-to:

1. Set aside 15–30 minutes to assemble your "salad bar" for the week. Depending on how many ingredients you decide to include, you may need a little more prep time.

2. Prep all of the ingredients and store them in inexpensive stackable clear containers so that it's easy to see what's in them. By stacking the containers, they don't take up too much refrigerator space. You can take some shortcuts by buying shelf-stable bags of cooked quinoa, carrots, or Brussels sprouts already grated or bagged broccoli or cauliflower florets. Just transfer the pre-prepped veggies into your stackable containers. (Another idea is to put the salad greens in a gallon resealable plastic bag and lay it on top of the stacked ingredients.)

3. Stack everything in one or two 9 × 13 pans, heavy-duty foil pans, or baking sheets with sides, along with favorite dressings. We even put ingredients that don't require refrigeration (like nuts, dried fruits, and foil-packed tuna) in the pan, too, so everything is right at your fingertips.

4. Then all you have to do is pull out the pan, pick what you want on your salad that day, and a superfoods salad is ready in moments.

The following ingredients are ideas of what you could include as part of your DIY salad bar (and you can certainly add other favorite salad ingredients to the mix). Superfoods are noted with an asterisk. The ingredient ideas can be mixed and matched for a variety of flavors, textures, and colors. For instance, Tami enjoys fresh sweet berries with the kale, which is more bitter. And while cheese isn't a traditional superfood, a sprinkle of reduced-fat feta or goat cheese adds a savory element and balances the sweet of the fruit. Chewy and tart dried cranberries or cherries, crunchy nuts or seeds, quinoa, mukimame (shelled form or edamame/green soybeans), and foil-packed tuna/salmon add protein and heartiness.

Some ingredients to include in your DIY superfoods salad bar

Nonstarchy vegetables

- Broccoli florets*
- Brussels sprouts, shaved/chopped, raw or roasted*
- Carrots, grated*
- Cauliflower florets*
- Curly kale, chopped*
- Mushrooms*
- Other salad greens that you prefer, such as spring mix, chopped romaine, or arugula
- Radishes, raw or roasted*
- Red onion, thinly sliced
- Spinach*
- Tomatoes* (cherry or grape means no prepping or chopping)
- Turnips, raw or roasted*

Carbohydrate foods

Starchy vegetables/legumes

- Black beans*
- Frozen peas, thawed*
- Garbanzo beans (chickpeas)*
- Kidney beans*
- Lentils, cooked*
- Mukimame*
- Pinto beans*
- Red beans*

Whole grains

- Cooked bulgur*

- Cooked quinoa (or fully cooked microwavable cups)*
- Cooked wheat berries*
- Corn

Fruit

- Blackberries*
- Blueberries*
- Dried cherries, no sugar added*
- Dried cranberries, reduced sugar*
- Mandarin orange slices packed in juice
- Pomegranate seeds*
- Raspberries*
- Strawberries*

Protein foods

- Boiled egg (grated, diced, or sliced)*
- Grilled flank steak, thinly sliced
- Roasted or grilled chicken, diced
- Roasted turkey, diced or shredded
- Salmon in foil packs*
- Shredded low-fat cheese
- Tuna in foil packs*

Healthy fats

- Avocado*
- Nuts: almonds, Brazil nuts, cashews, peanuts, pecans, pistachios, walnuts*
- Seeds: chia, flax, hemp, pumpkin, sunflower*
- Olive oil*
- Dressings with healthy fats. Find recipes for homemade dressings on the following pages, and page 280.

---

*Superfoods

OLIVE OIL–WHITE WINE VINAIGRETTE

Try making salad dressing at home to suit your taste and nutrition needs. This simple recipe is a great place to start. It's versatile, too! Toss it with salad greens, in pasta and vegetable salads, and as a marinade for chicken or pork.

THIS RECIPE CAN FIT IN THE FOLLOWING EATING PATTERNS: vegetarian, vegan, low- or very-low-carbohydrate, DASH, Mediterranean

NUMBER OF SERVINGS: 4 | **SERVING SIZE:** 2 Tbsp per serving
PREP TIME: 5 minutes

INGREDIENTS

- 1/4 cup extra-virgin olive oil
- 2 Tbsp dry white wine, such as Chardonnay
- 2 Tbsp cider vinegar
- 1 garlic clove, minced
- 2 tsp dried oregano
- 1/2 tsp onion powder
- 1 1/2 tsp hot pepper sauce, such as Franks
- 1/4 tsp salt

INSTRUCTIONS

1. Combine all ingredients in a small jar.
2. Secure with a lid and shake vigorously.

COOK'S SWAP

- Substitute wine with 1 Tbsp fresh lemon juice and 1 Tbsp water, if desired.

CHOICES: 3 Fat

BASIC NUTRITIONAL VALUES: Calories 130 | Calories from Fat 130 | **Total Fat** 14.0 g | Saturated Fat 1.9 g | Trans Fat 0.0 g | **Cholesterol** 0 mg | **Sodium** 220 mg | **Potassium** 25 mg | **Total Carbohydrate** 1 g | Dietary Fiber 0 g | Sugars 0 g | Added Sugars 0 g | **Protein** 0 g | **Phosphorus** 5 mg

CREAMY FRESH GARLIC DRESSING

This recipe is a cousin to Caesar dressing, but a much healthier cousin. Be sure to use fresh garlic (not the bottled variety or the powder) for this. You won't be disappointed!

THIS RECIPE CAN FIT IN THE FOLLOWING EATING PATTERNS: vegetarian, low- or very-low-fat, low- or very-low-carbohydrate, DASH

NUMBER OF SERVINGS: 5 | **SERVING SIZE:** 2 Tbsp per serving
PREP TIME: 5 minutes

INGREDIENTS

- 1/3 cup light mayonnaise
- 3 Tbsp 2% plain Greek yogurt
- 2 Tbsp 2% milk
- 1 Tbsp cider vinegar
- 2 tsp Dijon mustard
- 2 garlic cloves, minced
- 1/4 tsp black pepper

INSTRUCTIONS

1. Combine all ingredients in a small bowl. Whisk together until smooth.

Trick

- By adding the yogurt to the dressing, it "stretches" the flavor of the mayonnaise without the additional fat and sodium.

CHOICES: 1 Fat

BASIC NUTRITIONAL VALUES: Calories 50 | Calories from Fat 35 | **Total Fat** 4.0 g | Saturated Fat 0.5 g | Trans Fat 0.0 g | **Cholesterol** 4 mg | **Sodium** 160 mg | **Potassium** 40 mg | **Total Carbohydrate** 3 g | Dietary Fiber 0 g | Sugars 1 g | Added Sugars 1 g | **Protein** 1 g | **Phosphorus** 25 mg

RASPBERRY-GINGER VINAIGRETTE

Fruit-flavored salad dressing can often contain quite a bit of sugar and very little actual fruit. This vinaigrette has no added sugar and almost a cup of fiber-rich raspberries. Plus, it's simple to make! Just toss the ingredients in a jar and shake—the berries break down in the process. Try it on a fresh green salad topped with chicken or turkey, nuts, and a sprinkling of blue cheese, or on slices of cantaloupe or honeydew melon for a refreshing fruit salad.

THIS RECIPE CAN FIT IN THE FOLLOWING EATING PATTERNS: **vegetarian, vegan, low-fat, low- or very-low-carbohydrate, DASH**

NUMBER OF SERVINGS: 8 | **SERVING SIZE:** 2 Tbsp per serving
PREP TIME: 5 minutes

INGREDIENTS

- 2/3 cup fresh or frozen, thawed unsweetened raspberries
- 1/4 cup canola oil
- 1/4 cup balsamic vinegar
- 4 individual packets stevia
- 2 tsp grated ginger (see tips for using fresh ginger on page 50)
- 1/2 tsp salt

INSTRUCTIONS

1. Combine all ingredients in a small jar.
2. Secure with a lid and shake vigorously.

POINTER

- Substitute grated ginger with grated orange rind or grated lemon rind for a refreshing alternative.

CHOICES: 1 1/2 Fat

BASIC NUTRITIONAL VALUES: **Calories 70** | Calories from Fat 60 | **Total Fat** 7.0 g | Saturated Fat 0.5 g | Trans Fat 0.0 g | **Cholesterol** 0 mg | **Sodium** 150 mg | **Potassium** 25 mg | **Total Carbohydrate** 3 g | Dietary Fiber 1 g | Sugars 2 g | Added Sugars 0 g | **Protein** 0 g | **Phosphorus** 5 mg

COLESLAW WITH CHIA SEED DRESSING

Chia seeds contribute three ways in this salad. It's the ingredient that gives this coleslaw the texture of poppy seeds, it becomes a bit gelatinous so it helps to blend the other ingredients together, and it adds important dietary fiber even with the small amount used. That says a lot for 1 Tbsp of those tiny seeds.

THIS RECIPE CAN FIT IN THE FOLLOWING EATING PATTERNS: vegetarian, vegan, low- or very-low-carbohydrate, DASH

NUMBER OF SERVINGS: 4 | **SERVING SIZE:** 3/4 cup per serving
PREP TIME: 5 minutes

INGREDIENTS

- 3 cups coleslaw mix
- 1 cup matchstick carrots
- 1 Tbsp chia seeds
- 2 Tbsp extra-virgin olive oil
- 1 1/2 Tbsp cider vinegar
- 2 individual packets stevia
- 1/8 tsp crushed pepper flakes
- 1/8 tsp salt
- 1/8 tsp black pepper

INSTRUCTIONS

1. Combine all ingredients in a medium bowl and mix until blended.

POINTER

- Serve immediately for pronounced flavors and a crunchy texture, or cover and refrigerate 1 hour for a more blended flavor and softer texture.

CHOICES: 1 Nonstarchy Vegetable, 1 1/2 Fat

BASIC NUTRITIONAL VALUES: Calories 100 | Calories from Fat 70 | **Total Fat** 8.0 g | Saturated Fat 1.1 g | Trans Fat 0.0 g | **Cholesterol** 0 mg | **Sodium** 100 mg | **Potassium** 200 mg | **Total Carbohydrate** 6 g | Dietary Fiber 3 g | Sugars 2 g | Added Sugars 0 g | **Protein** 1 g | **Phosphorus** 45 mg

How to Roast Vegetables

Tami used to be fearful of roasting vegetables. "Would they turn out right? What if I messed them up?" She has since become a huge fan of roasted vegetables of all types and learned that there's no exact science to roasting vegetables. She's even become a fan of some vegetables roasted that she didn't particularly care for in the raw form, such as radishes. It's pretty hard to mess up roasted vegetables. There's a multitude of flavor combinations from which to choose. And roasted vegetables are tasty, healthy, and easy! See Table 3.7 for ideas on seasoning combinations and cooking times.

The secret formula for roasting vegetables

1. **Pick.** Pick your vegetables (about 2 lb or 8–10 cups). Wash and dry well (dryness is important so that vegetables roast and do not "steam" because of the moisture).
2. **Preheat.** Preheat the oven to 425°F.
3. **Portion.** Portion into 1–1 1/2 inch chunks (smaller pieces may take less time to roast and larger chunks more time).
4. **Place.** Place in a 1-gallon resealable plastic bag (or for a "greener" option, use a bowl and tongs).
5. **Drizzle.** Drizzle in 1 1/2–2 Tbsp olive oil.
6. **Season.** Select your seasonings and add to bag.
7. **Shake.** Shake bag and massage vegetables to coat well with oil and seasonings.
8. **Spread out.** Transfer vegetables to a baking sheet lined with a sheet of parchment paper or foil. Spread out in a single layer. This is important for even roasting. The parchment paper allows for quick cleaning. There's no need to scrub the roasting pan after cooking.
9. **Roast.** Place tray on an upper (not top) oven rack and roast until the edges are lightly browned and vegetables are tender when pierced with a fork (25–30 minutes for harder vegetables and 20–25 minutes for softer vegetables).
10. **Stir.** Stir once or twice during roasting to allow for even browning. Keep an eye on the vegetables during the final 5–10 minutes so they don't burn. Depending on the size of the vegetable pieces and the texture you prefer, you may want to roast a few minutes longer or a few minutes less.

Check out the ***Mixed Roasted Potatoes*** recipe on page 153 to see this formula in action. Also see ***Thyme Roasted Beans and Brown Onions*** on page 154, ***Roasted Carrots*** on page 290, and ***Garlic Roasted Brussels Sprouts*** on page 304.

3 Cook's Tips on Roasting Vegetables

1. **Mix vegetables with longer and shorter roasting times.** Start vegetables requiring a longer roasting time on one pan and then add vegetables with a shorter cooking time to the oven on another pan. When all are roasted, just toss together.

2. **Parboil longer-cooking vegetables to speed up roasting time.** Longer-cooking (harder) vegetables, such as potatoes, parsnips, or turnips, can be boiled about 5 minutes to soften and speed up roasting time if desired. Just drain them well and pat dry with a paper towel.

3. **Enjoy leftovers.** While roasted vegetables are the tastiest hot from the oven, we enjoy leftovers reheated in the microwave, or sometimes taken from the refrigerator and allowed to warm up slightly at room temperature. We also sometimes eat them straight from the refrigerator cold.

TABLE 3.7   VEGETABLE ROASTING TIMES AND SEASONING IDEAS

Vegetables Requiring Longer Roasting Time (25–30 minutes)	Vegetables Requiring Shorter Roasting Time (20–25 minutes)	Seasoning Ideas
• Broccoli florets • Brussels sprouts • Butternut squash chunks • Carrots • Cauliflower florets • Parsnips • Potatoes (white, red, yellow, sweet) • Radishes • Turnips	• Asparagus • Cherry or grape tomatoes • Green beans • Mushrooms • Onions • Peppers (green, orange, red, yellow, jalapeno, poblano) • Yellow squash • Zucchini	• Basil • Black pepper (fresh ground) • Cinnamon • Cloves • Coarse sea salt • Garlic or green garlic (fresh minced • Ginger (fresh grated) • Lemon pepper • Nutmeg • Parsley • Red pepper flakes • Rosemary • Soy sauce (lower sodium) • Sriracha sauce • Thyme

MIXED ROASTED POTATOES

Add a boost of nutrition to simple roasted potatoes by mixing in sweet potatoes! Sweet potatoes add a boost of fiber and a mega-dose of vitamin A.

THIS RECIPE CAN FIT IN THE FOLLOWING EATING PATTERNS: vegetarian, vegan, low-fat, DASH, Mediterranean

NUMBER OF SERVINGS: 6 | **SERVING SIZE:** About 3/4 cup per serving
PREP TIME: 10 minutes | **COOK TIME:** 30 minutes

INGREDIENTS

- 1 lb red potatoes, unpeeled and cut into 1-inch chunks
- 1 lb sweet potatoes, unpeeled and cut into 1-inch chunks
- 2 Tbsp extra-virgin olive oil
- 1 1/2 tsp dried rosemary
- 1/2 tsp dried oregano
- 1/2 tsp salt
- 1/4 tsp black pepper

INSTRUCTIONS

1. Preheat oven to 425°F.
2. Place all ingredients in a 1-gallon resealable plastic bag. Seal bag.
3. Shake bag and massage vegetables to coat well with oil and seasonings.
4. Transfer vegetables to a foil-lined baking sheet. Spread out in a single layer.
5. Place baking sheet on an upper (not top) oven rack. Stir and roast 15 minutes or until the edges are lightly browned and potatoes are tender when pierced with a fork.

POINTER

- Placing the potatoes in a single layer and not crowding is important for even roasting. The foil allows for quick cleanup rather than having to scrub the baking sheet.

CHOICES: 1 1/2 Starch, 1 Fat
BASIC NUTRITIONAL VALUES: Calories 150 | Calories from Fat 40 | **Total Fat** 4.5 g | Saturated Fat 0.7 g | Trans Fat 0.0 g | **Cholesterol** 0 mg | **Sodium** 220 mg | **Potassium** 630 mg | **Total Carbohydrate** 25 g | Dietary Fiber 3 g | Sugars 5 g | Added Sugars 0 g | **Protein** 3 g | **Phosphorus** 80 mg

THYME ROASTED BEANS AND BROWNED ONIONS

Green beans are an all-time versatile vegetable. Steamed, boiled, sautéed, or lightly roasted—any way you prepare them, they make a great side dish. These green beans are roasted with lots of onions and at a high temperature for deeper flavor and gorgeous browning.

THIS RECIPE CAN FIT IN THE FOLLOWING EATING PATTERNS: All

NUMBER OF SERVINGS: 8 | **SERVING SIZE:** About 2/3 cup per serving
PREP TIME: 10 minutes | **COOK TIME:** 30 minutes

INGREDIENTS

- 1 1/4 lb green beans, ends trimmed
- 12 oz onion, cut vertically, 1/4-inch wide
- 2 Tbsp olive oil
- 2 tsp dried thyme
- 1 tsp garlic powder
- 1/8 tsp black pepper
- 1/2 tsp salt

INSTRUCTIONS

1. Preheat oven to 425°F.
2. Place all ingredients, except the salt, in a 1-gallon resealable plastic bag. Seal bag.
3. Shake bag and massage vegetables to coat well with oil and seasonings.
4. Transfer vegetables to a foil-lined baking sheet. Spread out in a single layer.
5. Place baking sheet on an upper (not top) oven rack and roast 30 minutes, stirring every 10 minutes. Roast until the edges are lightly browned and beans are tender when pierced with a fork.
6. Sprinkle evenly with the salt. Using a fork, scrape up any browned bits and stir into the beans for added flavor.

CHOICES: 2 Nonstarchy Vegetable, 1/2 Fat

BASIC NUTRITIONAL VALUES: Calories 70 | Calories from Fat 30 | **Total Fat** 3.5 g | Saturated Fat 0.5 g | Trans Fat 0.0 g | **Cholesterol** 0 mg | **Sodium** 150 mg | **Potassium** 150 mg | **Total Carbohydrate** 9 g | Dietary Fiber 3 g | Sugars 3 g | Added Sugars 0 g | **Protein** 2 g | **Phosphorus** 30 mg

COOK'S SWAP

- As a low-carb alternative, use the roasted beans instead of rice with your next stir-fry.

POINTERS

- Serve warm or at room temperature.
- Cut or break beans into 2-inch pieces instead of roasting whole, if desired.

Protein Foods

Protein foods include a variety of animal and plant sources. Protein foods generally have minimal effect on blood glucose with type 2 diabetes, unless they are plant-based (such as soy proteins, tofu, and legumes) and contain carbohydrate that raises blood glucose. Fish, seafood, beef, pork, chicken, turkey, eggs, nuts, seeds, and soy products are all protein-rich foods. Beans and peas (legumes) are high in protein, but they are also higher in carbohydrate. They can be counted as either a carbohydrate food or a protein food.

Cheese and cottage cheese are often considered protein foods and dairy servings. For good health, vary your protein routine, including a variety of protein sources. Most people think "meat" when they think protein, but recipes like our *Black Bean and Yellow Quinoa* on page 156 can provide plant-based proteins without the meat. For eating plans other than vegetarian/vegan, try to choose fish and seafood twice a week. Keep meat and poultry lean by removing skin or cutting off fat. Choose low-fat dairy foods such as cheese or cottage cheese. For more information on proteins, refer to Chapter 2 (page 42).

BLACK BEAN AND YELLOW QUINOA

Quinoa is an ancient whole grain and a nutrient powerhouse! It's high in protein, high in fiber, and has a bonus of being gluten free! Quinoa is a great grain to use in plant-based dishes to add a boost of protein. In this recipe, turmeric is added to the water while cooking to give the quinoa a bright yellow color.

THIS RECIPE CAN FIT IN THE FOLLOWING EATING PATTERNS: vegetarian, low-fat, DASH

NUMBER OF SERVINGS: 4 | **SERVING SIZE:** 3/4 cups bean mixture plus 1/2 cup quinoa
PREP TIME: 15 minutes | **COOK TIME:** 20 minutes

INGREDIENTS

Quinoa:

- 1 1/2 cups water
- 3/4 cup uncooked quinoa
- 1/2 tsp ground turmeric
- 1/8 tsp salt

Beans:

- 2 Tbsp extra-virgin olive oil, divided use
- 2 cups chopped green bell pepper
- 1/2 cup chopped onion
- 1 (15-oz) can no-salt-added black beans, rinsed and drained
- 3/4 cup water
- 6 oz fresh salsa, about 2/3 cup
- 2 tsp ground cumin
- 1/4 tsp salt
- 1/2 cup 2% plain Greek yogurt

INSTRUCTIONS

1. Bring 1 1/2 cups water to a boil in a medium saucepan. Add the quinoa and turmeric, reduce heat, cover, and simmer 10 minutes. Remove from heat, let stand 5 minutes, and stir in 1/8 tsp salt.
2. Meanwhile, heat 1 1/2 tsp of the oil in a large non-stick skillet over medium-high heat. Tilt skillet to coat bottom slightly. Add peppers and onions. Cook 5 minutes or until peppers are tender.
3. Stir in the beans, 3/4 cup water, salsa, cumin, and 1/4 tsp salt; bring to a boil and cook 1 minute to heat through. Remove from heat. Stir in remaining 1 1/2 Tbsp oil.
4. Spoon equal amounts of the quinoa (about 1/2 cup) in four shallow bowls. Spoon the bean mixture over quinoa and top with yogurt.

CHOICES: 2 1/2 Starch, 1 Nonstarchy Vegetable, 1 Lean Protein, 1 Fat
BASIC NUTRITIONAL VALUES: Calories 320 | Calories from Fat 90 | **Total Fat** 10.0 g | Saturated Fat 1.6 g | Trans Fat 0.0 g | **Cholesterol** 0 mg | **Sodium** 240 mg | **Potassium** 750 mg | **Total Carbohydrate** 46 g | Dietary Fiber 8 g | Sugars 8 g | Added Sugars 0 g | **Protein** 14 g | **Phosphorus** 320 mg

COOK'S SWAPS

- For a lower-carb dish, substitute the quinoa and serve over shredded romaine lettuce with lime wedges.
- For a vegan dish, substitute the yogurt with a nondairy yogurt, or omit the yogurt entirely and serve with lime to squeeze over all.

POINTERS

- For a bit more spice, use poblano chili peppers instead of green bell pepper. They give a deeper "pepper" taste and a slight touch of heat. Do not discard the poblano pepper seeds if more heat is desired.
- Fresh salsa is sold in the deli and/or refrigerated section of the produce aisle. Look for the salsa that contains the lowest amount of sodium. And make sure you compare them equally. Sometimes a serving size on the label is 1 Tbsp, sometimes it's 2 Tbsp, and other times it's 1/4 cup . . . that's a big difference!

Trick

- Anytime you'd like to give your rice, grain, or even potato dish a pop of color, add 1/2 tsp ground turmeric to the water while cooking. It turns the food bright yellow without changing the flavor of the dish.

SHRIMP & BRUSSELS SPROUTS WITH SPICY LEMON DIPPING SAUCE

In recent years, Brussels sprouts have grown wildly popular! And shrimp is an all-time favorite seafood. Pair the two with a simple zesty lemon dipping sauce that has a bit of kick from fresh garlic and hot sauce, and you have a healthy appetizer or entrée.

THIS RECIPE CAN FIT IN THE FOLLOWING EATING PATTERNS: low- or very-low-fat, low- or very-low-carbohydrate, DASH, Mediterranean

NUMBER OF SERVINGS: 4 | **SERVING SIZE:** About 1 cup and 1 Tbsp sauce per serving
PREP TIME: 12 minutes | **COOK TIME:** 9 minutes

INGREDIENTS

- 4 cups water
- 8 oz frozen Brussels sprouts
- 12 oz raw peeled shrimp
- 1 large red bell pepper, cut into 1-inch cubes
- 2 Tbsp extra-virgin olive oil
- 2 tsp grated lemon rind
- 2 Tbsp fresh lemon juice
- 1 garlic clove, minced
- 2 tsp hot pepper sauce, such as Frank's

INSTRUCTIONS

1. Bring water to a boil in a medium saucepan over high heat, add Brussel sprouts, return to a boil, reduce heat to medium-low, cover, and cook 2 minutes. Add shrimp and return to a boil over high heat. Cook, uncovered, for 4 minutes or until shrimp are opaque in center.
2. Add the bell peppers to the pot with the shrimp and Brussels sprouts mixture.
3. Immediately drain the shrimp, pepper, and Brussels sprouts mixture in a colander and run under cold water to stop cooking process and to cool quickly. Drain well.
4. Whisk together the oil, lemon rind, juice, garlic, and hot sauce in a small bowl. Serve alongside shrimp, pepper, and Brussels sprouts mixture. Accompany with wooden picks for spearing and dipping.

CHOICES: 2 Nonstarchy Vegetable, 2 Lean Protein, 1/2 Fat
BASIC NUTRITIONAL VALUES: Calories 170 | Calories from Fat 60 | **Total Fat** 7.0 g | Saturated Fat 1.0 g | Trans Fat 0.0 g | **Cholesterol** 130 mg | **Sodium** 190 mg | **Potassium** 450 mg | **Total Carbohydrate** 8 g | Dietary Fiber 3 g | Sugars 3 g | Added Sugars 0 g | **Protein** 19 g | **Phosphorus** 205 mg

Carbohydrate Foods

Grains

Grains are a carbohydrate food and can be a good source of fiber and other nutrients. When it comes to grains, the best choices are *whole* grains. They have more nutrients and fiber than processed grains (such as white flour or white rice) and will likely not spike your blood glucose as quickly or as high. Dietary fiber from whole grains may help reduce blood cholesterol levels; may lower risk of heart disease, obesity, and type 2 diabetes; and may help reduce constipation.

Whole grains include the entire grain kernel, while refined grains have been processed, which removes dietary fiber, iron, and other nutrients. The following are examples of grain foods. Foods that are whole grain are designated with an asterisk:

- Whole-grain breads, such as 100% whole-wheat or rye*
- Whole-grain, high-fiber cereal*
- Cooked cereal such as oatmeal*, grits, hominy, or cream of wheat

*Whole-grain foods

- Rice, brown rice*, pasta, wheat tortillas, and corn tortillas*
- Low-fat crackers, snack chips, light popcorn*, and pretzels

Fruits

Fruits contain carbohydrate, so they are considered a "carbohydrate food" in the Diabetes Plate Method. Focus on whole fruits—they are your best bets. Whole fruits include fresh, canned, and unsweetened frozen varieties. If you choose whole fresh fruits that are in season, you can save money and increase variety. For instance, when oranges are in season, you can get variety in your fruits and increase nutrients by swapping in a blood orange or a Cara Cara orange, for instance.

Although 100% fruit juice can be part of a healthy eating pattern, it is much lower in dietary fiber than whole fruit, less satisfying, rapidly raises blood glucose, and, when consumed in excess, can contribute extra calories.

Milk/yogurt

Dairy foods are a great source of calcium, vitamin D, potassium, and protein. Milk and yogurt also contain carbohydrate, so they are considered a "carbohydrate food" in the Diabetes Plate Method. Choose dairy foods that are low-fat and fat-free, such as skim milk, fat-free yogurt, reduced-fat cheese, or light fortified soy beverage (commonly known as soymilk). For more information on carbohydrates, refer back to Chapter 2 (page 17).

Drink Water Instead of Sugary Beverages

With beverages, the goal is to go for drinks that are zero-calorie. Water is always the best choice. Here are 8 tips to help fit in more water:

1. Buy bottled water to easily grab a bottle and know exactly how much you started with and are drinking.
2. Keep a refillable water bottle or travel cup with you to keep water cold and to help you keep track of how much you're drinking.
3. Use an app to track your water intake.
4. Drink sparkling water or club soda if you prefer carbonation.
5. Add a calorie-free water-enhancer flavoring for variety.
6. Add a twist of lemon, lime, or orange for fresh flavor.
7. Make some creative ice cubes to add to water to give it visual appeal and light flavor. See the box "7 Creative Ice Cube Favorite Flavor Combinations" below.
8. Try flavor-infused water. Learn how to make **Lemony Spa Water** and **Watermelon Rosemary Refreshe**r on pages 37 and 38. Both are calorie-free and carbohydrate-free!

7 Creative Ice Cube Favorite Flavor Combinations

Chop the ingredients other than raspberries and blueberries into small pieces and sprinkle into ice trays. Fill with water and freeze.

1. Cucumber and basil
2. Cucumber and mint
3. Lime and mint
4. Fresh strawberries
5. Raspberries
6. Blueberries
7. Lemon

Healthy fat

You learned about healthy fats in Chapter 2 (page 54). To share a few more practical tips, here are 6 simple switches to healthy fat:

1. Switch cooking oils at home. Keep a variety in the pantry and rotate. There are many great flavored olive oils to switch up the flavor in dressings, for dipping and drizzling.
2. Top your morning whole-grain toast with almond butter, cashew butter, or peanut butter rather than butter.
3. Add crunch to a salad with almonds, pecans, pistachios, pumpkin seeds,

toasted sesame seeds, or sunflower seeds instead of bacon.

4. Switch in canola oil or corn oil for lard or shortening in cooking.

5. Lightly dip crusty bread in olive oil rather than slathering with butter.

6. Dip raw veggies in hummus rather than ranch-style dressing.

PRACTICAL METHODS AND TOOLS TO SIZE-UP AND MANAGE PORTIONS

Although following the Diabetes Plate Method helps manage portions automatically, following it every meal, every day, may not always be realistic or possible. Life happens. So, knowing

Rate Your Plate

After you create your plate, whether you're at a work potluck, church social, restaurant buffet, or in your own kitchen, take a close look at the foods and portions you've included. Then answer the following 5 questions:

1. **Is about 1/4 of your plate filled with carbohydrate foods, such as a starchy vegetables, grain, beans, fruit, or milk/yogurt?** That's about 30–45 g carbohydrate or 2–3 carbohydrate choices/servings.

2. **Is about 1/4 of your plate filled with a protein food, such as lean meat, poultry, fish, or plant-based protein?** Animal-based proteins are carbohydrate-free—unless they're breaded or have a carbohydrate-containing sauce or accompaniment. Plant-based protein foods, such as beans and legumes, do have carbohydrate that needs to be factored in.

3. **Is at least 1/2 of your plate filled with nonstarchy vegetables?** That's about 10–15 g carbohydrate or about 1 carbohydrate choice/serving.

4. **Is your plate colorful?** Having a colorfully portioned plate helps ensure you have a variety of foods and nutrients.

5. **Do you have a zero-calorie drink?**

The goal is to be able to answer "yes" to all of the questions above most of the time. Filling your plate in this manner helps manage carbohydrate and ensure that you're getting variety, a good balance of nutrients, and managed portions. Small changes add up.

how to measure and estimate portions, and becoming masterful at these skills, is important. Getting familiar with portion sizes can help you pinpoint how much you actually eat and whether you are meeting or exceeding your carbohydrate targets. The following are three methods to help you size-up and manage portion sizes.

Method #1: Use Measuring Tools

The most accurate way to get familiar with and assess portion sizes is to measure your food or beverage with measuring cups, measuring spoons, or a food scale. Be sure to use liquid measuring cups for liquids (they usually look like a small pitcher) and dry measuring cups for non-liquids—there *is* a difference. Most people

5 Top Tips for Measuring Portions

1. **Measure your drinking cups and mugs.** Fill your drinking cups and mugs with water and then pour it back into a liquid measuring cup to determine how many ounces they hold. You'll then know how much you're drinking when you fill the cup or mug all the way or just part of the way.

2. **Measure your bowls**. Fill your bowls with dry cereal and then measure the cereal with a dry measuring cup to identify how much the bowls hold and how much you eat when you fill them up.

3. **Measure your plate.** Use a tape measure. Is the plate 9 inches across? Or is it more like 11–12 inches?

4. **Use a measuring cup to serve foods** (such as soup, vegetables, casserole, or cereal) rather than using a spoon or ladle. You can then easily quantify the amount you eat and, from there, determine the carbohydrate count. Tami gleaned this tip from a client years ago, and it is now a favorite practice among many of her clients.

5. **When possible, measure out appropriate individual portions of foods.** For instance, use a measuring cup to put leftover casserole or chili into small plastic containers for reheating so you know exactly how much is in there. Better yet, purchase portion controlled 1-cup or 2-cup containers. There is no thinking required when you are ready to reheat for lunch or dinner. Or, measure appropriate portions of nuts, fruit, or other snacks and store them in resealable plastic bags or small airtight containers. That way, you have ready-made grab-and-go snacks.

are surprised to see how their actual portion sizes measure up against what they "thought" they were eating. These tips remind Tami of a gentleman she worked with who guessed his cereal bowl held about 1 cup. When he went home, poured cereal in to fill his bowl, and then measured what was in there with a dry measuring cup, he found it was actually 2 cups. He discovered he was routinely eating double what he thought.

Method #2: Use Hand Estimations

Although measuring cups and spoons certainly have their place, they aren't always convenient.

(Who wants to take measuring cups to a friend's house for dinner? Or to the deli at lunch?) One easy way to get in touch with portions is to use your hand. It's always with you.

Method #3: Visualize the Right Portion Size

A third method to become familiar with portion sizes is to compare them with everyday objects. Table 3.8 has some of our favorite common comparisons. Once you gain familiarity with standard portion sizes, you can easily compare them to common items and come up with other comparisons that work for you.

Using Your Hand to Estimate Portions*

Small adult fist = 1 cup

Palm of a woman's hand = 3 ounces
Palm of a man's hand = 5 ounces

*These are approximations and may vary slightly depending on the size of your hand.

Thumb tip to first joint = 1 tablespoon
Fingertip to first joint = 1 teaspoon
Whole thumb = 1 ounce

Compare your fist size to measuring cups to determine how many cups your fist equates to. Just hold your fist next to the measuring cup, and see how much of your fist will actually fit in the measuring cup. And compare your thumb and thumb tip to measuring spoons to determine how many teaspoons and tablespoons they equate to.

TABLE 3.8   COMMON COMPARISONS TO FIGURE OUT PORTION SIZES

Portion Size	Common Item
1 slice of whole-grain bread	DVD
3 oz meat	Deck of cards
3-oz fish fillet	Checkbook
2 Tbsp hummus or peanut butter	Ping pong ball
Medium-size piece of fruit	Tennis ball
1 cup salad greens	Baseball
1/2 cup beans, lentils, or cooked vegetables	1/2 baseball
1/4 cup nuts	Golf ball
1 tsp olive oil/healthy fat	A dice

You can then estimate portions and the associated carbohydrate content.

Summary

In summary, there are a variety of different eating patterns demonstrated to be beneficial in managing type 2 diabetes. Your personal preferences and goals are important considerations when choosing an eating pattern to embrace. The Diabetes Plate Method is an easy way to plan and portion meals to put your eating pattern of choice into practice. Work with your registered dietitian nutritionist to determine which eating pattern is the best for you. Small changes add up. The goal is to find your healthy eating style and maintain it for a lifetime.

Snack With Success

SNACKING: WHY, WHEN, AND WHAT?

In the past, typical meal plans for type 2 diabetes often called for two or three between-meal snacks each day. It was believed that snacks were necessary to help stabilize blood glucose levels. Now we know that not everyone with diabetes (particularly type 2 diabetes) routinely needs between-meal snacks, especially if three regular meals are part of the day. Extra calories and carbohydrate from unplanned or unnecessary snacks can translate into extra pounds and higher blood glucose. However, snacks may serve several positive purposes for people with diabetes. This chapter's focus is to bring clarity to 3 key topics and share a multitude of snack ideas so that you can snack with success:

1. **WHY** to snack
2. **WHEN** to snack
3. **WHAT** to snack on

Why to Snack

Planned snacks (the key word here is "planned") may serve several purposes:

1. To curb appetite and prevent over eating at mealtime
2. To head off hypoglycemia (low blood glucose)
3. To refuel between meals; when meals are delayed; and before, during, and/or after physical activity
4. To boost calorie intake if needed (although most adults with type 2 diabetes are focused on reducing calorie intake to manage weight)

When to Snack

As alluded to earlier in this chapter, snack times can vary from person to person. While one person may find that a late-morning nibble fuels the pre-lunch exercise class and helps head off hypoglycemia, another may need a small, midafternoon munchie to head off pre-supper hunger pangs. And yet another may find that a few bites near bedtime work best. Listen to your body and watch your blood glucose patterns; let them be your guide when it comes to snacking.

3 Questions to Ask Yourself When Considering a Snack

1. Are you truly hungry? Keep in mind that snacks add extra calories. So if weight loss is one of your goals, plan for those extra snack calories by trimming calories elsewhere in the day.
2. Do you need extra fuel for physical activity?
3. Do you need extra carbohydrate to keep blood glucose levels in range?

If the answer is "yes" to any of these questions, then it may be time for a snack.

5 Considerations to Help Size-up When You Need a Snack

#1: Weight goals

Do you need to lose weight, maintain weight, or gain weight?

- **If you want to lose or maintain weight**, a small, planned, between-meal snack can help curb your appetite and prevent overeating at mealtime. The key is to include the calories and carbohydrate in your daily eating plan to prevent weight gain and/or blood glucose spikes.
- **If you want to gain weight,** those extra calories from snacks can help you achieve your weight-gain goal. Keep in mind though that carbohydrate still needs to be tracked.

#2: Diabetes medications

If you take any diabetes medications, are you at risk for or do you experience hypoglycemia (low blood glucose) when your medication is at peak action? (If you're not sure, ask your diabetes health-care team or pharmacist.)

If the answer is "yes," a carbohydrate-containing snack can help prevent hypoglycemia. And as mentioned above, plan for those extra calories by trimming calories elsewhere in the day. Here are snacking guidelines to consider based on whether or not you take diabetes medications:

- **If you manage your diabetes with insulin or other diabetes medications,** mid-morning or mid-afternoon snacks may be an essential part of your meal plan to help provide energy and prevent hypoglycemia. A snack at bedtime may be called for if your blood glucose levels are below target range (generally <100 mg/dL) or if your blood glucose has a tendency to drop in the middle of the night. It may also be time for a snack if you know you will be eating your next meal later than usual or have unplanned physical activity. That extra bit of fuel will keep your blood glucose from falling too low. Consult your diabetes health-care team to determine if you should use snacks to prevent hypoglycemia, as well as if you find that you are having to frequently snack to prevent hypoglycemia. If you do experience and treat hypoglycemia, once blood glucose returns to normal, consuming a snack or meal can help prevent recurrence of hypoglycemia.

- **If you manage your type 2 diabetes exclusively through healthy eating and physical activity and eat regular meals,** between-meal snacks are not routinely necessary. Your blood glucose is not likely to drop too low, because you are not taking any diabetes medications. However, a snack could be in order for appetite control if your meals are small and hunger hits mid-morning or mid-afternoon, or if you need to fuel up after extra activity.

Consult your diabetes health-care team for guidance on whether snacks are necessary for you and how to fit them into your meal plan.

Hypoglycemia: What It Is and How to Treat It with Quick-Acting Carbohydrate

"Hypoglycemia" is the medical word for blood glucose that is below 70 mg/dL, which is too low. This condition is a "side effect" or risk of taking many of the diabetes medicines on the market today. If hypoglycemia is not treated, blood glucose may continue to fall to dangerous life-threatening levels. (For that reason, if you take a diabetes medicine with hypoglycemia as a potential side effect, it's always a good idea to check your blood glucose to make sure it's not low before driving, working on scaffolding, or placing yourself in other situations where your life or the lives of others may be put at risk). It can be challenging to balance carbohydrate intake (which raises blood glucose) with physical activity and any diabetes medications (which lower blood glucose), along with a variety of other factors that affect blood glucose.

Symptoms of hypoglycemia:

- Weakness or fatigue
- Shakiness
- Nervousness or anxiety
- Sweating
- Clamminess
- Irritability or impatience
- Confusion
- Rapid/fast heartbeat
- Lightheadedness or dizziness
- Hunger and nausea
- Sleepiness
- Blurred/impaired vision
- Tingling or numbness in the lips or tongue
- Headaches
- Anger, stubbornness, or sadness
- Lack of coordination
- Seizures
- Loss of consciousness (which can be life threatening)

What to do if you have hypoglycemia

If you feel like you may be hypoglycemic, check your blood glucose if possible to confirm where it is. For low blood glucose levels in the <70 mg/dL to 54 mg/dL range, use the Rule of 15 to help stabilize your blood glucose.

The Rule of 15:

1. Consume 15–20 g quick-acting carbohydrate (see examples that follow).
2. Wait 15 minutes and then recheck your blood glucose.
3. If blood glucose is still under 70 mg/dL, treat with another 15 g carbohydrate.
4. Once blood glucose returns to normal (that's >70 mg/dL), eat a meal or snack to prevent reoccurrence.

The following items provide 15–20 g quick-acting carbohydrate to treat hypoglycemia:

- Three to four glucose tablets (check package instructions)
- Glucose gel (check package instructions)
- 4 oz (1/2 cup) fruit juice or regular soda (not diet)
- 1 Tbsp honey, corn syrup, or sugar
- Three round hard candies (such as peppermint or butterscotch discs)
- Smarties candy, jellybeans, or gumdrops (check label on how many to consume for 15–20 g carbohydrate)
- 8 oz fat-free or 1% milk

What to do if you have hypoglycemia *(continued)*

If you are taking diabetes medications that put you at an increased risk for severe hypoglycemia (blood glucose levels <54 mg/dL), glucagon should be prescribed.

Generally, this rule would apply to individuals taking insulin, especially rapid-acting insulin. Glucagon is a hormone that's given by injection or dry nasal spray to rapidly raise blood glucose levels when a person is not able to swallow carbohydrate by mouth. Family, caregivers, and coworkers should know where it is and when and how to administer it.

Talk with your diabetes health-care team about a plan to manage your carbohydrate intake and any diabetes medications to keep your blood glucose from dropping too low, especially during physical activity.

#3: Blood glucose patterns

Does your blood glucose log or tracing show patterns of low blood glucose at certain times of day? If the answer is "yes," a snack may help head off that hypoglycemia. However, if you take diabetes medicines that can cause hypoglycemia, many health care providers prefer to try adjusting medication doses to prevent frequent hypoglycemia rather than encourage additional food intake, particularly if weight management is a concern. Ask your diabetes health-care team if this applies to you.

#4: Activity

Do you need extra carbohydrate to fuel physical activity and replenish your energy stores afterward?

- Extra carbohydrate is not usually needed to balance low to moderate physical activity of short duration, like a stroll around the block.
- For a higher-intensity and/or longer-duration activity, like a 30-minute jog or a 1-hour cycling class, a carbohydrate snack may in fact be needed before, during, or even after physical activity.

#5: Age

Do you need extra fuel based on your age and/or appetite?

- Children may need to eat every 3–4 hours because they have small stomachs.
- Teenagers may need extra calories from snacks during the day because they are growing and active.
- Adults may find that a small planned snack satisfies midday hunger, although

some adults can do without snacks. During pregnancy, several small snacks may be preferable and necessary.

- Older adults with small appetites may find they prefer eating small meals with several snacks in between.

What to Snack on

When hunger hits, you may not be sure what to eat. Should you avoid fruits for snacks? Do you have to eat protein with carbohydrate for a snack? Is a cookie off limits? The answer to all of these questions is "no!"

When considering potential snack foods, learn as much as you can about their nutrition profile and amount of carbohydrate in each serving. You can check out the Nutrition Facts label (learn more in Chapter 5), a mobile app, a free online database like Calorie King (www.calorieking.com), or one of many guidebooks, such as *The Diabetes Carbohydrate & Fat Gram Guide,* 5th edition, by Lea Ann Holzmeister, published by the American Diabetes Association. Take a look at the fat, sodium, and calories and try to keep those as low as possible. Compare the standard serving size to the portion size you actually plan to eat, and count the carbohydrate accordingly. Would you eat one serving? Or two?

Select Smart Snacks

When snack time hits, remember the 3 "S's"— Select Smart Snacks.

We've compiled a multitude of snack ideas gleaned from clients with diabetes that Tami has worked with over the years. We hope you enjoy them, too. Adjust the portion sizes to fit your needs. Snack on!

7 Smart snacks at home*

1. Frozen grapes: Remove grapes from stems. Wash and dry well and freeze them on a tray. Then place in a resealable plastic bag. They'll remind you of bites of sherbet or sorbet.

Are you unsure about whether you really need snacks or how to fit them into your eating plan to manage blood glucose?

Talk with your diabetes health-care team about if/when to incorporate snacks to best fuel your body and keep blood glucose levels in range based on your appetite, eating plan, physical activity, diabetes medications, and blood glucose trends. To see how a food and/or beverage affects your blood glucose, check your blood glucose 1 1/2–2 hours later and note the response.

---

*Carbohydrate content varies. Adjust portion sizes to fit your carbohydrate goals.

Snack Myth Busters

Myth: Fruit should not be eaten as a snack.

Fact: One serving of fruit (such as a small orange) is actually a convenient, nutritious, and delicious snack! It contains about 15 g carbohydrate—the ideal amount for a small snack.

Myth: If you eat carbohydrate for a snack, you must eat protein with it (such as peanut butter or cheese with crackers) to keep blood glucose levels stable.

Fact: Research shows that in individuals with type 2 diabetes, protein does not increase blood glucose levels or slow the digestion of carbohydrate. Therefore, protein does not have to be eaten with a carbohydrate snack to keep blood glucose stable. Furthermore, adding protein to a carbohydrate snack does not aid in the prevention or treatment of hypoglycemia. Although a little protein may help promote the feeling of satiety.

Myth: Sweet treats (such as a cookie) are off limits when you have diabetes.

Fact: Current nutrition guidelines for people with diabetes conclude that sugary foods do not have to be totally avoided, but the carbohydrate in sweets does have to be counted in your meal or snack to prevent out-of-range blood glucose. As reviewed in Chapter 2, sugar is just one type of carbohydrate. Research shows that if the carbohydrate in a sweet treat is counted in the meal or snack and kept within goal levels (or covered with insulin or other glucose-lowering medications), then blood glucose should not be significantly affected. For general good health, less sugar is better for anyone though.

2. Frozen 100% fruit juice bars
3. String cheese stick or dill pickle spear wrapped with turkey
4. Air-popped or light microwave popcorn
5. Salsa with cucumber slices for dipping
6. One piece of 100% whole-wheat bread spread with nut butter
7. Smoothie from the freezer (see our smoothie recipe ideas on pages 271 and 309)

Select Snacks with These 5 Criteria in Mind:

1. Help maintain blood glucose in range
2. Promote health (a great opportunity to work in a fruit or nonstarchy vegetable)
3. Tasty
4. Satisfying
5. Easy to prepare

. . . .

When snack time hits, remember the 3 "S's"—Select Smart Snacks.

. . . .

7 Smart 100-calorie snacks*

If calories are a concern and you're trying to keep them in check, try one of these 100-calorie snacks. All of these choices range from 80 to 120 calories:

1. One medium banana
2. 10 large shrimp with 2 Tbsp cocktail sauce
3. 2 Tbsp guacamole and 6 baked tortilla chips
4. Five olives and one mini Babybel light cheese
5. 1/2 cup cottage cheese with 1/4 cup berries (raspberries and blueberries pair well)
6. 15 almonds
7. 1/2 cup boiled/steamed edamame (green soybeans)

7 Smart snacks to go**

What do you do when you're on the run and hunger hits? Here are some ideas for portable snacks:

1. Small apple or tangerine
2. Hard-boiled egg
3. Unsalted or lightly salted soy nuts
4. Greek or Icelandic yogurt cup (both are naturally lower in carbohydrate and higher in protein than traditional yogurt)
5. String cheese and a few whole-grain crackers
6. One can of low-sodium tomato or vegetable juice
7. Cherry or grape tomatoes

7 Smart low-fat snacks**

1. Fat-free cottage cheese with a small wedge of cantaloupe or honeydew melon
2. Fresh or frozen mango cubes (Freeze cubed mango on a tray and then place in a resealable plastic bag to store in the freezer, or purchase a bag of frozen mango cubes.)
3. Cup of tomato soup
4. Sliced strawberries with a drizzle of balsamic vinegar
5. Whole-grain pretzel sticks
6. Baked or air-fried apple chips
7. Raw cauliflower with a squeeze of lime and sprinkle of ground cumin

----

*These snacks are based on calories, not carbohydrate content.
**Carbohydrate content varies. Adjust portion sizes to fit your carbohydrate goals.

7 Smart snacks for the workday**

Stock your desk or workspace with smart snacks that can rescue you when you're stranded with no sign of lunch in sight.

1. Microwavable containers of vegetable, tomato, bean, or lentil soup
2. Unsweetened applesauce cups
3. Fruit cups packed in juice or water
4. Individual packages of nuts (choose heart-healthy almonds, walnuts, pistachios, or peanuts)
5. Foil packs or mini cans of water-packed tuna or salmon
6. Instant oatmeal (plain is lower in carbohydrate)
7. High-fiber cereal bars

7 Smart "free" snacks***

If you want to squash hunger without raising blood glucose, try one of the "free" snacks. They're considered "free" because they contain 5 grams or fewer of carbohydrate and fewer than 20 calories per serving.

1. 1/2 cup diced tomato drizzled with 1 tsp fat-free Italian dressing
2. 1 cup sugar-free gelatin with 1 tsp light whipped topping
3. 1/2 cup baby carrots
4. 1/4 cup blackberries
5. Flavor-infused water (such as ***Lemony Spa Water*** or ***Watermelon Rosemary Refresher*** on pages 37 and 38)
6. Mug of low-sodium broth or bouillon
7. Two homemade frozen pops made from a sugar-free fruit drink (such as sugar-free Kool-Aid or Crystal Light)

**Carbohydrate content varies. Adjust portion sizes to fit your carbohydrate goals.

***Hunger can be a symptom of hypoglycemia. If you take a medication that may cause hypoglycemia, when hunger hits, check your blood glucose if possible to rule out hypoglycemia. If your blood glucose is low, you will need to treat it with a source of quick-acting carbo-hydrate. If trying to avoid excessive calories, glucose

7 DASH-style snacks*

1. Pecans
2. Walnuts
3. Broccoli florets
4. Strawberries over low-fat Greek yogurt
5. Oats topped with blueberries
6. Apple slices with peanut butter
7. Grilled pineapple slice

7 Mediterranean-style snacks*

1. Canned sardines (they work in a fish serving and are portable with the pop-top can)
2. Olives
3. Toothpick skewer of cherry tomato, mozzarella ball, and basil leaf
4. Hummus with baby carrots
5. Baba ganoush with whole-wheat pita bread
6. Walnuts or roasted chickpeas
7. Avocado slices drizzled with olive oil and balsamic vinegar and a sprinkle of sunflower seeds

*Carbohydrate content varies. Adjust portion sizes to fit your carbohydrate goals.

7 Plant-based snacks*

1. Kale chips
2. Red, orange, and yellow pepper strips
3. Almonds
4. Sunflower seeds
5. Pear slices with almond butter
6. Low-fat popcorn
7. Plum

7 Very-low-carbohydrate (sometimes called "keto") snacks**

1. Single serving packets of nut butter
2. Carrot or celery sticks
3. Cucumber boats (split lengthwise, scoop out seeds, and stuff with tuna, turkey, or lean ham)
4. Lower-sodium beef jerky or turkey jerky
5. String cheese
6. Deviled egg
7. Turkey meatballs with marinara

*Carbohydrate content varies. Adjust portion sizes to fit your carbohydrate goals.
**All contain minimal carbohydrate. Adjust portion sizes to fit your needs. If you take a medication with hypoglycemia as a side effect, carry a source of fast-acting sugar, such as glucose tablets in the event that your blood glucose drops too low.

FROZEN BLACKBERRY YOGURT SWIRL

Fruit and yogurt is nothing new, but using frozen fruit creates an ice cold, creamy treat similar to soft serve ice cream. Enjoy it as a high-protein, low-carb dessert, or a sweet breakfast on a hot summer day.

THIS RECIPE CAN FIT IN THE FOLLOWING EATING PATTERNS: vegetarian, low- or very-low-fat, low- or very-low-carbohydrate, DASH, Mediterranean

NUMBER OF SERVINGS: 4 | **SERVING SIZE:** 2/3 cup per serving
PREP TIME: 5 minutes | **STAND TIME:** 10 minutes

INGREDIENTS

- 1 1/3 cups plain fat-free Greek yogurt
- 5 individual packets stevia
- 1/2 tsp almond extract
- 2 cups frozen blackberries

INSTRUCTIONS

1. Combine the yogurt, stevia, and almond extract in a medium bowl, stirring well.
2. Stir in the frozen berries.
3. Let stand 10 minutes to allow the berries to thaw slightly and release some juices.

Trick

- Don't want to wait 10 minutes? To keep a frozen texture to the dish, but bring out some of the juices of the berries, place the frozen berries in a microwave-safe bowl and microwave on high setting for 15 seconds or until "partially" thawed, but still mostly frozen. Then gently stir into the yogurt.

COOK'S SWAPS

- Get creative! Substitute frozen blackberries with your favorite frozen fruit. Blueberries and raspberries also work well.
- For a vegan dish, use a plant-based, nondairy yogurt.

(Trick on following page)

CHOICES: 1 Fruit, 1 Lean Protein
BASIC NUTRITIONAL VALUES: Calories 90 | Calories from Fat 5 | **Total Fat** 0.5 g | Saturated Fat 0.1 g | Trans Fat 0.0 g | **Cholesterol** 1 mg | **Sodium** 30 mg | **Potassium** 210 mg | **Total Carbohydrate** 15 g | Dietary Fiber 4 g | Sugars 11 g | Added Sugars 0 g | **Protein** 9 g | **Phosphorus** 125 mg

AVOCADO STACK-UP CUPS

Smash the avocado right in its skin and top by stacking up salsa, black beans, and a squeeze of lime.

THIS RECIPE CAN FIT IN THE FOLLOWING EATING PATTERNS: vegetarian, vegan, low- or very-low-carbohydrate, DASH, Mediterranean

---

NUMBER OF SERVINGS: 4 | **SERVING SIZE:** 1/2 avocado plus about 1/3 cup bean and salsa mixture per serving

PREP TIME: 10 minutes | **COOK TIME:** 16 minutes | **STAND TIME:** 30 minutes

INGREDIENTS

- 2 ripe avocados
- 2 Tbsp fresh lime or lemon juice
- 6 oz fresh salsa (2/3 cup)
- 1 cup no-salt-added black beans, rinsed and drained

INSTRUCTIONS

1. Cut each avocado in half and remove pits. Roughly mash each avocado half (in its shell). Place each avocado half in a small bowl. Top with equal amounts of the lime juice, salsa, and beans.

POINTER

- Serve immediately or cover and refrigerate up to 8 hours.

CHOICES: 1/2 Starch, 1/2 Fruit, 2 1/2 Fat

BASIC NUTRITIONAL VALUES: Calories 180 | Calories from Fat 100 | **Total Fat** 11.0 g | Saturated Fat 1.6 g | Trans Fat 0.0 g | **Cholesterol** 0 mg | **Sodium** 190 mg | **Potassium** 620 mg | **Total Carbohydrate** 19 g | Dietary Fiber 8 g | Sugars 2 g | Added Sugars 0 g | **Protein** 5 g | **Phosphorus** 115 mg

QUICK-FIX BRUSCHETTA

Store the tomato mixture in small individual containers and any chips or crackers in snack-size resealable plastic bags to have a portion-controlled portable snack at the ready when snack time arrives. NOTE: chips, crackers, bread, and other pairings are not included in the Nutrition Information.

THIS RECIPE CAN FIT IN THE FOLLOWING EATING PATTERNS: vegetarian, vegan, low-fat, low- or very-low-carbohydrate, DASH, Mediterranean

---

NUMBER OF SERVINGS: 4 | **SERVING SIZE:** 1/3 cup plus 1 oz chips per serving
PREP TIME: 5 minutes | **STAND TIME:** 30 minutes

INGREDIENTS

- 1 1/4 cups chopped tomatoes
- 1 Tbsp finely chopped red onion
- 1 1/2 Tbsp capers, drained
- 1 Tbsp dried basil
- 1 Tbsp red wine vinegar
- 2 tsp extra-virgin olive oil

INSTRUCTIONS

1. Combine all ingredients in a small bowl. Stir well.
2. Let stand 30 minutes to absorb flavors. See below for serving ideas.

POINTERS

- Cover and refrigerate leftover tomato mixture up to 4 days. If it needs a bit of a lift, stir in a very small amount of vinegar to brighten it back up!

SERVING IDEAS

- To keep this a lower-carb snack, serve with sweet potato chips or other low-carb crackers.
- To keep this a lower-fat dish, serve on sliced, toasted bread or whole-grain crackers, like Triscuits.

CHOICES: NA

BASIC NUTRITIONAL VALUES: Calories 35 | Calories from Fat 20 | **Total Fat** 2.5 g | Saturated Fat 0.3 g | Trans Fat 0.0 g | **Cholesterol** 0 mg | **Sodium** 80 mg | **Potassium** 150 mg | **Total Carbohydrate** 3 g | Dietary Fiber 1 g | Sugars 2 g | Added Sugars 0 g | **Protein** 1 g | **Phosphorus** 15 mg

ORANGE-ZESTED TRAIL MIX

Some people store trail mix in a resealable plastic bag, some store it in a plastic container, but our preference is a large mason jar. It fits easily in a pantry shelf and doesn't get lost, you can see what's in the jar instantly, and the jar seals airtight to maintain freshness.

THIS RECIPE CAN FIT IN THE FOLLOWING EATING PATTERNS: vegetarian, vegan, DASH

NUMBER OF SERVINGS: 8 | **SERVING SIZE:** 1/2 cup per serving
PREP TIME: 10 minutes | **COOK TIME:** 16 minutes | **STAND TIME:** 30 minutes

INGREDIENTS

- 2 2/3 cups Wheat Chex–style cereal
- 3/4 cup roasted, salted, shelled pumpkin seeds
- 1 1/2 Tbsp canola oil
- 1 Tbsp grated orange zest
- 1 Tbsp ground cinnamon
- 1/4 tsp salt
- 1/2 cup dried fruit, such as dried cranberries or cherries

INSTRUCTIONS

1. Preheat the oven to 300°F.
2. Place the cereal and pumpkin seeds on a large rimmed baking sheet. Drizzle with the oil and toss until well coated. Spread in a single layer.
3. Bake for 8 minutes, stir, spread back in a single layer, and bake 8 minutes more.
4. Remove from oven. Sprinkle with the remaining ingredients. Toss until well blended. Let stand 30 minutes for peak flavors and texture. Allow to completely cool before storing.

POINTERS

- Store completely cooled leftovers in an airtight container at room temperature up to 2 weeks.
- This trail mix is not just for snacking! Sprinkle on top of yogurt for a quick breakfast option.

CHOICES: 1 Starch, 1/2 Fruit, 1 1/2 Fat

BASIC NUTRITIONAL VALUES: Calories 190 | Calories from Fat 70 | **Total Fat** 8.0 g | Saturated Fat 1.2 g | Trans Fat 0.0 g | **Cholesterol** 0 mg | **Sodium** 220 mg | **Potassium** 190 mg | **Total Carbohydrate** 27 g | Dietary Fiber 4 g | Sugars 7 g | Added Sugars 5 g | **Protein** 5 g | **Phosphorus** 215 mg

SMOKY ALMONDS

Almonds are a simple, filling, portable snack, packed with protein and healthy fats that can tide you over between meals. Smoked paprika gives these almonds a savory, smoky flavor.

THIS RECIPE CAN FIT IN THE FOLLOWING EATING PATTERNS: **vegetarian, vegan, low- or very-low-carbohydrate, DASH, Mediterranean**

NUMBER OF SERVINGS: 4 | **SERVING SIZE:** 1/4 cup per serving
PREP TIME: 5 minutes | **COOK TIME:** 10 minutes

INGREDIENTS

- 4 oz whole almonds
- 1 1/2 tsp canola oil
- 1/2 tsp smoked paprika
- 1/8 tsp garlic powder
- Pinch cayenne pepper (about 1/16 tsp)
- 1/4 tsp salt

INSTRUCTIONS

1. Preheat oven to 350°F.
2. Place almonds on baking sheet, drizzle oil over all, and toss until well coated.
3. Sprinkle the remaining ingredients over evenly and toss until well blended. Arrange almonds in a single layer.
4. Bake 5 minutes, stir, arrange in a single layer again, and bake 5 minutes more.

POINTERS

- Allow to cool completely before storing in an airtight container. Store at room temperature up to 2 weeks for peak flavors.
- Pre-portion almonds into snack-size resealable plastic bags so no thought is required when hunger hits.

CHOICES: 1/2 Carbohydrate, 1 Lean Protein, 2 1/2 Fat
BASIC NUTRITIONAL VALUES: Calories 190 | Calories from Fat 150 | **Total Fat** 17.0 g | Saturated Fat 1.3 g | Trans Fat 0.0 g | **Cholesterol** 0 mg | **Sodium** 150 mg | **Potassium** 210 mg | **Total Carbohydrate** 6 g | Dietary Fiber 3 g | Sugars 1 g | Added Sugars 0 g | **Protein** 6 g | **Phosphorus** 140 mg

tablets are a quick treatment.

Top 20 Snacking Strategies

1. **Plan, plan, and plan.** The best snack is one that's incorporated into your eating plan.
2. **Keep an eye on calories.** If you're trying to lose or maintain weight, keep an eye on the calories in the snack portions you eat. For instance, 1/4 cup nuts are a healthy snack option and only 180 calories. But if you eat 1 cup, that adds nearly 800 calories.
3. **Snack with a reason.** Try to snack only when you're truly hungry or need extra carbohydrate to fuel physical activity or head off hypoglycemia.
4. **Be on guard against stress eating.** When the urge to snack hits you, ask yourself if you are truly hungry (does your stomach feel empty or is it growling?). Eating out of boredom or in response to stress may lead to weight gain and rising blood glucose levels.
5. **Establish a snacking zone.** Eat only at the kitchen table so other locations won't serve as food cues. For instance, if you snack in the recliner in front of the TV, each time you sit there, you may find you want to eat something.
6. **Do away with distractions.** It is too easy to mindlessly overeat while engaged in another activity like working on the computer, playing video games, watching a movie, or watching TV. When eating, eliminate distractions and focus on your food to help you feel satisfied more quickly and avoid overeating.
7. **If in doubt, keep it out.** If there's a snack food that's too much of a temptation and triggers you to overeat, keep it out of the house. If chips are a weakness, but there aren't any in the house, fresh fruits or veggies in the fridge may seem more desirable.
8. **Out of sight, out of mind.** Keep snack foods out of sight so you aren't tempted to nibble for no reason.
9. **Make snacks count.** Make snack time an opportunity to work in a fruit, vegetable, milk/milk substitute, or whole-grain serving.
10. **Satisfy sweet cravings with fruit.** When you're craving a sweet and cool treat, try frozen grapes or frozen banana chunks. They are an easy way to satisfy your sweet tooth and work in a fruit serving.
11. **Broaden your snacking horizons.** Try something new for snacks. Maybe try soy nuts, or whole-wheat pita bread or jicama with hummus.
12. **Keep snacking simple and convenient.** Have nutritious, prepared, and ready-to-eat snack options at your fingertips. If fruit and vegetable chunks are conveniently precut, prepared, and in the fridge, you might be more likely to grab them if they're ready to eat.

13. **Love leftovers.** A small serving of last night's entrée or veggie could make an easy, tasty snack.

14. **Watch out for portion distortion.** What is commonly considered a "portion" is often actually more than enough. Many people think of a bag of microwave popcorn as one "portion." But if you eat the whole bag, that one "portion" actually has 50–60 g carbohydrate. Ask yourself whether you really need that many calories or that much carbohydrate.

15. **Keep snacks "snack size."** Smaller, carbohydrate-controlled, snack-size portions can curb hunger without sending blood glucose out of range.

16. **Snack outside the package.** Measure snacks and put an appropriate portion in a bowl or resealable plastic bag so you know exactly how much you are eating. If you eat directly from a large bag or box, then it's difficult to know exactly how much you've eaten. Did you just eat 10 peanuts or 30? It can be hard to keep track! Studies show that when people eat from bulk-size bags, they eat more.

17. **Single-size can be wise.** Buy snacks in single-serving packages to easily manage portions.

18. **Check out label lingo.** Don't be fooled by labeling claims. Foods marketed as "low fat" or "fat-free" can still be high in calories and carbohydrate. Check the Nutrition Facts label to find out the whole story.

19. **Make a perfect match.** Match snack calories and carbohydrate to your activity and blood glucose. A marathon runner can consume more calories and carbohydrate than someone who is sedentary.

20. **Enjoy your snack!** Choose snacks that you enjoy! If you don't like raw broccoli, then don't force yourself to eat it.

Plan Smart, Shop Smart, Cook Smart

As you've learned in the previous chapters, what you eat is core to managing diabetes and prediabetes, as well as keeping you healthy and strong. Without a doubt, eating well takes some time and thought. Our goal in this chapter is to help take the stress level down. We'll share tips and recipes to help you plan Diabetes Plate Method meals (whichever eating pattern you're following), shop for those foods, and cook smart. Let's get started!

PLAN SMART

All "meal planning" really means is that you decide ahead of time what you'll be eating. You decide how you'll fill the different sections of your Diabetes Plate Method plate. Investing a few minutes to map out your meals and snacks and use them as a guide can have a big payoff.

Planning Meals: 4 Tried-and-True Tips to Get You Started

1. **Get familiar with the eating pattern you will be embracing.** As a refresher, you can learn more about the different eating patterns to help manage blood glucose in Chapter 3. Although this book provides an abundance of basic guidance, we recommend a visit with a registered dietitian nutritionist (RDN), who can review your health and nutrition history, medications, blood glucose patterns, lifestyle, and personal preferences and goals and then work with you to design

4 Important Benefits of Planning Meals in Advance and Reasons to Do So

1. **Healthier food choices.** Taking the time to plan meals in advance can result in meals that align with your eating pattern of choice and follow the Diabetes Plate Method.
2. **Time savings.** A 5- to 10-minute time investment up front to plan meals (and even snacks) will yield greater time savings in the end because planning enables you to shop for groceries efficiently and avoid extra trips to the store for missing items.
3. **Money savings.** Planning meals ahead means you can create a grocery list and buy only what you need, in the proper package size, so there's less food wasted from extra ingredients you don't know what to do with. Also, eating at home, rather than paying for meals out, saves even more money.
4. **Energy savings.** Planning meals in advance not only saves mental energy because you don't have to sweat over what to have for dinner, it saves on fuel costs by limiting extra trips to pick up forgotten ingredients. We find that cooking is much more enjoyable when we're prepared.

an individualized plan. For instance, maybe you've decided to eat more Mediterranean style, but are unsure exactly how many fruits, dairy, and grain foods to aim for each day. An RDN can provide guidance. Once you know the number of servings of each type of food to try to include, you have a basic outline of your daily meal plan. That outline then translates into your menus (or what you'll eat at each meal and snack), which then leads to your grocery list.

2. **Plan a week in advance if at all possible.** We find it easiest to start by planning dinner. The goal is to plan at least five dinner meals each week, knowing that we may have a meal somewhere else at least one night a week, and the other night we'll repurpose any leftovers (although we do often enjoy leftovers from dinner at lunch the next day). Each chapter concludes with menu ideas and coordinated recipes to give you a place to start.

3. **Plan with a fresh mind.** Tami usually plans meals on Saturday mornings when her mind is fresh. Then she grocery shops Saturday or Sunday afternoon. She's found if she tries to plan meals after a day at work she's tired and not thinking clearly or creatively. What day and time might work for you to get in the habit of planning, if you're not already doing so?

4. **Rely on favorites.** Start by thinking about some of your favorite meals and recipes. Note how they fit into your eating patterns. (Refer back to Chapter 2 for many ideas on recipe renewal if you need tips on how to improve the nutritional value of some of those recipes.) These foods will be the heart of your meal plan. We usually plan meals for the week including two or three that are quick, assembly-type meals (you can learn more about that later in this chapter) and two or three that may require a little more cooking for the nights we have more time to spend in the kitchen. We also frequently incorporate "planned overs," which you can learn more about a little later in this chapter, too. There are a variety of recipe and menu-planning websites and mobile apps. Some even generate a grocery list for you to simplify things further. The recipes incorporated into menus throughout this book may spark your meal-planning creativity.

How to Plan Diabetes Plate Method Meals in 5 Steps

1. Create 3 columns, either on a piece of paper or electronically. (Many like to use Excel or a Word document on the computer, so they can easily save the menus and access them to recycle later on.)
2. In the first column, list five or more non-starchy vegetables you enjoy.

3. In the second column, list five or more favorite protein foods ("main dishes") you can prepare.
4. In the third column, list carbohydrate foods you'd like to fit in, including grains, starchy vegetables, fruit, and milk/yogurt to fit within your carbohydrate goals and eating pattern.
5. Mix and match the items in each column to plan five meals. Once you have the food combinations, you can adjust portion sizes of each to fit the Diabetes Plate Method or your eating pattern.

Expand these meal-planning lists over time with new recipes and other family favorites.

4 Strategies to Simplify Meal Planning: Assembly Meals, Batch Cooking, "Planned Overs," and Backup Meals

When planning meals for the week, we love "assembly meals," and batch cooking with "planned overs" in mind. All three trim time, yet lend a healthy meal that we know our families will enjoy.

Strategy 1: assembly meals

There will be those days when you just don't feel like spending a lot of time preparing a meal. That's when we turn to assembly meals, which can take on different forms. Maybe it's a meal prep kit shipped to the front door with a recipe and all the tasty ingredients to prepare it.

Maybe it's a similar meal prep kit purchased at a local market, which is increasingly popular. Or maybe it's a few items you have on hand to pull together a meal in minutes without a lot of preparation. Here are 6 assembly meal ideas, which you can tweak to suit you:

1. **Mediterranean-style stuffed sweet potato.** Microwave a small sweet potato. Split it and top with a foil packet of tuna or reduced-fat feta cheese, sliced red onion, red chilies for a little heat, a squeeze of lime juice, and a dollop of Greek yogurt. Round out the meal with a couple of handfuls of prepared bagged salad greens and a vinaigrette. Try the recipe for *Mediterranean Stuffed Sweet Potato* on page 190.

2. **Rotisserie chicken meal.** Purchased rotisserie chicken, steam-in-the-bag fresh or frozen veggies, bagged kale salad topped with blueberries or strawberries and vinaigrette. Try the recipe for *Kale-Berry Salad* on page 191.

3. **Avocado Caprese salad.** This recipe is great during the summer months when tomatoes are in season. It may sound fancy, but you just layer on your plate sliced tomato, sliced avocado, sliced fresh mozzarella or mozzarella balls, a few fresh basil leaves or dollops of pesto from a jar, and drizzle with balsamic vinaigrette (or olive oil and balsamic vinegar) and sprinkle with black pepper. To get in a whole grain, this can be layered over chilled leftover quinoa or shelf-stable fully cooked quinoa, or crusty whole-grain bread. Try the recipe for *Knife and Fork Avocado Caprese Salad* on page 193.

4. **Plant-based burrito bowl.** Packaged microwavable quinoa or brown rice (it comes in small microwavable pouches and individual serving cups) topped with canned beans (such as black or pinto), salsa (we like to buy and keep fresh salsa or pico de gallo on hand), reduced-fat cheese (dairy or nondairy), diced avocado, dollop of reduced-fat sour cream or fat-free Greek yogurt, and a dash of hot sauce if you like heat. Try the recipe for *Pico Pinto Bowls* on page 195.

5. **Salad with chicken, tuna, or salmon.** Bagged salad greens (like kale, spinach, arugula, or spring mix), cherry or grape tomatoes, purchased fully cooked quinoa (from a cup or pouch), shredded rotisserie chicken or foil-packed tuna or salmon, sliced almonds, and bottled vinaigrette. Try the recipe for *Tuna-Quinoa Layered Salad* on page 196.

6. **Stuffed pita sandwich.** Pita bread is great for making quick sandwiches. When you cut it in half, you can carefully separate the two sides of the bread to make a "pocket" that you can stuff with your favorite sandwich ingredients.

Add plenty of vegetables like spinach or other greens, or diced tomatoes or cucumbers, etc. And add a protein like a chopped hard-boiled egg, hummus, or beans. Add flavor with a drizzle of olive oil and vinegar. Try the recipe for ***Egg and Hummus–Stuffed Pitas*** on page 198.

There will be those days when you just don't feel like spending a lot of time preparing a meal. That's when you turn to assembly meals.

Let's Practice Using the Diabetes Plate Method

LOW-CARBOHYDRATE MEXICAN-STYLE MEAL
On the menu: *Pork taco with black beans and guacamole*

NONSTARCHY VEGETABLES
- Lettuce
- Peppers
- Onions
- Pico de gallo

CARBOHYDRATES
- Corn tortilla
- Black beans

PROTEIN
- Shredded pork loin

ZERO-CALORIE DRINK
- Sparkling water with lime

HEALTHY FAT
- Guacamole

MEDITERRANEAN-STYLE MEAL
On the menu: *Grilled trout over couscous with steamed broccoli, arugula salad, and fresh figs*

NONSTARCHY VEGETABLES
- Tomato
- Cucumber
- Arugula salad with lemon olive oil vinaigrette
- Steamed broccoli

CARBOHYDRATES
- Couscous
- 2 small fresh figs

PROTEIN
- Grilled trout

ZERO-CALORIE DRINK
- Water

HEALTHY FAT
- Olive oil on salad

DASH-STYLE MEAL
On the menu: *Herb grilled chicken with wild rice, green beans, roasted carrots, and mixed berries*

NONSTARCHY VEGETABLES
- Fresh steamed green beans with salt-free seasoning mix
- Roasted carrots

CARBOHYDRATES
- Wild rice
- Mixed berries

PROTEIN
- Herb grilled chicken breast

ZERO-CALORIE DRINK
- Herbal unsweetened iced tea

HEALTHY FAT
- Olive oil on roasted carrots

CARBOHYDRATES
- Chickpeas mixed in with zucchini
- Clementine or mandarin orange sections

NONSTARCHY VEGETABLES
- Cooked spiralized zucchini tossed with pesto

PROTEIN
- Steamed mussels

ZERO-CALORIE DRINK
- Unsweetened iced tea

HEALTHY FAT
- Olive oil in pesto

LOW-FAT MEAL
On the menu: *Steamed mussels over spiralized pesto zucchini and chickpeas, with clementine orange*

VEGETARIAN/PLANT-BASED MEAL
On the menu: *Black bean burger with toppings and mashed avocado and roasted Brussels sprouts*

NONSTARCHY VEGETABLES
- Lettuce
- Tomato
- Onion
- Jalapeno slice topping
- Roasted Brussels sprouts

CARBOHYDRATES
- Whole-wheat bun

PROTEIN
- Black bean burger

ZERO-CALORIE DRINK
- Green tea

HEALTHY FAT
- Mashed avocado

NONSTARCHY VEGETABLES
- Green salad
- Marinara for spaghetti

CARBOHYDRATES
- Spaghetti

PROTEIN
- Ground turkey meatballs

ZERO-CALORIE DRINK
- Unsweetened iced tea

HEALTHY FAT
- Italian or Caesar dressing

MIXED MEAL: SPAGHETTI DINNER
On the menu: *Spaghetti with turkey meatballs and sauce and a green salad*

MEDITERRANEAN STUFFED SWEET POTATO

THIS RECIPE CAN FIT IN THE FOLLOWING EATING PATTERNS: **vegetarian, low- or very-low-fat, low-carbohydrate, DASH, Mediterranean**

NUMBER OF SERVINGS: 4 | **SERVING SIZE:** 1 stuffed potato half per serving
PREP TIME: 8 minutes | **COOK TIME:** 18 minutes

INGREDIENTS

- 2 medium sweet potatoes (about 6–8 oz each), pierced in several areas with a fork
- 3 oz feta cheese, crumbled
- 1/4 cup finely chopped green onion
- 1/8 tsp crushed pepper flakes
- 1/2 cup plain fat-free Greek yogurt

INSTRUCTIONS

1. Wrap each potato in a damp paper towels. Microwave on high setting for 18 minutes or until fork-tender. Remove paper towels and cut each in half lengthwise. Fluff potatoes with a fork.
2. Top with equal amounts of the remaining ingredients.

POINTER

- Microwaves vary in power, so check your food a few minutes before instructed times.

CHOICES: 2 1/2 Starch, 1 Medium-Fat Protein

BASIC NUTRITIONAL VALUES: Calories 240 | Calories from Fat 45 | **Total Fat** 5.0 g | Saturated Fat 2.8 g | Trans Fat 0.2 g | **Cholesterol** 15 mg | **Sodium** 310 mg | **Potassium** 940 mg | **Total Carbohydrate** 40 g | Dietary Fiber 6 g | Sugars 14 g | Added Sugars 0 g | **Protein** 10 g | **Phosphorus** 210 mg

KALE-BERRY SALAD

THIS RECIPE CAN FIT IN THE FOLLOWING EATING PATTERNS: **vegetarian, low-fat, low- or very-low-carbohydrate, DASH, Mediterranean**

NUMBER OF SERVINGS: 4 | **SERVING SIZE:** 2 cups per serving
PREP TIME: 7 minutes

INGREDIENTS

Salad:

- 1 (4.5-oz) package kale mix, such as Dole Power Up Greens Baby Kale
- 1 cup matchstick carrots
- 1 cup fresh or frozen, thawed blueberries
- 1 oz salted, roasted pumpkin seeds
- 1 oz reduced-fat blue cheese, crumbled

Vinaigrette:

- 2 Tbsp red wine vinegar
- 1 Tbsp extra-virgin olive oil
- 1 individual packet stevia
- 1/8 tsp salt

INSTRUCTIONS

1. Combine the salad ingredients in a salad bowl.
2. Combine the vinaigrette ingredients in a small jar, secure with lid, and shake vigorously. Drizzle vinaigrette over the salad and toss gently, yet thoroughly until well coated.

(Cook's Swap and Pointers on following page)

CHOICES: 1/2 Fruit, 1 Nonstarchy Vegetable, 1 1/2 Fat
BASIC NUTRITIONAL VALUES: Calories 130 | Calories from Fat 70 | **Total Fat** 8.0 g | Saturated Fat 2.0 g | Trans Fat 0.0 g | **Cholesterol** 8 mg | **Sodium** 240 mg | **Potassium** 330 mg | **Total Carbohydrate** 10 g | Dietary Fiber 3 g | Sugars 5 g | Added Sugars 0 g | **Protein** 5 g | **Phosphorus** 140 mg

COOK'S SWAP

- For a vegan option, substitute blue cheese with 1 avocado, peeled and chopped, and an additional 1/8 tsp salt.

POINTERS

- Substitute berries with 1 cup chopped apple (you can buy packaged, precut apples), if desired.
- It takes less than 2 minutes to shake together a vinaigrette in a small jar (one of our favorite tips to mix up dressing!).

KNIFE AND FORK AVOCADO CAPRESE SALAD

***THIS RECIPE CAN FIT IN THE FOLLOWING EATING PATTERNS:* vegetarian, low-carbohydrate, DASH, Mediterranean**

NUMBER OF SERVINGS: 4 | **SERVING SIZE:** 1 oz bread, 1 cup vegetables and cheese, plus 1 Tbsp dressing per serving
PREP TIME: 10 minutes

INGREDIENTS

- 4 oz crusty whole-grain loaf bread, thinly sliced
- 3 oz fresh mozzarella, thinly sliced
- 4 Roma tomatoes, sliced crosswise into rounds
- 2 avocados, peeled, pitted, and sliced
- 1/4 cup chopped fresh basil leaves
- 1/4 cup low-fat balsamic dressing, such as Newman's Own Light Balsamic Vinaigrette
- 1/8 tsp salt
- 1/4 tsp black pepper

INSTRUCTIONS

1. Place equal amounts of the bread slices, overlapping slightly, on each of four plates. Top with equal amounts of the mozzarella, tomatoes, avocado, and basil. Spoon 1 Tbsp dressing over each serving. Sprinkle salt and black pepper over all.

(Tricks and Pointers on following page)

CHOICES: 1 Starch, 1/2 Fruit, 1 Medium-Fat Protein, 2 1/2 Fat
BASIC NUTRITIONAL VALUES: Calories 280 | Calories from Fat 160 | **Total Fat** 18.0 g | Saturated Fat 4.7 g | Trans Fat 0.0 g | **Cholesterol** 10 mg | **Sodium** 400 mg | **Potassium** 620 mg | **Total Carbohydrate** 23 g | Dietary Fiber 8 g | Sugars 5 g | Added Sugars 0 g | **Protein** 10 g | **Phosphorus** 195 mg

Tricks

- Cut the bread into 12 thin slices if possible. Thinner slices make the serving size look larger to the eye, and the "taste balance" is better as the bread soaks up flavors from the other ingredients.
- If you don't plan on serving all four portions at one time, store ingredients individually—then it's ready when you are. Prevent the cut avocado from browning by squeezing lemon juice or lime juice over it, covering with plastic wrap, and refrigerating until needed (up to 24 hours), or wait to cut the avocado until right before eating.

POINTERS

- Fresh mozzarella is not the same as other mozzarella cheeses. It is a fresh, semi-soft cheese; has a higher water content; and is mild in flavor. And because it is low in fat and low in sodium, it is considered to be one of the healthiest cheeses. It's best to serve at room temperature for peak flavors and texture. Fresh mozzarella is sold in packages of water or whey and should be stored in its liquid in the refrigerator. Use this cheese within 2–3 days of opening the package.
- While any tomato can be used, Roma tomatoes are preferred over regular tomatoes because they have less water content. It helps to keep the salad from becoming "watery."

PICO PINTO BOWLS

THIS RECIPE CAN FIT IN THE FOLLOWING EATING PATTERNS: **vegetarian, low- or very-low-fat, low-carbohydrate, DASH**

NUMBER OF SERVINGS: 4 | **SERVING SIZE:** 1 1/2 cups per serving
PREP TIME: 4 minutes | **COOK TIME:** 2 minutes

INGREDIENTS

- 1 (8.8-oz) package precooked brown rice, such as Uncle Ben's Ready Rice (or 1 3/4 cups cooked brown rice)
- 1 (15.5-oz) can no-salt-added pinto beans, rinsed and drained
- 3/4 cup fresh salsa or pico de gallo, such as Tostado brand
- 1 cup plain 2% Greek yogurt
- 1 avocado, peeled, pitted, and chopped

INSTRUCTIONS

1. Prepare rice according to package directions.
2. Spoon equal amounts of the rice into four bowls. Top each serving of rice with beans and salsa and heat in the microwave (up to two bowls at a time) 1–2 minutes or until heated through. Top with yogurt and avocado.

COOK'S SWAP

- For a vegan dish, omit the yogurt or use a plant-based nondairy yogurt.

POINTER

- Pico de gallo is a fresh salsa, sold most often in the refrigerated produce section. It is typically a blend of chopped tomato, onion, serrano, or jalapeno pepper, with a hint of fresh lime juice and cilantro.

CHOICES: 2 Starch, 1/2 Carbohydrate, 1 Lean Protein, 1 Fat
BASIC NUTRITIONAL VALUES: Calories 290 | Calories from Fat 70 | **Total Fat** 8.0 g | Saturated Fat 1.7 g | Trans Fat 0.0 g | **Cholesterol** 8 mg | **Sodium** 220 mg | **Potassium** 690 mg | **Total Carbohydrate** 42 g | Dietary Fiber 10 g | Sugars 5 g | Added Sugars 0 g | **Protein** 14 g | **Phosphorus** 265 mg

TUNA-QUINOA LAYERED SALAD

***THIS RECIPE CAN FIT IN THE FOLLOWING EATING PATTERNS:* low- or very-low-carbohydrate, DASH, Mediterranean**

NUMBER OF SERVINGS: 4 | **SERVING SIZE:** 2 cups per serving
PREP TIME: 6 minutes

INGREDIENTS

- 1 (4.5-oz) package baby kale mix
- 1/3 cup light Caesar salad dressing, such as Newman's Own
- 1 (4.4-oz) cup fully cooked quinoa, such as Minute Organic White and Red Quinoa (or 3/4 cup cooked quinoa)
- 4 oz slivered almonds
- 1 cup grape tomatoes
- 2 (2.6-oz) pouches low-sodium albacore white tuna in water, or 1 (5-oz) can water-packed albacore tuna, rinsed and drained
- 1/4 tsp black pepper

INSTRUCTIONS

1. Combine the greens and dressing in a salad bowl. Toss gently until well coated. Divide equally into four plates or salad bowls.
2. Sprinkle evenly with the quinoa, almonds, and tomatoes. Flake the tuna and sprinkle evenly over all. Sprinkle with black pepper.

COOK'S SWAP

- Substitute Caesar dressing with another light salad dressing.

CHOICES: 1/2 Starch, 1/2 Carbohydrate, 2 Lean Protein, 3 1/2 Fat

BASIC NUTRITIONAL VALUES: Calories 310 | Calories from Fat 180 | **Total Fat** 20.0 g | Saturated Fat 2.2 g | Trans Fat 0.0 g | **Cholesterol** 15 mg | **Sodium** 370 mg | **Potassium** 680 mg | **Total Carbohydrate** 19 g | Dietary Fiber 6 g | Sugars 4 g | Added Sugars 1 g | **Protein** 18 g | **Phosphorus** 295 mg

POINTER

- Not all canned tuna is the same! Albacore tuna has more heart-healthy omega-3 fat than "chunk light" tuna. Choose canned tuna packed in water, and look for low-sodium options to stock your pantry.

Trick

- Want a nuttier, more pronounced flavor from your almonds? Toast them! On the stovetop, heat a large skillet over medium-high heat, add nuts, and cook 3–4 minutes or until beginning to lightly brown. Remove from heat and let cool a few minutes before adding to the salad. Or, toast in a toaster for a few minutes. Keep your eye on them—they can burn very quickly!

EGG AND HUMMUS–STUFFED PITAS

THIS RECIPE CAN FIT IN THE FOLLOWING EATING PATTERNS: **vegetarian, low-fat, low-carbohydrate, DASH, Mediterranean**

NUMBER OF SERVINGS: 4 | **SERVING SIZE:** 1 stuffed pita half per serving
PREP TIME: 10 minutes

INGREDIENTS

- 1 cup prepared hummus
- 2 (6-inch each) whole-wheat pita rounds, warmed
- 2 cups packed spring mixed greens
- 4 hard-boiled eggs, peeled and chopped
- 4 tsp red wine vinegar
- 4 tsp extra-virgin olive oil

INSTRUCTIONS

1. Cut pitas in half crosswise, and carefully pull apart the layers to make a pocket. Spoon 1/4 cup hummus into each pita pocket.
2. Top with equal amounts of greens and chopped egg. Drizzle vinegar and oil over all. Sprinkle with black pepper to taste.

COOK'S SWAPS

- Instead of a pita pocket, try serving open-faced. Carefully cut the pitas in half horizontally so you have two thin pita rounds. Top each with the remaining ingredients.
- For a vegetarian and/or vegan option, substitute each egg with 2 Tbsp drained and rinsed canned beans like chickpeas or cannellini beans.
- For even more fiber and protein, and a little less carbohydrate and sodium, substitute two full pita rounds with four pieces whole-wheat pocket bread, such as Toufayan brand Smart Pockets.

CHOICES: 2 Starch, 1 Lean Protein, 2 1/2 Fat

BASIC NUTRITIONAL VALUES: Calories 310 | Calories from Fat 140 | **Total Fat** 16.0 g | Saturated Fat 3.1 g | Trans Fat 0.0 g | **Cholesterol** 185 mg | **Sodium** 490 mg | **Potassium** 330 mg | **Total Carbohydrate** 28 g | Dietary Fiber 6 g | Sugars 5 g | Added Sugars 0 g | **Protein** 15 g | **Phosphorus** 275 mg

Trick

- You can make hard-boiled eggs at home. They're easy to batch-cook, and you can store them unpeeled in a bowl in the refrigerator. Or, to save even more time, purchase cooked, peeled eggs in your deli or dairy aisle at your grocers.

Strategy 2: batch cooking

Have you heard of batch cooking? Or ever tried it out? Batch cooking means making the most of your time in the kitchen by cooking extra of a food for use later. Batch cooking is a great opportunity to stock the freezer for days when you don't have time to cook or don't feel like cooking. Some foods are better suited to freezing and reheating than others. (Later in this chapter on page 259, find lists of a few foods that fare well in the freezer, followed by a few that are best suited *not* to freeze.) Batch cooking can also be used with the intent to make "planned overs," which you'll learn more about later in this chapter as well.

3 Examples of Batch Cooking

1. Prepare a double batch of spaghetti sauce. Use half and freeze the remainder to pull out on another day, and dinner will be a few microwave minutes away. Our **Chunky Marinara Sauce** on page 200 is perfect for this.
2. Make two of a favorite casserole, assembling one in a disposable foil pan. Enjoy one now, and freeze the other in the disposable pan to pull out and bake another day. Tami does this with a favorite chicken and broccoli casserole.
3. While you have the blender out, make a double batch of smoothies, or two different flavors. Portion into small jars with lids and pop in the freezer to thaw and enjoy later if you are on the run. Try the recipes for **Lean Green Pineapple Smoothie** (on page 309) and **Cherry Berry Banana Smoothie** (on page 271).

CHUNKY MARINARA SAUCE

Make the most of your time in the kitchen through batch cooking. Make a batch of this simple marina sauce and serve some over pasta the first night. Then save some for another time, by either freezing or turning into a completely different dish, like the **Heat-and-Go Italian Soup** *on page 202.*

THIS RECIPE CAN FIT IN THE FOLLOWING EATING PATTERNS: **vegetarian, vegan, low-fat, low-carbohydrate, DASH**

NUMBER OF SERVINGS: 8 | **SERVING SIZE:** 1/2 cup per serving
PREP TIME: 7 minutes

INGREDIENTS

- 1/4 cup extra-virgin olive oil, divided use
- 1 cup chopped onion
- 8 garlic cloves, minced
- 3 (14.5-oz) cans no-salt-added diced tomatoes
- 1 cup water
- 3 Tbsp tomato paste
- 2 Tbsp balsamic vinegar
- 1 1/2 Tbsp dried oregano
- 1/2 cup chopped fresh basil
- 1 tsp salt

INSTRUCTIONS

1. Heat 1 Tbsp of the oil in a large nonstick skillet over medium heat. Add onion and cook 3 minutes or until translucent. Add garlic and cook 30 seconds, stirring constantly.

2. Add tomatoes, water, paste, vinegar, and oregano. Reduce heat and simmer, uncovered, for 30 minutes or until onions are very tender, stirring occasionally.

3. Remove from heat, stir in the basil, remaining 3 Tbsp of the oil, and salt.

4. Store in an airtight container in the fridge for up 4 days, or freeze for up to 2 months.

CHOICES: 1 Starch, 1 Fat

BASIC NUTRITIONAL VALUES: Calories 120 | Calories from Fat 60 | **Total Fat** 7.0 g | Saturated Fat 1.0 g | Trans Fat 0.0 g | **Cholesterol** 0 mg | **Sodium** 320 mg | **Potassium** 440 mg | **Total Carbohydrate** 12 g | Dietary Fiber 3 g | Sugars 6 g | Added Sugars 0 g | **Protein** 2 g | **Phosphorus** 50 mg

Serving Ideas

- Serve marinara sauce over 1 cup whole-wheat pasta with 1 Tbsp grated Parmesan for a classic spaghetti.
- Spoon over cooked chicken breasts, top with part-skim mozzarella, and broil until the cheese is melted.
- Transform into an Italian-style sloppy joe with lean ground beef or ground turkey.
- Use as a filling for baked mushrooms.

Tricks

- Don't want to deal with or handle 8 cloves of fresh garlic? Use the bottled minced variety sold in jars in the produce section. 1/2 tsp is equal to 1 garlic clove.
- Don't mind handling that much fresh garlic, but don't know how to get rid of the smell on your fingertips? Wash your hands in warm soapy water, dry them, and then rub your fingers on a chrome faucet or chrome handles. The chrome neutralizes the garlic smell!

POINTER

- This is an ideal make-ahead recipe because the flavors intensify as it is stored in the fridge, making it even better the next day.

HEAT-AND-GO ITALIAN SOUP

This recipe might be the easiest soup you will ever make! Just combine **Chunky Marinara Sauce** *(see page 200) with beans and water, bring it to a boil, and top with a little cheese. It's healthy in a hurry, and can be a "planned over"!*

THIS RECIPE CAN FIT IN THE FOLLOWING EATING PATTERNS: vegetarian, low-fat, low-carbohydrate, DASH

NUMBER OF SERVINGS: 4 | **SERVING SIZE:** 1 cup per serving

PREP TIME: 3 minutes | **COOK TIME:** 5 minutes

INGREDIENTS

- 2 cups reserved *Chunky Marinara Sauce* (page 202) (or store-bought marinara)
- 1/2 (15-oz) can no-salt-added navy beans, rinsed and drained
- 1 1/2 cups water
- 2 oz shredded part-skim mozzarella cheese
- 2 tsp grated Parmesan cheese

INSTRUCTIONS

1. Combine marinara sauce, beans, and water in a medium saucepan. Bring to a boil over medium-high heat.
2. Remove from heat, pour equal amounts into each of four soup bowls, and top evenly with mozzarella and Parmesan cheeses.

COOK'S SWAP

- Try serving over sautéed veggies, such as zucchini slices or yellow crookneck squash, or over grilled or broiled portobello mushroom caps or eggplant slices for a quick and interesting side dish.

CHOICES: 1 1/2 Starch, 1 Lean Protein, 1 1/2 Fat

BASIC NUTRITIONAL VALUES: Calories 210 | Calories from Fat 90 | **Total Fat** 10.0 g | Saturated Fat 2.9 g | Trans Fat 0.1 g | **Cholesterol** 10 mg | **Sodium** 410 mg | **Potassium** 540 mg | **Total Carbohydrate** 22 g | Dietary Fiber 6 g | Sugars 6 g | Added Sugars 0 g | **Protein** 9 g | **Phosphorus** 175 mg

Strategy 3: planned overs

Few people want to eat the same meal day after day, but what we call "planned overs" can become another go-to strategy when planning meals. Basically, you plan ahead by intentionally making more of an ingredient than you'll eat in one meal and save it to use as part of another meal later in the week. Planned overs can be used for breakfast, lunch, or dinner meals. Several planned-over recipes follow. Eat planned overs within 3–4 days or freeze for later use.

Here are 7 examples of how to create and incorporate planned overs:

1. **Roast a turkey breast or cook in a slower cooker.** Enjoy as an entrée one day and use the extra meat for turkey pot pie a day or two later.
2. **Roast a chicken or buy a rotisserie chicken.** Enjoy it as an entrée one day, as topping for a salad another day for a quick assembly meal, and in chicken enchiladas the next day.
3. **When you have the grill fired up, grill some extra chicken breasts.** Cool and freeze in a resealable plastic bag, and then thaw later to warm and enjoy on a salad, in a wrap, or as a main dish.
4. **Cook a pork loin.** Enjoy a portion today. Shred some and toss with barbecue sauce to enjoy as pork barbecue at lunch another day.
5. **Cook a large roast in the slow cooker.** Eat part one day and then shred and freeze the rest to incorporate in a beef vegetable soup another day.
6. **Sauté extra spinach or steam extra broccoli.** Enjoy at dinner one night and in an egg scramble the next morning.
7. **Cook extra quinoa, millet, farro, or other whole grain.** Enjoy the grain as a side dish one day, as an addition to Greek-style salad the next, and add to vegetable soup the third day.

The recipes on pages 202–209 are designed to help you put "planned overs" into practice.

INSTANT POT HERB PROVENCAL CHICKEN THIGHS

Batch cooking doesn't have to be reserved for the stovetop or oven. Take advantage of an Instant Pot and cook up a bunch of chicken thighs, serve some with a simple tomato caper topping, and reserve the rest of the cooked chicken for a casserole or skillet dish another night. For example, use in the **Green Chile Chicken Casserole** *recipe on page 206.*

THIS RECIPE CAN FIT IN THE FOLLOWING EATING PATTERNS: low- or very-low-carbohydrate, DASH, Mediterranean

NUMBER OF SERVINGS: 4 (plus 4 chicken thighs reserved for *Green Chile Chicken Casserole*)
SERVING SIZE: 1 thigh plus 1/4 cup tomato mixture per serving | **PREP TIME:** 15 minutes
COME TO PRESSURE TIME: 5 minutes | **COOK TIME:** 18 minutes

INGREDIENTS

Chicken Thighs:

- 1 Tbsp dried oregano
- 1 1/2 tsp garlic powder
- 1 tsp paprika
- 1/2 tsp black pepper
- 1 Tbsp extra-virgin olive oil
- 8 (4-oz each) boneless, skinless chicken thighs
- 1 cup water
- 1 lemon, sliced

Tomato Topping:

- 1 cup chopped tomatoes
- 2 Tbsp capers, drained
- 1/8 tsp salt
- 1 Tbsp extra-virgin olive oil

INSTRUCTIONS

1. Combine the oregano, garlic powder, paprika, black pepper, and 1 Tbsp oil in a large bowl. Whisk together until well blended, add chicken, and toss until well coated.

2. Press the Sauté button on the Instant Pot, then press the Adjust button to "More" or "High." When the display says "Hot," add half of the chicken, smooth side down, and cook 5 minutes on one side only. Remove from pot and set aside. Repeat with remaining half of the chicken. Remove from pot.

3. Add water and lemon slices to pot, top with the thighs overlapping slightly. Seal the lid, close the valve, press Cancel button, and reset to Manual/Pressure Cook for 8 minutes.

(continued)

INSTANT POT HERB PROVENCAL CHICKEN THIGHS (*continued*)

4. Use a quick pressure release. When valve drops, carefully remove the lid. Remove chicken and lemon slices from pot, discarding lemon slices only.
5. Reserve 4 thighs and 1/2 cup of the liquid for the Green Chile Chicken Casserole recipe. Cover and refrigerate up to 2 days.
6. Combine the tomatoes, capers, salt, and 1 Tbsp oil in a small bowl. Top the remaining thighs with the tomato mixture and serve.

CHOICES: 3 Lean Protein, 1 Fat

BASIC NUTRITIONAL VALUES: Calories 190 | Calories from Fat 110 | **Total Fat** 12.0 g | Saturated Fat 2.5 g | Trans Fat 0.0 g | **Cholesterol** 105 mg | **Sodium** 240 mg | **Potassium** 340 mg | **Total Carbohydrate** 3 g | Dietary Fiber 1 g | Sugars 1 g | Added Sugars 0 g | **Protein** 19 g | **Phosphorus** 180 mg

GREEN CHILE CHICKEN CASSEROLE

Prepackaged individual servings of brown rice and quinoa can be found at most supermarkets. Using them in this recipe means it takes only 7 minutes to prepare! If quinoa is new to you, a great way to introduce it is to mix it with rice for more protein, fiber, and a unique ingredient combination. This is a "planned over" recipe incorporating reserved chicken and broth from **Instant Pot Herb Provencal Chicken Thighs** *recipe on page 204.*

THIS RECIPE CAN FIT IN THE FOLLOWING EATING PATTERNS: low-carbohydrate, DASH

NUMBER OF SERVINGS: 4 | **SERVING SIZE:** 1 cup per serving

PREP TIME: 7 minutes | **COOK TIME:** 35 minutes

INGREDIENTS

- 4 cooked chicken thighs (from the reserved **Instant Pot Herb Provencal Chicken Thighs** recipe)
- 1/2 cup broth (reserved broth from **Instant Pot Herb Provencal Chicken Thighs** recipe)
- 1 (8.8-oz) package precooked brown rice, such as Uncle Ben's Ready Rice (or 1 1/2 cups cooked brown rice)
- 1 (4.4-oz) container precooked quinoa, such as Minute White and Red Organic Quinoa (or 3/4 cup cooked quinoa)
- 1 tsp ground cumin
- 2 (4-oz) cans chopped green chilies
- 3 oz shredded reduced-fat sharp cheddar cheese
- 1/4 cup 2% plain Greek yogurt

INSTRUCTIONS

1. Preheat oven to 350°F.
2. Shred the reserved chicken and place in a medium bowl with the reserved broth, rice, quinoa, and cumin. Stir gently until well blended. Spoon into an 8 × 8-inch baking dish, and spoon chilies evenly over all.
3. Cover with foil and bake 30–35 minutes or until heated through. Top with cheese. Let stand 5 minutes to absorb flavors and allow cheese to melt slightly. Serve topped with yogurt.

POINTER

- It's important to read the labels on precooked, ready-to-serve quinoa varieties. They can vary greatly in sodium and fat content. Choose the lowest sodium and lowest fat content available.

CHOICES: 2 Starch, 3 Lean Protein, 1 1/2 Fat

BASIC NUTRITIONAL VALUES: Calories 380 | Calories from Fat 140 | **Total Fat** 15.0 g | Saturated Fat 5.0 g | Trans Fat 0.0 g | **Cholesterol** 120 mg | **Sodium** 530 mg | **Potassium** 480 mg | **Total Carbohydrate** 33 g | Dietary Fiber 4 g | Sugars 3 g | Added Sugars 0 g | **Protein** 29 g | **Phosphorus** 420 mg

SIMPLE STEAMED BROCCOLI

Steamed broccoli is a perfect simple side dish when you need to add some vegetables to your plate. While you are making it, you may as well cook a large batch as planned overs for another dish, like quick and easy **Corn and Broccoli Soup** *on page 208.*

***THIS RECIPE CAN FIT IN THE FOLLOWING EATING PATTERNS:* All**

NUMBER OF SERVINGS: 4 (plus 2 cups broccoli reserved for *Corn and Broccoli Soup*)
SERVING SIZE: 1/2 cup broccoli with lemon wedge | **PREP TIME:** 5 minutes
COOK TIME: 4 minutes

INGREDIENTS

- 4 cups broccoli florets (from about 1 1/2 heads broccoli or 12-oz package fresh broccoli florets)
- 1 lemon, cut into wedges

INSTRUCTIONS

1. Bring about 1 inch of water to a boil in the bottom of a large saucepan. Place steamer basket in bottom of pan. Place florets in the steamer basket, cover, and cook until tender-crisp, about 4 minutes.
2. Set aside 2 cups of broccoli to cool, and then store in an airtight container in the fridge for up to 5 days.
3. Serve the remaining broccoli in 1/2-cup portions with fresh lemon wedges.

> **POINTER**
>
> - Serve steamed broccoli alongside a meat-based entrée like ***Tandoori-Style Chicken with Fresh Mint*** (page 217) to add nonstarchy vegetables to your plate.

CHOICES: 1 Nonstarchy Vegetable

BASIC NUTRITIONAL VALUES: Calories 25 | Calories from Fat 0 | **Total Fat** 0.0 g | Saturated Fat 0.0 g | Trans Fat 0.0 g | **Cholesterol** 0 mg | **Sodium** 15 mg | **Potassium** 260 mg | **Total Carbohydrate** 5 g | Dietary Fiber 2.5 g | Sugars 1 g | Added Sugars 0 g | **Protein** 3 g | **Phosphorus** 90 mg

CORN AND BROCCOLI SOUP

The next time you prepare steamed broccoli (such as on page 207), cook extra as planned overs for this quick and easy soup! Soup can take time to chop, sauté, and simmer. But not this recipe! Using frozen and precooked veggies means the whole recipe takes just 15 minutes from start to finish.

THIS RECIPE CAN FIT IN THE FOLLOWING EATING PATTERNS: vegetarian, low-fat, low-carbohydrate, **DASH**

NUMBER OF SERVINGS: 4 | **SERVING SIZE:** 1 cup per serving
PREP TIME: 5 minutes | **COOK TIME:** 10 minutes

INGREDIENTS

- 2 cups frozen corn kernels
- 1 1/2 cups chopped red bell pepper
- 1/2 cup water
- 1 1/2 cups 2% milk
- 2 cups reserved steamed broccoli florets
- 1/2 cup chopped green onion
- 3 oz shredded reduced-fat sharp cheddar cheese
- 1/2 tsp salt
- 1/4 tsp black pepper
- 1/4 cup chopped fresh parsley

INSTRUCTIONS

1. Combine corn, bell pepper, and water in a medium saucepan. Bring to a boil, reduce heat, cover, and simmer 5 minutes or until peppers are tender. Add the milk, broccoli, and green onion.
2. Cover and cook 2 minutes or until heated.
3. Remove from heat, stir in the remaining ingredients, except the parsley. Serve topped with parsley.

CHOICES: 1 Starch, 1/2 Reduced-Fat Milk, 1 Nonstarchy Vegetable, 1 Lean Protein, 1/2 Fat
BASIC NUTRITIONAL VALUES: Calories 200 | Calories from Fat 60 | **Total Fat** 7.0 g | Saturated Fat 3.9 g | Trans Fat 0.1 g | **Cholesterol** 20 mg | **Sodium** 520 mg | **Potassium** 600 mg | **Total Carbohydrate** 25 g | Dietary Fiber 4 g | Sugars 10 g | Added Sugars 0 g | **Protein** 12 g | **Phosphorus** 305 mg

POINTER

- Substitute red bell pepper with green bell pepper, if desired.
- 2% milk is used instead of nonfat to lend a little more creaminess, while still keeping the fat far lower than a traditional cream soup.

Tricks

- Using a small amount of water to cook the vegetables initially is the best way to cook the vegetables for a "cream"-based soup. The milk is added near the end and just cooked long enough to heat through, preventing it from curdling.
- The cheese is added *after* the soup has been removed from the heat to prevent curdling as well.

HERBED QUINOA

When you're cooking quinoa for a simple savory side one night, prepare an extra 2 cups (cooked) and use that as part of a main dish the next night. See what can be done with the rest as planned overs in **Chickpea and Feta Quinoa Salad** *on the next page.*

THIS RECIPE CAN FIT IN THE FOLLOWING EATING PATTERNS: vegetarian, vegan, low-fat, low-carbohydrate, DASH, Mediterranean

---

NUMBER OF SERVINGS: 4 (plus 2 cups reserved for *Chickpea and Feta Quinoa Salad*)
SERVING SIZE: 1/2 cup per serving | **PREP TIME:** 5 minutes | **COOK TIME:** 15 minutes
STAND TIME: 5 minutes

INGREDIENTS

- 2 1/2 cups water
- 1 1/4 cups uncooked quinoa
- 2 Tbsp extra-virgin olive oil
- 1 Tbsp dried oregano
- 1/2 tsp salt

INSTRUCTIONS

1. Bring water to a boil in a medium saucepan. Stir in the quinoa and reduce heat, cover, and simmer 15 minutes or until liquid is absorbed.
2. Remove from heat and let stand 5 minutes, covered. Stir in oil, oregano, and salt.
3. Save 2 cups quinoa for Chickpea and Feta Quinoa Salad. Store in an airtight container in the fridge for up to 4 days or in the freezer for up to 2 months.

CHOICES: 1 Starch, 1 Fat
BASIC NUTRITIONAL VALUES: Calories 130 | Calories from Fat 45 | **Total Fat** 5.0 g | Saturated Fat 0.7 g | Trans Fat 0.0 g | **Cholesterol** 0 mg | **Sodium** 150 mg | **Potassium** 150 mg | **Total Carbohydrate** 18 g | Dietary Fiber 2 g | Sugars 2 g | Added Sugars 0 g | **Protein** 4 g | **Phosphorus** 120 mg

CHICKPEA AND FETA QUINOA SALAD

This recipe with fresh Mediterranean flavor incorporates planned-over **Herbed Quinoa** *from the previous page.*

THIS RECIPE CAN FIT IN THE FOLLOWING EATING PATTERNS: vegetarian, DASH, Mediterranean

NUMBER OF SERVINGS: 4 | **SERVING SIZE:** 1 3/4 cups per serving
PREP TIME: 7 minutes

INGREDIENTS

- 2 cups reserved Herbed Quinoa (or other cooked grains)
- 2 cups chopped kale
- 1/2 (15.5-oz) can no-salt-added chickpeas, rinsed and drained
- 1/2 (14-oz) can quartered artichoke hearts, drained
- 3 oz feta cheese crumbled
- 1 cup chopped cucumber
- 1/2 cup chopped red onion
- 2 Tbsp cider vinegar
- 1 Tbsp extra-virgin olive oil

INSTRUCTIONS

1. Combine all ingredients in a large bowl. Toss until well blended.

POINTERS

- No need to peel the cucumber. The skin provides a bit more fiber and color to the dish . . . and it's one less thing to do!
- Substitute kale with spinach, if desired.
- Try batch cooking other grains to incorporate into future meals. This process will save time, steps, and energy.

CHOICES: 2 Starch, 1 Nonstarchy Vegetable, 1 Medium-Fat Protein, 1 1/2 Fat

BASIC NUTRITIONAL VALUES: Calories 300 | Calories from Fat 130 | **Total Fat** 14.0 g | Saturated Fat 4.0 g | Trans Fat 0.2 g | **Cholesterol** 15 mg | **Sodium** 480 mg | **Potassium** 440 mg | **Total Carbohydrate** 35 g | Dietary Fiber 7 g | Sugars 7 g | Added Sugars 0 g | **Protein** 12 g | **Phosphorus** 285 mg

Strategy 4: backup meals

You may find it helpful to have ingredients for a few backup meals on hand to pull together a meal when life doesn't go as planned, as it often does. One night, Tami's family had planned to grill cedar plank salmon but arrived home from work to a torrential downpour. The salmon stayed in the refrigerator until the next day, and they headed for a backup meal. Another day, they'd planned to have a "planned-over" meal with previously grilled chicken on a green salad. Tami opened the bag of seemingly fresh salad greens to find many were spoiled. Time for another backup meal! The ***Grilled Veggie and Cheese Sandwich*** on page 213 is perfect for nights just like this.

7 Backup Meal Ideas that May Inspire You

1. Foil packet of tuna or salmon, whole-grain crackers, and microwavable vegetable or tomato soup
2. Nut butter on whole-grain crackers, baby carrots, and a small piece of fresh fruit or fruit canned in juice
3. Fully cooked shrimp (thaw under cool water and drain well), ready-to-heat quinoa or brown rice, and steam-in-the-bag frozen vegetable
4. Scrambled egg or egg "fried" in a nonstick skillet; ready-to-heat quinoa or brown rice; frozen vegetables such as spinach, chopped broccoli, onion, or peppers (we keep diced onion and peppers in the freezer for occasions like this). Top with salsa or avocado if you have any on hand.
5. Panini or oven-toasted sandwich made with whole-grain bread, reduced-fat cheese, fresh vegetables (think tomato, onion, cucumber, zucchini, artichoke hearts, kale, spinach, mushrooms, peppers, etc.), or fresh fruit (such as apples or pears)
6. Healthy frozen packaged meal
7. A planned backup homemade freezer meal. We often stash single servings of leftover bean or lentil soups or chili in the freezer for occasions like this. Or when making a favorite casserole, split a 9 × 13-inch pan into two square 8 × 8-inch pans and freeze one to have on hand for a backup meal.

GRILLED VEGGIE AND CHEESE SANDWICH

Some days, things just don't go as planned and the meal you thought you were going to have just doesn't happen. That's why it's helpful to keep some staples on hand to pull together a satisfying backup meal like this piled high sandwich (which flattens slightly as it grills). The cheese on the top and bottom helps hold it together and give you a cheesy bite all the way through!

THIS RECIPE CAN FIT IN THE FOLLOWING EATING PATTERNS: vegetarian, low-fat, low-carbohydrate, DASH

NUMBER OF SERVINGS: 4 | **SERVING SIZE:** 1 sandwich per serving
PREP TIME: 12 minutes | **COOK TIME:** 5 minutes

INGREDIENTS

- 8 oz crusty whole-grain loaf bread, cut in half lengthwise
- 8 ultra-thin slices baby Swiss cheese, such as Sargento
- 1 cup thinly sliced red or green bell pepper
- 1 cup chopped kale
- 1/4 cup thinly sliced onion
- 2 Tbsp extra-virgin olive oil
- 1 Tbsp cider vinegar
- 1 Tbsp dried basil
- 1/4 tsp salt

INSTRUCTIONS

1. Coat uncut sides of bread with nonstick cooking spray and place bread, cut side up, on a cutting board. Top the bottom half with the 4 cheese slices, bell pepper, kale, onion, and top with remaining 4 cheese slices.

2. In a small bowl, whisk together the oil, vinegar, basil, and salt. Spoon evenly over the cut side of the top half of the bread.

3. Place the top bread half on top of the vegetables and press down firmly to adhere slightly. Cut into fourths, forming four sandwiches.

4. Heat a large nonstick skillet over medium-low heat. Cook sandwiches for 2–3 minutes on each side, pressing down with a spatula to flatten, or until cheese melts slightly and bread is lightly browned, turning sandwiches carefully.

(Cook's Swap and Pointers on following page)

CHOICES: 1 1/2 Starch, 1 Nonstarchy Vegetable, 1 Medium-Fat Protein, 1 1/2 Fat
BASIC NUTRITIONAL VALUES: Calories 300 | Calories from Fat 140 | **Total Fat** 15.0 g | Saturated Fat 4.8 g | Trans Fat 0.2 g | **Cholesterol** 15 mg | **Sodium** 430 mg | **Potassium** 240 mg | **Total Carbohydrate** 28 g | Dietary Fiber 5 g | Sugars 5 g | Added Sugars 0 g | **Protein** 14 g | **Phosphorus** 260 mg

COOK'S SWAP

- For a vegan dish, substitute cheese with 1/2 cup hummus and serve hot or cold.

POINTERS

- Use loaf bread rather than sliced bread for best results.
- Keep a bread loaf or two in the freezer to have on hand so you can make a sandwich like this any time as a back-up meal.
- Don't have any Swiss cheese on hand? Use 4 oz of any reduced-fat cheese (shredded cheese works, too). Replace bell pepper with roma tomatoes, bottled roasted peppers, or any other chopped vegetables you have on hand (get creative!). Instead of kale, you could use any leafy greens like spinach, lettuce, or arugula.

35 Foods in a Well-Stocked Kitchen You Can Use to Pull Together a Quick Meal

No time to cook? Healthy eating is easier if you keep a variety of basic staple foods on hand to pull together quick and healthy meals and snacks. Then you can add fresh ingredients as needed. The following list includes 35 foods and ingredients to spark your thinking about what you can keep on hand to make quick meals. Tailor these foods to your preferences and health goals.

1. Applesauce, unsweetened
2. Artichoke hearts
3. Beans, canned (no-salt-added if possible)
4. Canned tomatoes (crushed, whole, diced, tomato sauce)
5. Cheese, reduced-fat varieties
6. Chicken, frozen fully cooked, diced, or sliced
7. Coffee
8. Eggs or liquid egg substitutes
9. Fruits, in juice (canned or individual serving cups) or frozen without sugar

(continued)

35 Foods in a Well-Stocked Kitchen You Can Use to Pull Together a Quick Meal *(continued)*

10. Fruit spreads, 100% fruit or reduced-sugar
11. Herbs and spices
12. Lentils
13. Marinara
14. Mussels, frozen microwavable varieties
15. Nonstick cooking spray
16. Nuts, including almonds, peanuts, pecans, pistachios, and walnuts
17. Nut butter, such as almond butter and peanut butter
18. Oatmeal
19. Oil, such as canola, olive, or corn
20. Olives
21. Olive tapenade/spread
22. Pasta, whole-wheat or fiber-enriched
23. Red bell peppers, roasted
24. Salmon, canned in water or foil packed
25. Salsa
26. Shrimp, frozen fully cooked
27. Soups, reduced-sodium and reduced-fat
28. Tea
29. Tuna, canned in water or foil-packed
30. Turkey meatballs, fully cooked frozen
31. Vegetables, a variety of canned or frozen (no-salt-added if possible)
32. Vinegars, including balsamic, red wine, and white wine
33. Whole grains, fully cooked in micro-wavable pouches or individual cups (such as brown rice or quinoa)
34. Whole-grain bread and crackers
35. Yogurt, fat-free or low-fat

Meal Planning for One

Cooking for one can seem challenging. Check out our next four recipes designed to feed one or two people. And, here are 5 tips that have helped clients Tami has worked with over the years who meal-plan for themselves.

1. **Look for recipes that serve one.** While in years gone by most recipes were designed to feed multiple people, there are now a variety of recipes designed as single servings. Check out the *Bountiful Breakfast Sandwich* on page 262

2. **Freeze extra portions.** If buying poultry, fish, or meat for instance, take out what you'll eat and freeze the rest in single servings (we use resealable plastic freezer bags) to pull out for easy use in future meals. Or if making chili, soup, or a casserole, store leftovers in single-serving containers for easy heat-and-eat meals.

3. **Use a toaster oven.** Instead of heating up the big oven, a toaster oven is small, convenient, and quick to heat. It's perfect for roasting a chicken breast, fish, or

vegetables; baking muffins; and warming leftover portions.

4. **Grocery shop at the salad bar.** At the salad bar, you can choose exactly the amount you want and will use of a variety of vegetables. You can even find things like chickpeas and beets when you'd like some, but don't need a whole can.

5. **Cook once, enjoy twice.** With versatile ingredients like quinoa, cook a little extra to enjoy in a different way (the "planned overs" concept). For instance, an extra cup or two of cooked quinoa can be enjoyed as a savory side dish, a grain salad for lunch, or a breakfast cereal topped with fruit. (See *Herbed Quinoa* recipe on page 210 earlier in this chapter.)

TANDOORI-STYLE CHICKEN WITH FRESH MINT

Tandoori-style basically involves marinated meat being cooked over an intense fire in a clay oven called a tandoor. This recipe achieves the "tandoori-style" without a clay oven. Marinating chicken breast marinated in yogurt and citrus overnight produces chicken that is so tender you can cut it with a fork! Plus, you'll spoon some reserved marinade over the chicken as it cooks for a rich flavor. This is a planned over recipe—reserve part of this chicken for **Chicken and Fresh Mandarin Thai Salad** *on page 219.*

THIS RECIPE CAN FIT IN THE FOLLOWING EATING PATTERNS: low- or very-low-fat, low- or very-low-carbohydrate, DASH

NUMBER OF SERVINGS: 2 (plus 2 chicken breasts reserved for *Chicken and Fresh Mandarin Thai Salad*) | **SERVING SIZE:** 3 oz cooked chicken per serving
PREP TIME: 12 minutes plus marinate time: 8 hours | **COOK TIME:** 10 minutes

INGREDIENTS

- 2/3 cup 2% plain Greek yogurt
- 2 Tbsp fresh lemon juice
- 1 Tbsp grated ginger (see tips for using fresh ginger on page 50)
- 2 tsp curry powder
- 1/2 tsp garlic powder
- 4 (4-oz) boneless, skinless chicken breasts, flattened to 1/2-inch thickness
- 1/8 tsp salt
- 2 Tbsp chopped fresh mint leaves

INSTRUCTIONS

1. Whisk together the yogurt, lemon juice, ginger, curry powder, and garlic powder in a medium bowl to make marinade. Reserve 1/4 cup yogurt marinade in a separate container. Add the chicken to the remaining yogurt marinade in the bowl, and toss several times until well coated. Cover and refrigerate overnight or at least 8 hours.
2. Preheat broiler.
3. Place a baking rack coated with nonstick cooking spray on a foil-lined baking pan. Place the chicken pieces on the baking rack, reserving any remaining marinade. Broil about 6 inches away from heat source 5 minutes. Turn chicken pieces, spoon the reserved marinade on top of each breast, and broil 5 minutes or until no longer pink in center.

(continued)

TANDOORI-STYLE CHICKEN WITH FRESH MINT (*continued*)

4. Reserve 2 breasts for *Chicken and Fresh Mandarin Thai Salad* (page 219). Cover with plastic wrap and refrigerate up to 48 hours.
5. Sprinkle the remaining 2 breasts with the salt and mint, and serve.

POINTERS

- Flattening the chicken has two benefits: it tenderizes the chicken and it provides for even cooking.
- To flatten chicken easily, place a sheet of plastic wrap on the kitchen countertop or work surface. Arrange the chicken breasts on top at least 2 inches apart. Top with another sheet of plastic wrap. Using the smooth side of a meat mallet or heavy bottle, gently pound to an even 1/2-inch thickness, being careful not to pound any thinner than that.

CHOICES: 4 Lean Protein

BASIC NUTRITIONAL VALUES: Calories 160 | Calories from Fat 30 | **Total Fat** 3.5 g | Saturated Fat 1.3 g | Trans Fat 0.0 g | **Cholesterol** 65 mg | **Sodium** 220 mg | **Potassium** 300 mg | **Total Carbohydrate** 4 g | Dietary Fiber 1 g | Sugars 2 g | Added Sugars 0 g | **Protein** 28 g | **Phosphorus** 235 mg

CHICKEN AND FRESH MANDARIN THAI SALAD

A fresh mandarin is the real name for those little "Cuties" or "Halos" you see in the produce aisle. They are so easy to peel and have on hand for a quick salad with personality that goes beyond the typical lettuce and tomato variety. This is a "planned over" recipe incorporating reserved chicken from **Tandoori-Style Chicken with Fresh Mint** *on page 217.*

THIS RECIPE CAN FIT IN THE FOLLOWING EATING PATTERNS: low-fat, low-carbohydrate, DASH

NUMBER OF SERVINGS: 2 | **SERVING SIZE:** 3 cups per serving
PREP TIME: 6 minutes

INGREDIENTS

- 4 cups baby kale mix
- 1 cup matchstick carrots
- 1 fresh mandarin orange, peeled and sectioned
- 2 cooked chicken breasts (reserved from ***Tandoori-Style Chicken with Fresh Mint***)
- 1/4 cup chopped red onion
- 1 oz unsalted dry roasted peanuts
- 1/4 cup sesame ginger dressing, such as Newman's Own Sesame Ginger
- 2 Tbsp chopped fresh mint

INSTRUCTIONS

1. Divide the kale mix, carrots, and orange sections between two shallow bowls.
2. Chop the reserved chicken and sprinkle over all. Top with equal amounts of the remaining ingredients.

POINTER

- To bring out the "nuttiness" of the peanuts, toast them quickly by heating a medium skillet over medium-high heat, add the peanuts, and cook 4 minutes or until beginning to lightly brown, stirring frequently.

CHOICES: 1 Carbohydrate, 2 Nonstarchy Vegetable, 4 Lean Protein, 1 Fat
BASIC NUTRITIONAL VALUES: Calories 350 | Calories from Fat 120 | **Total Fat** 13.0 g | Saturated Fat 2.5 g | Trans Fat 0.0 g | **Cholesterol** 65 mg | **Sodium** 420 mg | **Potassium** 900 mg | **Total Carbohydrate** 28 g | Dietary Fiber 6 g | Sugars 15 g | Added Sugars 4 g | **Protein** 34 g | **Phosphorus** 365 mg

SKILLET PORK WITH ORANGE-BALSAMIC REDUCTION

This recipe is easy, of course, but it tastes so complex thanks to the simple pan sauce drizzled on top. The pan sauce is made by adding orange juice and balsamic vinegar to the same pan cooking the pork chops. The liquid dissolves all the caramelized bits of meat and seasoning stuck to the pan, and then the flavors are concentrated by quickly boiling the sauce over high heat. This is another recipe illustrating the concept of "planned overs" with one pork chop reserved for **Almond Pork "Fried" Quinoa** *on page 222.*

THIS RECIPE CAN FIT IN THE FOLLOWING EATING PATTERNS: low-fat, low- or very-low-carbohydrate, DASH

NUMBER OF SERVINGS: 2 (plus 1 pork chop reserved for *Almond Pork "Fried" Quinoa*)
SERVING SIZE: 3 oz cooked pork and 1 Tbsp sauce per serving | **PREP TIME:** 6 minutes
COOK TIME: 9 minutes

INGREDIENTS

- 3 (4-oz each) boneless loin pork chops, trimmed of fat
- 1 tsp curry powder
- 1/2 tsp paprika
- 1/4 tsp black pepper
- 2 tsp canola oil
- 1/4 cup 100% orange juice
- 1 1/2 Tbsp balsamic vinegar
- 1/8 tsp salt

INSTRUCTIONS

1. Season both sides of the pork chops with the curry powder, paprika, and black pepper.
2. Heat oil in large nonstick skillet over medium-high heat. Tilt skillet to lightly coat bottom. Add pork chops and cook 4 minutes on each side or until the pork reaches an internal temperature of 165°F.
3. Reserve 1 pork chop for Almond Pork "Fried" Quinoa. Once it is cool, cover with plastic wrap and refrigerate up to 48 hours.
4. Place remaining pork chops on separate plates.
5. To pan residue, add the orange juice, vinegar, and salt. Bring to a boil over medium-high heat and continue to boil for 30–45 seconds or until reduced to 2 Tbsp. Spoon over two pork chops.

CHOICES: 1/2 Carbohydrate, 3 Lean Protein, 1 Fat
BASIC NUTRITIONAL VALUES: Calories 210 | Calories from Fat 90 | **Total Fat** 10.0 g | Saturated Fat 2.8 g | Trans Fat 0.0 g | **Cholesterol** 60 mg | **Sodium** 200 mg | **Potassium** 400 mg | **Total Carbohydrate** 6 g | Dietary Fiber 0 g | Sugars 4 g | Added Sugars 0 g | **Protein** 21 g | **Phosphorus** 185 mg

COOK'S SWAP

- Substitute pork with chicken breasts, flattened to 1/2-inch thickness, if desired.
- See how to easily flatten chicken breasts in the Pointers on page 218.

POINTER

- When boiling the orange juice mixture, watch closely so it doesn't burn—it reduces faster than you might think!

ALMOND PORK "FRIED" QUINOA

Just a simple swap from brown rice to quinoa bumps up the fiber from 5 grams to 7 grams and reduces carbohydrate by about 7 grams. You can certainly use 1 cup of precooked brown rice, but why not give quinoa a try? It's lighter in taste and texture, comes in a variety of colors and is a healthy addition to your pantry staples, too! This is a "planned over" recipe incorporating a pork chop reserved from **Skillet Pork with Orange Balsamic Reduction** *on page 220.*

THIS RECIPE CAN FIT IN THE FOLLOWING EATING PATTERNS: low- or very-low-carbohydrate, DASH

NUMBER OF SERVINGS: 2 | **SERVING SIZE:** 1 cup per serving
PREP TIME: 6 minutes | **COOK TIME:** 9 minutes

INGREDIENTS

- 1 cooked pork chop (reserved from *Skillet Pork with Orange-Balsamic Reduction*)
- 1 tsp canola oil
- 1 (4.4-oz) container precooked quinoa (or 3/4 cup cooked quinoa)
- 1/4 cup slivered almonds
- 1/2 cup chopped green onions
- 1/2 cup fresh or thawed frozen shelled edamame
- 1 large egg, beaten
- 1 Tbsp reduced-sodium soy sauce

INSTRUCTIONS

1. Chop pork into 1/2-inch cubes and set aside.
2. Heat a medium nonstick skillet over medium heat. Add oil and tilt skillet to coat bottom lightly. Cook quinoa and almonds 4 minutes or until almonds begin to brown on the edges, stirring frequently.
3. Stir in the pork, onions, and edamame; cook 2 minutes, stirring frequently. Drizzle the egg over all and cook 45 seconds or until egg is cooked, stirring constantly.
4. Remove from heat and drizzle soy sauce over all.

CHOICES: 1 1/2 Starch, 1/2 Carbohydrate, 3 Lean Protein, 2 Fat
BASIC NUTRITIONAL VALUES: Calories 380 | Calories from Fat 180 | **Total Fat** 20.0 g | Saturated Fat 3.3 g | Trans Fat 0.0 g | **Cholesterol** 120 mg | **Sodium** 440 mg | **Potassium** 970 mg | **Total Carbohydrate** 27 g | Dietary Fiber 8 g | Sugars 3 g | Added Sugars 0 g | **Protein** 25 g | **Phosphorus** 385 mg

COOK'S SWAPS

- Use 1/4 cup liquid egg substitute instead of the egg to lower cholesterol in the dish.

POINTER

- This is a fast-moving recipe, so have everything prepped before starting.
- Edamame is a shelled green soybean that looks similar to a small lima bean but is lower in carbohydrate than beans or peas.

BEEF BURGERS WITH AVOCADO SPREAD

Avocados have exploded in popularity—and there's a reason for that! Not only do they taste great, but avocado is low in carbohydrate, rich in fiber, and full of filling, healthy fats. This recipe illustrates the concept of "planned overs," with one burger reserved to make **Pizza Flats** *on page 226.*

THIS RECIPE CAN FIT IN THE FOLLOWING EATING PATTERNS: low-carbohydrate, DASH

NUMBER OF SERVINGS: 2 (plus 1 patty reserved for *Pizza Flats*) | **SERVING SIZE:** 3-oz beef patty, 1 bun, plus about 2 Tbsp avocado spread per serving

PREP TIME: 10 minutes | **COOK TIME:** 8 minutes

INGREDIENTS

- 12 oz 95% lean ground beef
- 2 garlic cloves, minced
- 2 tsp Worcestershire sauce
- 1/8 tsp salt
- 1/8 tsp black pepper
- 1/2 avocado, peeled and mashed
- 1/2 tsp hot sauce, such as Frank's
- 4 rings of green bell pepper, divided use
- 2 whole-wheat hamburger buns, warmed
- 1/4 cup sliced red onion
- 2 romaine lettuce leaves

INSTRUCTIONS

1. Combine the ground beef, garlic, Worcestershire sauce, and salt in a bowl. Shape into three patties, about 4 inches in diameter.
2. Heat a medium nonstick skillet coated with nonstick cooking spray over medium-high heat. Sprinkle black pepper over patties and cook 3–4 minutes on each side or until lightly pink in the center.
3. Meanwhile, combine the avocado and hot sauce in a small bowl and mash. Set aside.
4. Reserve one patty plus two bell pepper rings for Pizza Flats.
5. Place remaining two patties on bottom of buns. Top with equal amounts of onion, bell pepper rings, and lettuce. Spoon avocado mixture evenly over the remaining bun halves.
6. Cover reserved patty and pepper rings with plastic wrap and refrigerate up to 48 hours.

CHOICES: 1 1/2 Starch, 1 Nonstarchy Vegetable, 3 Lean Protein, 2 Fat

BASIC NUTRITIONAL VALUES: Calories 350 | Calories from Fat 140 | **Total Fat** 15.0 g | Saturated Fat 4.3 g | Trans Fat 0.4 g | **Cholesterol** 70 mg | **Sodium** 480 mg | **Potassium** 740 mg | **Total Carbohydrate** 29 g | Dietary Fiber 6 g | Sugars 5 g | Added Sugars 0 g | **Protein** 27 g | **Phosphorus** 325 mg

COOK'S SWAPS

- Substitute ground beef with lean ground turkey, if desired.
- Don't like bell pepper? Use 1/4 cup sliced mushrooms instead (save some for the Pizza Flats recipe on the next page).
- For a very-low-carb dish, ditch the burger bun or use lettuce leaves as a "bun" instead.

POINTER

- For soft, warm buns, place in the microwave on high setting for 15–20 seconds, *or* for a crunchier version, place them in a toaster or toaster oven (cut side up) and toast until lightly browned.

Trick

- Store the reserved patty in a resealable plastic sandwich bag; it will make it easy to prep for the Pizza Flat recipe. Simply crumble the patty in the bag . . . no need to get your fingers messy!

PIZZA FLATS

When you think of flour tortillas, you may think of burritos, but here we use tortillas as a thin crust for traditional pizza toppings. There are many low-carb tortilla options in the store today—look for a low-carb, high-fiber, whole-wheat flour tortilla for a more diabetes-friendly option. This is a "planned over" recipe incorporating a reserved burger and pepper rings from the **Beef Burgers with Avocado Spread** *recipe on page 224.*

THIS RECIPE CAN FIT IN THE FOLLOWING EATING PATTERNS: low-fat, low-carbohydrate, very-low-carbohydrate, DASH

NUMBER OF SERVINGS: 2 | **SERVING SIZE:** 1 pizza flat per serving
PREP TIME: 10 minutes | **COOK TIME:** 8 minutes

INGREDIENTS

- 2 bell pepper rings (reserved from *Beef Burgers with Avocado Spread*)
- 1 cooked burger patty (reserved from *Beef Burgers with Avocado Spread*)
- 2 (8-inch) low-carb, high-fiber, whole-wheat flour tortillas
- 1/4 tsp garlic powder
- 1/4 cup no-salt-added tomato sauce
- 1 oz shredded part-skim mozzarella cheese
- 2 tsp dried oregano
- 1/2 tsp dried fennel seed or dried basil
- 1/8 tsp crushed pepper flakes
- 1 Tbsp grated Parmesan cheese

INSTRUCTIONS

1. Preheat oven to 400°F.
2. Chop pepper rings and crumble reserved patty.
3. Coat both sides of the tortillas with nonstick cooking spray and place on baking sheet. Sprinkle with garlic powder. Spread tomato sauce evenly over both tortillas. Top with the remaining ingredients, except the Parmesan cheese.
4. Bake 5 minutes or until tortilla edges are lightly golden. Sprinkle with Parmesan cheese. Cut each in four wedges.

COOK'S SWAPS

- Instead of tomato sauce, you could use a layer of thinly sliced tomatoes under your pizza toppings.

CHOICES: 1 Starch, 1/2 Carbohydrate, 3 Lean Protein
BASIC NUTRITIONAL VALUES: **Calories 220** | Calories from Fat 100 | **Total Fat** 11.0 g | Saturated Fat 4.8 g | Trans Fat 0.3 g | **Cholesterol** 45 mg | **Sodium** 510 mg | **Potassium** 370 mg | **Total Carbohydrate** 23 g | Dietary Fiber 16 g | Sugars 2 g | Added Sugars 0 g | **Protein** 21 g | **Phosphorus** 355 mg

SHOP SMART

Once you have a plan, it's time to shop! In this section, you'll learn tips to save money and time, and use the Nutrition Facts food label to get the healthy ingredients you need to prepare healthy meals in your kitchen.

4 Time-Savers of Savvy Shoppers

- **"Click list" shopping**. Large and small retailers alike offer "click list" shopping, which allows customers to order and purchase groceries online and then pick them up at the store at a designated time, where they are delivered to the car.
- **Mail-order shopping.** You can buy almost anything online these days, including groceries. In many areas, shoppers can now order groceries online (such as from Amazon) and have them delivered to their doorstep. Or shoppers can use an app to order groceries from select local stores and have them delivered to their home.
- **Mail-order meal kit delivery**. These meal kits include recipes with the ingredients and are delivered to your door. Many grocery stores now sell meal kits, typically found in the deli area or fresh foods section.
- **CSA memberships**. Community-supported agriculture (CSA) is a way to buy local food directly from a farmer. You purchase a "share" and become a farm "member." You then receive a box of vegetables or other farm products regularly throughout the growing season. Not only is it convenient, it may help you to eat more vegetables.

6 Money-Saving Tips of Savvy Shoppers

Money-Saving Tip 1: Search for bargains in more than one type of store

- Visit a warehouse club once a month, for instance, to stock up on non-perishable staples in large sizes, and a supercenter for low everyday prices.
- Check your local food co-op for near-wholesale prices on beans, grains, and other bulk foods.

Money-Saving Tip 2: Minimize the number of minutes spent in the store to save money

- Food marketing research has found that shoppers pay almost $2 for every minute spent inside the grocery store, so getting in and out as efficiently as possible is the goal.

Money-Saving Tip 3: Shop with a list

- The first step to reducing shopping minutes in the store is shopping with a list to guide you.

- As you make your list, keep the Diabetes Plate Method in mind. So, the goal is that about one-half of what's on the list should be nonstarchy vegetables, one-fourth carbohydrate foods (grains, starchy vegetables, beans and lentils, fruits, and dairy), and one-fourth protein foods, with the add-on of healthy fats and zero-calorie drinks or water.
- Try keeping a running list on your phone's Notes or on the refrigerator door to add to as you realize you need items. Some clients Tami has worked with create a "template" list of items they typically buy and then add items, or mark off those not needed that week.
- Organizing your list to match the layout of your grocery store can get you through the store more efficiently and save even more money. It can prevent time doubling back to pick up forgotten items.

Money-Saving Tip 4: Buy when foods are on sale

- Most grocery stores have predictable sales cycles; for example, perhaps ground beef or certain canned goods are on sale every 6 weeks. Make a note of these sales dates and then stock up and plan your menus around them.
- Find out when stores mark down big-ticket items like meat, fish, and poultry. We've found that these markdowns often happen on Sundays. If you have adequate freezer space, you can buy and freeze for later use.
- Buy "in season" produce. Some fruits and vegetables grow better in the spring and summer, for instance, and cost more during the winter months when they're not as easily grown. See Table 4.1 for examples of seasonal produce. In-season produce is usually less expensive and at peak flavor. For instance, think about the flavor and price of tomatoes in the summer versus the winter months, when they are less flavorful and more expensive. You may find some good buys at the local farmer's market (while supporting your local farmers). Buy only what you can use or freeze before it spoils.

Money-Saving Tip 5: Join your store's loyalty program

- Typically, signup for a loyalty program is free. You then receive electronic coupons and savings when you provide your contact information.

Money-Saving Tip 6: Take advantage of specials, coupons, and store brands

- You may find huge deals on specials such as "buy one, get one free."

TABLE 4.1   EXAMPLES OF SEASONAL PRODUCE

This list is not all-inclusive, but does cover a lot of the seasonal produce you can find at grocery stores and farmer's markets.

Spring Season	Summer Season	Fall Season	Winter Season
Apricots	Blackberries	Apples	Chestnuts
Artichokes	Blueberries	Butternut squash	Grapefruit
Asparagus	Broccoli	Cauliflower	Kale
Avocados	Cantaloupes	Cranberries	Leeks
Carrots	Cherries	Figs	Lemons
Celery	Cucumbers	Garlic	Mandarins
Chives	Grapes	Ginger	Oranges
Collards	Green beans	Mushrooms	Radishes
Fava beans	Nectarines	Pears	Rutabaga
Fennel	Plums	Pomegranates	Tangerines
Mangos	Raspberries	Potatoes	Turnips
Mustard greens	Strawberries	Pumpkins	
Peaches	Tomatoes	Quince	
Pineapples	Watermelons	Radicchio	
Rhubarb	Yellow squash	Sweet potatoes	
Strawberries	Zucchini squash	Swiss chard	

- Coupons save money if you use them on items you normally buy. For extra motivation, note the amount you save each week and use that to treat yourself to a massage, movie, or something else you enjoy.
- Consumer research shows that store brands or generic versions of products can be of equal or superior quality as name brands and cost 15–30% less. Many of the store brands are made by the same companies that make the big-brand foods.
- Table 4.2 shows more smart shopping selections to save money.

TABLE 4.2   5 SMART SHOPPING SELECTIONS THAT SAVE MONEY

Instead of this . . .	Buy this . . .	And save . . .	Takeaway message
Pre-shredded carrots $0.19/oz	Whole carrots shredded at home $0.06/oz	$0.13/oz	Convenience costs more.
Marinated pork tenderloin $4.26/lb	Plain pork tenderloin with spices added at home $3.94/lb	$0.32/lb	Convenience costs more.
Brand-name whole-grain toasted oat cereal $0.21/oz	Store-brand whole-grain toasted oat cereal $0.14/oz	$0.07/oz	Brand names cost more.
Brand-name olive oil $0.46/oz	Store-brand olive oil $0.15/oz	$0.31/oz	Brand names cost more.
100-calorie snack pack of unsalted almonds $0.77/oz	Bulk packed unsalted almonds $0.35/oz	$0.42/oz	Individual servings cost more.

Quick Tips on How to Use the Nutrition Facts Label to Guide Your Food Choices

Do you ever find yourself feeling a bit bewildered as you navigate all of the food and beverage options out there? As you embrace making decisions about what to buy, the Nutrition Facts label is a powerful tool to help guide your choices. The Nutrition Facts label makes it easier to make more informed food and beverage choices and can help build carbohydrate awareness.

The Nutrition Facts label contains a wealth of useful information. As you check out the Nutrition Facts, begin to explore the following:

- How many servings are in the container?
- What is the serving size? (The serving size appears in large, bold font. On the last label update, serving sizes were updated to better reflect the amount people typically eat and drink.)

Nutrition Facts

8 servings per container

Serving Size   **2/3 cup (55g)**

Amount per serving

Calories   230

	% Daily Value*
Total Fat 8g	**10%**
Saturated Fat 1g	**5%**
Trans Fat 0g	
Cholesterol 0mg	**0%**
Sodium 160mg	**7%**
Total Carbohydrate 37g	**13%**
Dietary Fiber 4g	**14%**
Total Sugars 12g	
Includes 10g Added Sugars	**20%**
Protein 3g	
Vitamin D 2mcg	10%
Calcium 260mg	20%
Iron 8mg	45%
Potassium 235mg	6%

*The % Daily Value (DV) tells you how much a nutrient in a serving of food contributes to a daily diet. 2,000 calories a day is used for general nutrition advice.

- How many calories are in one serving? (Calories are now displayed in large, bold font.)
- How much Total Carbohydrate is in one serving? (Added sugars are now listed, too; see Table 4.3 for more information.)
- How many servings will you eat?

These questions are important because if you discover you will eat two or three servings,

that means you will consume two or three times the Total Carbohydrate and other nutrients.

See Table 4.3 for some quick-tip reminders about the key nutrients listed on the Nutrition Facts label that affect your diabetes to provide a point of reference, cut through any confusion, and focus on the information you need to know to make the best choices for you.

Using the Nutrition Facts label can help you discover many healthy swaps to align with the eating pattern you are embracing. See Table 4.4 for a few examples.

In addition to the Nutrition Facts label, check out the **ingredient list,** looking specifically for familiar healthy ingredients. Typically, the shorter the ingredient list, the better. **Label claims** can also help direct you toward foods that may work for you. Examples include "low-fat," "fresh," "high in fiber," and "a good source of."

Discovery that comes from building awareness through using food labels can drive positive behavior change. Over time, once you've identified the best-for-you choices, future shopping trips will go faster.

COOK SMART

You don't have to be a chef to prepare healthy meals. While cooking is a skill, it is a skill that gets better with time and practice. This section includes tips on finding good recipes and making the most of your time in the kitchen. We're fans of recipes with five ingredients or less. Using less ingredients can make cooking seem more manageable.

TABLE 4.3   NUTRITION FACTS QUICK TIPS

Nutrient	Quick Tip
Calories Calories are especially important to factor in when trying to lose weight or maintain a healthy weight.	Guide to calories in a single serving of a food: • 40 calories is low • 100 calories is moderate • 400 or more calories is high
Fats The types and amount of fat is particularly important in relation to cardiovascular health.	Lower is better for: • Saturated fat • Trans fat
Sodium Give sodium extra attention if you're concerned about high blood pressure.	Aim for 2,300 mg/day or less.
Total Carbohydrate This is an important number to know because carbohydrate foods have the greatest impact on blood glucose.	Focus on Total Carbohydrate rather than grams of sugars, since Total Carbohydrate is what affects your blood glucose most directly. The grams of Total Carbohydrate listed on the Nutrition Facts label already include starch, fiber, sugars, and sugar alcohols—you don't have to count those separately or add those to Total Carbohydrate. If you count carbohydrate choices (servings), approximately 15 g Total Carbohydrate = 1 carbohydrate choice (serving). **Added Sugars** listed under Total Carbohydrate indicates sugars added during the processing of food. The goal is to minimize consuming foods and beverages with added sugars. Added sugars are included in the Total Carbohydrate and do not need to be counted separately.
Dietary Fiber Dietary fiber aids digestion, promotes bowel regularity and colon health, and lowers the risk of some diseases, including heart disease and cancer.	Foods containing >3 g dietary fiber per serving are a significant source of fiber, whereas those with 5 or more grams of dietary fiber are excellent sources.

TABLE 4.4   DISCOVERIES MADE BY USING THE NUTRITION FACTS LABEL TO GUIDE FOOD CHOICES

Eating Pattern	Choose this . . .	Instead of this . . .	And you get . . .
Mediterranean-style	Olive oil–based vinaigrette	Creamy salad dressing	Healthier fats
DASH-style	Whole-grain bread	White bread	Whole grains and more fiber
Plant-based	Unsweetened almond milk	Unsweetened soymilk	Less calories and carbohydrate
Low-carbohydrate	Light cheddar cheese	Regular cheddar cheese	Less fat and calories
Paleo	Wild-caught tuna canned in water	Wild-caught tuna canned in oil	Less fat and calories
Low-fat	Oatmeal	Cream of wheat	More fiber

Reliable Recipes

One key to being a good cook is having a good recipe—one that "works" and tastes good, aside from being "good for you." This book equips you with many of these types of recipes!

In general, when checking out recipes, ask yourself the following 5 questions. The goal is to be able to answer "yes" to most or all of the questions.

1. Does the recipe appeal to your sense of taste?
2. Will the recipe fit into your eating pattern? (See Tables 4.5–4.8, which show several swaps to make the recipe match in certain eating patterns.)
3. Is a nutrient analysis of the recipe provided to help you see if/how it fits in your goals?
4. Does the recipe include common familiar ingredients? (Or does it have exotic ingredients that you might only use once or twice?)
5. Does the time required to prep and cook the recipe fit into your schedule?

3 Tried-and-True Cooking Tips

When Tami was teaching her son some basic cooking, she quickly learned the importance of sharing the following 3 tips. They may seem simple, but they can help ensure a successful outcome.

1. Read through the recipe at least twice before diving into preparing it. Check to make sure you have all the ingredients on

TABLE 4.5   8 SWAPS TO MAKE A RECIPE MORE MEDITERRANEAN-STYLE

All of these swaps may not work in every instance, but they give you ideas.

Recipe Ingredient	Healthy Swap
Beef	Chicken or fish
Butter	Olive oil
Vegetable oil	Olive oil
Butter or melted cheese on vegetables	Tomato sauce with herbs or marinara
Sandwich roll or bun	Whole-wheat pita
Jelly or jam	Fresh berries
Salt	Basil, mint, ginger, paprika
Mayonnaise as a spread	Mashed avocado

TABLE 4.6   6 SWAPS TO MAKE A RECIPE MORE PLANT-BASED

All of these swaps may not work in every instance, but they give you ideas.

Recipe Ingredient	Healthy Swap
Butter	Blended or mashed avocado
Cow's milk	Unsweetened almond or soymilk
Dairy yogurt	Soy yogurt
Ground beef	Beans and legumes
Sour cream– or mayonnaise-based dip	Hummus
Beef or chicken broth	Vegetable broth

TABLE 4.7   5 SWAPS TO REDUCE CARBOHYDRATE IN RECIPES

All of these swaps may not work in every instance, but they give you ideas.

Recipe Ingredient	Healthy Swap
Pasta	Zucchini noodles or spaghetti squash
White rice	Riced cauliflower
Bread crumbs	Almond meal
Banana in a smoothie	1/2 an avocado
Tortilla, sandwich bun, or bread	Lettuce leaf wrap

hand or if you need to make any swaps for health benefits. Also make sure you understand the steps.

2. Check if you need to do any pre-prep (such as marinating meat) or prepare part of the recipe ahead (such as making a dressing and refrigerating to allow flavors to blend).

3. If the recipe requires an oven or grill, they usually need to be preheated.

Kitchen Tools to Have On Hand

Having the right kitchen tools at your fingertips makes cooking easier and more enjoyable. There is no one ideal list of kitchen tools

TABLE 4.8   6 SWAPS TO REDUCE FAT IN RECIPES

All of these swaps may not work in every instance, but they give you ideas.

Recipe Ingredient	Healthy Swap
Oil in baked goods	Puréed fruit (such as banana, applesauce, pumpkin, or avocado)
Oil to fry	Nonstick cooking spray and nonstick skillet or air fryer
Peanut butter	Powdered peanut butter
Whole milk or half-and-half	Skim or 1% milk; fat-free half-and-half
Buttermilk	Low-fat plain yogurt
Ground beef	Ground sirloin (90–92% lean)

because the utensils and appliances you need depend on what and how you like to cook. Here are some basic tools to have on hand to start with:

- Baking dishes, glass and nonstick metal
- Baking sheets, nonstick
- Can opener
- Cutting boards (plastic for meat, wooden for other items)
- Food thermometer
- Grater (box or handheld)
- Kitchen scale
- Knives (a variety)
- Measuring cups and spoons
- Mixing bowls
- Pastry brush
- Potholders/hot pads
- Pots (several sizes)
- Roasting pan with rack
- Slotted spoons
- Spatulas
- Strainer

Appliances that can be worth their space

In addition to kitchen tools, the following appliances can be worth their space. We've provided a description of common uses for each.

- **Air fryer.** If you're someone who enjoys the crisp of fried foods, an air fryer, which "fries" without added fat, may be worth the cabinet space to you.

- **Blender.** Blenders are great for making smoothies, but can be used for a variety of other purposes. For instance, you can use a blender to turn cauliflower into riced cauliflower, frozen bananas into **Banana "Soft Serve"** (see recipe on page 274), cooked black beans or pinto beans into purée for bean burgers, and peanuts or almonds into nut butters.

- **Electric countertop grill.** A countertop grill allows for indoor grilling of most any food that could be cooked on a gas or charcoal grill outdoors. A plus is the fat and juices that cook out can be drained off. Electric grills can also be used to make paninis or other grilled sandwiches.

- **Food processor.** Using a food processor is a fast way to chop, slice, dice, and shred. Other uses include making quick dressings, sauces, and salsas.

- **Microwave.** A standard appliance in most kitchens these days, microwave ovens can be used for thawing, reheating, and cooking countless foods.

- **Instant pot.** An instant pot is a super speedy pressure cooker that can be used to prepare a variety of foods and meals in minutes. Most models not only pressure cook, but also slow cook, steam, and sauté; cook rice and grains; and keep food warm. Check out the recipes using an instant pot on pages 204, 238, and 240.

- **Slow cooker.** Slow cookers can be used to prepare a variety of foods with the convenience of putting the food in and then leaving it to cook slowly at a low temperature for several hours. Slow cookers are not only good for soups: because of the long, low temperature, they help tenderize less expensive cuts of meat (such as roasts), as well as turkey breasts, chicken, and pork, and even cook oatmeal. Find two slow-cooker recipes on pages 242 and 244.

- **Toaster oven.** If you are cooking for one or two, a toaster oven adds the convenience of being able to toast, bake, broil, and warm without heating up the kitchen with the regular oven.

INSTANT POT LEMON HERB TURKEY BREAST

Turkey isn't just for Thanksgiving! Instead of a whole turkey, purchase a bone-in turkey breast—which is much easier to handle and smaller when you don't need to prepare a feast. Cooking in an Instant Pot seals in all of the richly seasoned juices, and then you can cook down the juices (also known as "au jus") in the pot for a rich and simple gravy to spoon on top.

THIS RECIPE CAN FIT IN THE FOLLOWING EATING PATTERNS: low- or very-low-fat, low- or very-low-carbohydrate, DASH, Mediterranean

NUMBER OF SERVINGS: 12 | **SERVING SIZE:** 3 oz cooked turkey plus 2 Tbsp *au jus* per serving
PREP TIME: 12 minutes | **COME TO PRESSURE** 14 minutes
COOK TIME: 43 minutes plus 10 minutes natural release | **STAND TIME:** 15 minutes

INGREDIENTS

- 2 Tbsp extra-virgin olive oil
- 1 (5 1/2 lb) frozen bone-in turkey breast, thawed, rinsed, and patted dry
- 2 tsp poultry seasoning
- 1 tsp dried rosemary
- 2 tsp onion powder
- 2 tsp paprika
- 1 tsp garlic powder
- 1/2 tsp salt
- 1/4 tsp black pepper
- 1 1/3 cups water
- 1 large lemon, cut into six wedges

INSTRUCTIONS

1. Brush oil evenly over the turkey. In a small bowl, combine the poultry seasoning, rosemary, onion powder, paprika, garlic powder, salt, and pepper. Sprinkle evenly over the turkey.
2. Place the water and lemon wedges in the bottom of the Instant Pot. Top with the turkey breast (cavity side up). Seal the lid, close the valve, and set the Manual/Pressure Cook button to 33 minutes.
3. Use the natural pressure release for 10 minutes followed by a quick pressure release. When the valve drops, carefully remove the lid. Remove the turkey and set aside on a cutting board. Let stand for 15 minutes and then remove the skin and slice.
4. Meanwhile, remove lemon wedges and discard. Press the Cancel button and set to Sauté. Then press the Adjust button to "More" or "High." Bring the cooking liquid to a boil and boil for 13–15 minutes or until reduced to 1 1/2 cups liquid. Serve with sliced turkey.

CHOICES: 3 Lean Protein
BASIC NUTRITIONAL VALUES: Calories 150 | Calories from Fat 35 | **Total Fat** 4.0 g | Saturated Fat 0.8 g | Trans Fat 0.0 g | **Cholesterol** 70 mg | **Sodium** 180 mg | **Potassium** 230 mg | **Total Carbohydrate** 1 g | Dietary Fiber 0 g | Sugars 0 g | Added Sugars 0 g | **Protein** 26 g | **Phosphorus** 200 mg

POINTERS

- This cooks up *a lot* of turkey, putting batch-cooking into practice. Divide it up into smaller portions and freeze it.
- You can use this turkey in most any recipe that calls for cooked chicken or turkey—don't limit yourself just to turkey sandwiches!

INSTANT POT SHREDDED SAVORY BEEF BRISKET

Cooking beef brisket in the Instant Pot makes this tough cut of meat so tender that it falls apart when you stir it at the end. Coffee granules in this recipe may seem like an odd addition, but they gives the brisket a richer, meatier flavor.

THIS RECIPE CAN FIT IN THE FOLLOWING EATING PATTERNS: low- or very-low-fat, low- or very-low-carbohydrate, DASH

NUMBER OF SERVINGS: 12 | **SERVING SIZE:** 1/2 cup | **PREP TIME:** 20 minutes
COME TO PRESSURE 15 minutes | **COOK TIME:** 1 hour and 15 minutes

INGREDIENTS

- 1 Tbsp canola oil
- 2 1/2 lb trimmed flat cut beef brisket, cut into 3-inch pieces
- 1 (14-oz) package frozen peppers and onions
- 1 cup water
- 2 Tbsp balsamic vinegar
- 1 Tbsp instant coffee granules
- 2 tsp smoked paprika
- 1/4 cup tomato paste
- 1 tsp salt
- 1/2 tsp black pepper

INSTRUCTIONS

1. On the Instant Pot, press the Sauté button and then press the Adjust button to "More" or "High." When the display says "Hot," add the oil and tilt the pot to lightly coat the bottom. Working in two batches, add half of the beef and cook for 5 minutes on one side only. Remove and set aside. Repeat with the remaining beef.
2. Return the beef, browned sides up, and any accumulated juices to the pot along with the topping of frozen pepper and onion mixture, water, balsamic vinegar, instant coffee granules, and smoked paprika.
3. Seal the lid, close the valve, press the Cancel button, and set to Manual/Pressure Cook for 75 minutes.
4. Use a quick pressure release. When the valve drops, carefully remove the lid. Place a colander over a bowl and drain the beef mixture, reserving 2 cups of the cooking liquid.
5. Return drained beef mixture to pot. Whisk together the reserved liquid, tomato paste, salt, and pepper and return to the pot. Using a fork, stir the beef mixture until the beef shreds.

CHOICES: 2 Lean Protein, 1 Fat

BASIC NUTRITIONAL VALUES: Calories 150 | Calories from Fat 50 | **Total Fat** 6.0 g | Saturated Fat 1.7 g | Trans Fat 0.0 g | **Cholesterol** 60 mg | **Sodium** 230 mg | **Potassium** 270 mg | **Total Carbohydrate** 4 g | Dietary Fiber 1 g | Sugars 2 g | Added Sugars 0 g | **Protein** 21 g | **Phosphorus** 140 mg

COOK'S SWAP

- Serve as is, over warmed corn tortillas, as part of a taco salad, in lettuce wraps, over riced veggies, over veggie spirals, on baked potato halves, or in a grain bowl . . . the uses are endless!

Trick

- Why brown one side only? That's all you'll need to bring out the flavor of the beef.

POINTERS

- When purchasing large cuts of beef or pork, always buy about 8 oz more than you need. You will lose some of the weight after the meat is trimmed of fat.
- Leftovers freeze well. Freeze in individual portions for easy thawing and to help in managing portions.

SLOW-COOKER HEARTY WHITE BEAN & SMOKED SAUSAGE SOUP

No need to soak the dried beans for this recipe—they cook right along with the other ingredients. Adding the browned sausage and the parsley near the end helps to elevate the taste of the sausage so it doesn't "get lost" in the bean mixture, and the parsley adds freshness to every bite.

THIS RECIPE CAN FIT IN THE FOLLOWING EATING PATTERNS: low- or very-low-fat, low-carbohydrate

---

NUMBER OF SERVINGS: 6 | **SERVING SIZE:** 1 cup per serving
PREP TIME: 15 minutes | **COOK TIME:** 5 hours and 35 minutes | **STAND TIME:** 15 minutes

INGREDIENTS

- 1 cup dried large white beans, such as Great Northern or Lima, rinsed and drained
- 4 cups frozen peppers and onions, thawed
- 1 cup frozen sliced carrots, thawed
- 4 cups water, divided use
- 1 Tbsp sodium-free chicken bouillon granules
- 2 dried bay leaves
- 1 tsp dried thyme
- 1/4 tsp crushed pepper flakes
- 8 oz smoked turkey sausage, chopped
- 1/2 cup chopped fresh parsley
- 2 Tbsp extra-virgin olive oil
- 1/4 tsp salt

INSTRUCTIONS

1. Coat a 3 1/2- to 4-quart slow cooker with nonstick cooking spray.
2. Stir in the beans, peppers and onions, carrots, 3 1/2 cups water, bouillon, bay leaves, thyme, and pepper flakes.
3. Cover and cook on high for 5 1/2–6 hours and on low for 10–12 hours.
4. When done, heat a medium nonstick skillet coated with nonstick cooking spray over medium-high heat. Add sausage and cook 4 minutes or until browned on edges. Stir remaining 1/2 cup water into the skillet to release any browned bits and add to the bean mixture with the parsley, oil, and salt. Cover and let stand for 15 minutes to absorb flavors. Remove bay leaves before serving.

CHOICES: 1 Starch, 1 Nonstarchy Vegetable, 1 Lean Protein, 1 1/2 Fat
BASIC NUTRITIONAL VALUES: Calories 230 | Calories from Fat 80 | **Total Fat** 9.0 g | Saturated Fat 1.8 g | Trans Fat 0.0 g | **Cholesterol** 20 mg | **Sodium** 500 mg | **Potassium** 740 mg | **Total Carbohydrate** 24 g | Dietary Fiber 7 g | Sugars 5 g | Added Sugars 1 g | **Protein** 13 g | **Phosphorus** 220 mg

POINTERS

- There's no prep work involved when using frozen veggies and they're waiting in the freezer for you.
- To thaw frozen vegetables quickly, place the frozen pepper mixture and the frozen carrots in a large colander and run under cold water 30–45 seconds or until they are pliable. Drain well.

SLOW-COOKER PEPPERY PORK TENDERLOIN WITH FENNEL

This serves four, but it's a nice size for one or two people, leaving leftovers for later in the week. Cooking tenderloins in a slow cooker not only helps to keep them moist but you don't have to heat up the oven or your kitchen either. Don't be tempted to swap in plain praprika: Smoked paprika has tons of flavor!

THIS RECIPE CAN FIT IN THE FOLLOWING EATING PATTERNS: low-fat, low- or very-low-carbohydrate, DASH

NUMBER OF SERVINGS: 4 | **SERVING SIZE:** 3 oz cooked pork plus about 1 1/2 Tbsp *au jus* per serving | **PREP TIME:** 10 minutes
COOK TIME: 1 hour 15 minutes | **STAND TIME:** 5 minutes

INGREDIENTS

- 2 tsp chili powder
- 1 tsp garlic powder
- 1/2 tsp smoked paprika
- 1/4 tsp black pepper
- 1/4 tsp salt
- 1/8 tsp dried fennel
- 1/8 tsp cayenne pepper
- 1 lb pork tenderloin
- 1/4 cup water
- 1 Tbsp tomato paste
- 1 Tbsp extra-virgin olive oil

INSTRUCTIONS

1. Combine chili powder, garlic powder, smoked paprika, black pepper, salt, fennel, and cayenne in a small bowl. Sprinkle generously onto the pork and press down with fingertips so it sticks to all sides of the pork.
2. Add water and tomato paste to a 3 1/2- to 4-quart slow cooker and whisk until well blended. Top with the pork.
3. Cover and cook on low for 2 1/2 hours or on high for 1 hour and 15 minutes or until the internal temperature of the pork registers 165°F on a meat thermometer. Transfer to a cutting board. Let stand 5 minutes before slicing.
4. While the pork is resting, increase the heat on slow cooker to high (if cooking on low). Whisk the oil into the pan drippings and cook for 5–10 minutes until slightly reduced. Serve pork with the *au jus* (the juices in the slow cooker from cooking).

CHOICES: 3 Lean Protein
BASIC NUTRITIONAL VALUES: Calories 160 | Calories from Fat 60 | **Total Fat** 7.0 g | Saturated Fat 1.5 g | Trans Fat 0.0 g | **Cholesterol** 60 mg | **Sodium** 200 mg | **Potassium** 440 mg | **Total Carbohydrate** 2 g | Dietary Fiber 1 g | Sugars 1 g | Added Sugars 0 g | **Protein** 22 g | **Phosphorus** 210 mg

POINTER

- A great way to store unused tomato paste is to put the paste in a sandwich baggie, press to flatten tomato paste as much as possible, seal the bag, and freeze. When ready to use, simply break off a portion. To thaw frozen paste, microwave on high for 20–30 seconds or until thawed.

Sheet Pan Suppers

We're fans of sheet pan suppers. They make for easier meal prep because there's only one pan! They also save time, save dishwashing, and allow the oven do the work. Not to mention, sheet pan suppers are tasty and visually pleasing. You'll find six sheet pan recipes that follow, built around each of the healthy eating patterns. The Teriyaki Salmon and Broccoli Sheet Pan for Two recipe on page 305 at the end of this chapter is another flavorful sheet pan dish.

Here are the basics of how to get started with sheet pan suppers:

1. **Select a sheet pan with sides.** A baking sheet will not work because baking juices will flow off the pan. A 9 × 13-inch baking pan is too deep to allow airflow for roasting.

2. **Pick a protein.** Chicken, beef, pork, fish, and cubed tofu all work well. Or even mini meatloaves.

3. **Vary your vegetables to round out the meal.** How many vegetables you use is up to you. Make sure though that the pieces are dry (so they roast, not steam) and are about the same size to allow for even cooking. See more on roasting vegetables on pages 151–155, 288–209, and 302–303.

4. **Pick your flavorings.** These flavoring can include a variety of herbs, garlic, lemon juice, flavored vinegars, or vinaigrette dressings for starters.

5. **Opt for an oil.** A little oil is necessary to coat the vegetables and promote browning. Olive oil works well and adds flavor, but you could use a variety of other oils.

6. **Roast at 400°F** until everything is cooked through and the vegetable edges are browned. This typically takes 20–40 minutes depending on the vegetables and protein you choose and the size of the pieces. If the meat is bone-in, cooking time will be longer than for boneless meat. To allow for even cooking, typically start the meat and hard vegetables together, and add the quicker-cooking vegetables a little later. Take special care to make sure pork and poultry is fully cooked. We keep a digital meat thermometer handy to do a quick check. Pork should be cooked to at least 145°F (with a 3-minute rest time after baking) and chicken to 165°F. Poultry and pork meat juices should run clear when fully cooked.

Check out Table 4.9 for some favorite food combinations to use in sheet pan cooking.

TABLE 4.9   SOME FAVORITE SHEET PAN SUPPER COMBOS TO GET YOU THINKING

Protein	Vegetables	Flavorings
Sheet pan fajitas: Flat iron steak or top sirloin; or boneless, skinless chicken breast cut in strips	Red bell pepper Yellow bell pepper Onion chunks	Reduced-sodium fajita seasoning
Chicken breast	Asparagus, mushrooms	Lemon and garlic
Chicken thighs	Cherry tomatoes, green beans	Pesto, balsamic vinegar, garlic
Sliced pork loin	Carrots, Brussels sprouts, red onion, sweet potatoes	Rosemary or sage, garlic
Salmon fillets or shrimp	Broccoli, red potatoes	Lemon wedges, Italian dressing (instead of olive oil)

2 Tips for Perfect Sheet Pan Suppers

- Another great thing about sheet pan suppers is you can often do some of the prep work ahead of time. Store the ingredients in resealable plastic bags in the refrigerator and pull out when it's time to get cooking.
- While parchment paper or foil are not absolutely necessary, it does keep things from sticking to the pan, making clean up a lot easier. And for serving, you can simply lift the parchment or foil off the hot pan onto a serving platter. You'll find parchment paper near the foil and plastic wrap in the grocery.

ROASTED FISH, POTATOES AND BEANS WITH CAPERS AND FETA

Fingerling potatoes are appropriately named because they are actually shaped like fingers! They're fun to eat, have a concentrated rich potato flavor, and they cook quickly . . . especially when cut in half (lengthwise).

THIS RECIPE CAN FIT IN THE FOLLOWING EATING PATTERNS: **low-fat, low-carbohydrate, DASH, Mediterranean**

NUMBER OF SERVINGS: 4 | **SERVING SIZE:** 3 oz cooked fish and about 1 1/2 cups vegetables per serving

PREP TIME: 15 minutes | **COOK TIME:** 27 minutes

INGREDIENTS

- 1 lb fingerling potatoes, cut in half lengthwise
- 12 oz green beans, ends trimmed
- 2 Tbsp extra-virgin olive oil, divided use
- 4 (4-oz) cod fillets, rinsed and pat dry
- 1 Tbsp dried dill
- 1 1/2 tsp dried oregano
- 1/2 tsp salt
- 1/4 tsp black pepper
- 1 lemon, quartered
- 1 oz crumbled feta cheese
- 2 tsp capers, drained
- 2 Tbsp chopped fresh parsley

INSTRUCTIONS

1. Preheat oven to 425°F.
2. Line two baking sheets with foil. Top one with potatoes and beans, drizzle with 1 Tbsp of the oil, and toss to coat. Spread into a single layer. Arrange the cod on the other baking sheet. Drizzle the remaining 1 Tbsp oil over fish. Sprinkle the dill, oregano, salt, and pepper evenly over the fish and vegetables.
3. Bake the vegetables for 15 minutes. Stir vegetables and place the fish baking pan in the oven along with the vegetable baking sheet. Bake both for 12 minutes or until fish flakes with a fork.
4. Stir the vegetables and serve topped with the fish. Squeeze lemon juice evenly over all and sprinkle with the feta, capers, and parsley.

(Cook's Swap and Trick on following page)

CHOICES: 1 Starch, 2 Nonstarchy Vegetable, 3 Lean Protein, 1/2 Fat

BASIC NUTRITIONAL VALUES: Calories 280 | Calories from Fat 80 | **Total Fat** 9.0 g | Saturated Fat 2.1 g | Trans Fat 0.1 g | **Cholesterol** 55 mg | **Sodium** 490 mg | **Potassium** 890 mg | **Total Carbohydrate** 26 g | Dietary Fiber 5 g | Sugars 4 g | Added Sugars 0 g | **Protein** 25 g | **Phosphorus** 245 mg

COOK'S SWAP

- Substitute cod with mahi mahi or boneless, skinless chicken breasts, flattened to 1/2-inch thickness, if desired. (See flattening instructions on page 218.)

Trick

- Cutting the potatoes in half lengthwise not only allows the potatoes and the beans to cook evenly because they are closer in thickness, it also "stretches" the potatoes, making it look as though there is more. Even better, this method allows the potatoes to take on more flavor from the other ingredients.

BEAN AND TORTILLA CHIP STACK UP

Craving nachos? This vegetarian sheet pan supper will satisfy your craving for your favorite Tex-Mex nachos, with smart swaps to make them healthier: black beans instead of beef, plain Greek yogurt instead of sour cream, and extra vegetables.

***THIS RECIPE CAN FIT IN THE FOLLOWING EATING PATTERNS:* vegetarian, low-carbohydrate**

NUMBER OF SERVINGS: 4 | **SERVING SIZE:** 1/4 recipe (or 1 oz chips, 3/4 oz cheese plus about 1/2 cup vegetables per serving)
PREP TIME: 10 minutes | **COOK TIME:** 6 minutes

INGREDIENTS

- 4 oz restaurant-style corn tortilla chips, such as Santitas
- 3 oz shredded reduced-fat sharp cheddar cheese
- 1 1/2 tsp chili powder
- 1 tsp ground cumin
- 1 cup no-salt-added black beans, rinsed and drained
- 1 poblano chili pepper, seeded and finely chopped
- 2 oz sliced ripe olives
- 1 Roma tomato, finely chopped
- 1 avocado, diced
- 1/4 cup chopped fresh cilantro
- 1/2 cup fat-free plain Greek yogurt
- 1 lime, quartered

INSTRUCTIONS

1. Preheat oven to 425°F.
2. Arrange chips in a single layer on a foil-lined baking sheet, top with the cheese, chili powder, cumin, beans, chili pepper, and olives. Bake 6 minutes or until cheese melts slightly and edges of tortilla chips begin to lightly brown.
3. Remove from oven. Sprinkle tomatoes, avocado, and cilantro evenly over all. Using a teaspoon, top with yogurt and serve with lime wedges.

POINTER

- Roma (or plum) tomatoes have less liquid, so when chopped, they do not water down the other ingredients.
- Rinsing the black beans provides a cleaner taste and texture and helps reduce sodium.

CHOICES: 2 Starch, 1/2 Carbohydrate, 1 Lean Protein, 3 Fat
BASIC NUTRITIONAL VALUES: Calories 380 | Calories from Fat 170 | **Total Fat** 19.0 g | Saturated Fat 4.2 g | Trans Fat 0.0 g | **Cholesterol** 15 mg | **Sodium** 390 mg | **Potassium** 580 mg | **Total Carbohydrate** 39 g | Dietary Fiber 8 g | Sugars 3 g | Added Sugars 0 g | **Protein** 16 g | **Phosphorus** 325 mg

CHICKEN THIGHS WITH THYME, SWEET POTATOES & CAULIFLOWER

This comforting dish features roasted sweet potatoes, richly browned onion, and tender chicken thighs. Best of all, you can prepare the whole thing on a foil-lined sheet pan, with no other dishes to wash!

THIS RECIPE CAN FIT IN THE FOLLOWING EATING PATTERNS: low-carbohydrate, DASH, Mediterranean

---

NUMBER OF SERVINGS: 4 | **SERVING SIZE:** 3 oz cooked chicken and 1 1/2 cups vegetables per serving

PREP TIME: 15 minutes | **COOK TIME:** 27 minutes | **STAND TIME:** 10 minutes

INGREDIENTS

- 2 medium sweet potatoes (about 1 lb), cut in 1-inch chunks
- 4 oz onion, cut in 1/2-inch wedges (about 1 medium)
- 12 oz cauliflower florets, about 1-inch pieces (from 1/2 head of cauliflower, or 12-oz package of precut cauliflower florets)
- 1 1/2 Tbsp extra-virgin olive oil
- 4 (4-oz) boneless, skinless chicken thighs
- 1 tsp dried thyme
- 1/2 tsp garlic powder
- 1/2 tsp paprika
- 1/2 tsp salt
- 1/4 tsp black pepper

INSTRUCTIONS

1. Preheat oven to 425°F.
2. Place the sweet potatoes, onion, and cauliflower on a foil-lined baking sheet, drizzle the vegetables with oil, and toss until well coated. Arrange in a single layer on one side of the baking sheet. Arrange the chicken on the other side of the baking sheet and sprinkle the remaining ingredients evenly over all.
3. Bake 27 minutes or until chicken reaches 165°F.
4. Remove from oven. Gently lift the foil on the vegetable end of the baking sheet and fold the vegetables over onto the chicken. Press the foil down gently to cover and let stand for 10 minutes.

CHOICES: 1 Starch, 2 Nonstarchy Vegetable, 2 Lean Protein, 1 1/2 Fat

BASIC NUTRITIONAL VALUES: Calories 300 | Calories from Fat 110 | **Total Fat** 12.0 g | Saturated Fat 2.6 g | Trans Fat 0.0 g | **Cholesterol** 105 mg | **Sodium** 420 mg | **Potassium** 960 mg | **Total Carbohydrate** 27 g | Dietary Fiber 5 g | Sugars 9 g | Added Sugars 0 g | **Protein** 22 g | **Phosphorus** 265 mg

POINTER

- Don't skip the last step! It's very important to the overall flavors of the dish. This technique allows the chicken and the vegetables to absorb the flavor of the ingredients and provides moisture to the overall dish. It also helps to release the browned bits on the foil, which adds tons of flavor.

RED PEPPER AND GREEN PEPPER SHRIMP TORTILLA FLATS

Just because you're watching your carbs doesn't mean you have to give up warm corn tortillas. Here you'll enjoy tortillas smothered with broiled veggies and shrimp tossed with cilantro and cumin— keeping the overall recipe pretty low in carbs, but high in taste!

THIS RECIPE CAN FIT IN THE FOLLOWING EATING PATTERNS: low-fat, low-carbohydrate, DASH

NUMBER OF SERVINGS: 4 **|** **SERVING SIZE:** 1 cup shrimp mixture plus 2 tortillas per serving
PREP TIME: 10 minutes **|** **COOK TIME:** 10 minutes

INGREDIENTS

- 1 lb raw peeled shrimp
- 1 red bell pepper, cut in strips
- 1 green bell pepper, cut in strips
- 1 (4-oz) onion, cut vertically
- 1 Tbsp canola oil
- 2 tsp chili powder
- 1 tsp ground cumin
- 1/2 tsp salt
- 1/2 cup chopped fresh cilantro
- 8 small (4-inch) corn tortillas, warmed
- 1 lime, quartered

INSTRUCTIONS

1. Preheat oven to 425°F.
2. Combine shrimp, red and green peppers, onion, oil, chili powder, cumin, and salt in a large bowl. Toss until well coated. Place equal amounts on each on two baking pans in a single layer. Bake 10 minutes or until shrimp are opaque in the center.
3. Remove from oven. Sprinkle with the cilantro and toss gently. Place two tortillas on each of four dinner plates. Spoon equal amounts of the shrimp mixture on each tortilla and serve with lime wedges. Serve open-face with a knife and fork.

COOK'S SWAP

- For an even lower carb meal, substitute the corn tortillas and serve on 4 cups shredded romaine lettuce or 8 large romaine lettuce leaves plus 1 avocado, chopped.

CHOICES: 1/2 Starch, 2 Nonstarchy Vegetable, 3 Lean Protein
BASIC NUTRITIONAL VALUES: Calories 210 | Calories from Fat 45 | **Total Fat** 5.0 g | Saturated Fat 0.5 g | Trans Fat 0.0 g | **Cholesterol** 170 mg | **Sodium** 420 mg | **Potassium** 510 mg | **Total Carbohydrate** 18 g | Dietary Fiber 4 g | Sugars 4 g | Added Sugars 0 g | **Protein** 24 g | **Phosphorus** 315 mg

BASIL-TOMATO CHICKEN WITH WHITE BEANS

This recipe couldn't be easier to prepare—the only thing you need to chop is the basil! And, everything is prepared on a foil-lined sheet pan, making cleanup a breeze.

THIS RECIPE CAN FIT IN THE FOLLOWING EATING PATTERNS: **low-fat, low- or very-low-carbohydrate, DASH, Mediterranean**

NUMBER OF SERVINGS: 4 | **SERVING SIZE:** About 3 oz cooked chicken plus about 1 cup vegetables per serving
PREP TIME: 10 minutes | **COOK TIME:** 16 minutes

INGREDIENTS

- 1 (10-oz) container grape tomatoes
- 12 oz asparagus, broken into 2-inch pieces
- 1/2 tsp salt, divided use
- 8 chicken tenderloins, about 1 1/4 lb total
- 1/2 tsp paprika
- 1/4 tsp black pepper
- 1/2 (15-oz) can no-salt-added cannellini beans, rinsed and drained
- 1/2 cup chopped fresh basil
- 1 oz sliced Kalamata olives
- 2 tsp extra-virgin olive oil

INSTRUCTIONS

1. Preheat oven to 425°F.
2. Place tomatoes and asparagus on a foil-lined baking pan. Coat vegetables with nonstick cooking spray and toss gently. Arrange in a single layer and sprinkle with 1/4 tsp of the salt. Top the vegetables with the chicken. Sprinkle paprika, pepper, and remaining 1/4 tsp salt over all.
3. Place baking pan on an upper oven rack (not the top rack) and cook 13 minutes or until chicken is no longer pink in center.
4. Sprinkle the beans, basil, olives, and oil over all and cook 3 minutes.

(Cook's Swap, Trick, and Pointer on following page)

CHOICES: 1/2 Starch, 1 Nonstarchy Vegetable, 5 Lean Protein
BASIC NUTRITIONAL VALUES: Calories 270 | Calories from Fat 70 | **Total Fat** 8.0 g | Saturated Fat 1.4 g | Trans Fat 0.0 g | **Cholesterol** 80 mg | **Sodium** 480 mg | **Potassium** 760 mg | **Total Carbohydrate** 15 g | Dietary Fiber 5 g | Sugars 4 g | Added Sugars 0 g | **Protein** 35 g | **Phosphorus** 330 mg

COOK'S SWAP

- For a very-low-fat dish, substitute olives with 2 Tbsp drained capers and omit olive oil.

POINTER

- Substitute chicken with 1 lb raw peeled shrimp.

Trick

- When you want a dish to have a bit of browned color, but don't want to use oil, sprinkle the dish with a small amount of paprika to give color without affecting the flavors of the other ingredients.

HERBED PORK CHOPS WITH BUTTERNUT SQUASH AND APPLES

Butternut squash is packed with vitamin A and dietary fiber. Buy precut squash in the produce section to cut down on the time and effort it takes to prepare this meal.

THIS RECIPE CAN FIT IN THE FOLLOWING EATING PATTERNS: low-carbohydrate, DASH

NUMBER OF SERVINGS: 4 | **SERVING SIZE:** About 4 1/2 oz cooked pork plus 1 cup vegetable mixture per serving
PREP TIME: 13 minutes | **COOK TIME:** 31 minutes | **STAND TIME:** 5 minutes

INGREDIENTS

- 1 lb butternut squash cubes, about 3/4 inch in size
- 1 cup chopped onion
- 8-oz apple (about 2 small or 1 large), such as Honey Crisp, halved, cored, and cut into 1-inch chunks (about 2 cups total)
- 1/4 tsp dried rosemary leaves
- 1 Tbsp canola oil
- Four (6-oz) boneless pork chops, trimmed of fat
- 1 1/2 tsp paprika
- 1 tsp dried thyme leaves
- 3/4 tsp salt
- 1/4 tsp black pepper
- 1 1/2 oz roasted, salted, shelled pumpkin seeds

INSTRUCTIONS

1. Preheat oven to 425°F.
2. Combine the squash, onions, and apples on a foil-lined baking sheet. Sprinkle with rosemary and drizzle oil over all. Toss until well coated. Place in a single layer and cook 15 minutes.
3. Meanwhile, sprinkle both sides of the pork with the paprika and thyme.
4. Push the vegetables and fruit to one side of the baking sheet and sprinkle with the pumpkin seeds. Arrange the pork chops in a single layer on the other side of the baking sheet. Bake 8 minutes, turn pork chops, and cook 8 more minutes or until pork is slightly pink in center and internal temperature reaches 165°F with a meat thermometer.
5. Remove from oven. Sprinkle the salt and pepper evenly over all. Cover with a sheet of foil and let stand 5 minutes to develop flavors and release natural juices.

(Cook's Swap and Pointer on following page)

CHOICES: 1 Starch, 1/2 Fruit, 1 Nonstarchy Vegetable, 5 Protein, 2 Fat
BASIC NUTRITIONAL VALUES: Calories 420 | Calories from Fat 180 | **Total Fat** 20.0 g | Saturated Fat 5.1 g | Trans Fat 0.0 g | **Cholesterol** 85 mg | **Sodium** 540 mg | **Potassium** 1070 mg | **Total Carbohydrate** 27 g | Dietary Fiber 5 g | Sugars 10 g | Added Sugars 0 g | **Protein** 37 g | **Phosphorus** 445 mg

COOK'S SWAP

- Substitute pumpkin seeds with chopped pecans, if desired.

POINTER

- Be sure to buy a slightly thicker cut of pork chops for this recipe for peak texture and flavors. If a thin cut is purchased, it will be tough and flavorless.

Keep Cooking Safe

Keep your kitchen safe by properly storing, cooking, and handling your food.

The U.S. Department of Agriculture (USDA) recommends 4 easy steps to keep your foods safe:

1. **Clean.** Wash your hands, utensils, and cutting boards often—especially before and after contact with raw meat, poultry, seafood, and eggs. Many don't realize or think about this. If, for instance, you take raw chicken out of the package to put on the grill, wash your hands immediately or that raw chicken juice on your hands can contaminate everything you touch with salmonella (a common culprit of foodborne illness).

2. **Separate.** Keep raw meat, poultry, and seafood away from foods that won't be cooked. Use separate utensils, dishes, and cutting boards for raw food and cooked foods. Plastic, acrylic, or glass cutting boards are best for meat, since they can be easily washed (wooden cutting boards can absorb raw meat juices).

3. **Cook.** Use a food thermometer. The USDA website provides safe cooking temperatures for different foods. You can't tell whether food has been safely cooked just by how it looks. Tami will never forget the Thanksgiving her husband smoked a turkey and it looked golden brown, so he declared it done then took a picture of his prized turkey. But, when he carved into it, it was still raw in the center (although it "looked" cooked from the outside)!

4. **Chill.** Chill leftovers and takeout foods promptly. Discard anything left out at room temperature over 2 hours to prevent foodborne illness. Keep the refrigerator at a safe 40°F or slightly below.

Foods to Freeze or Not to Freeze

A Few Freezer-Friendly Foods

Most cooked dishes will keep for 2–3 months in the freezer. All of the following foods stand up to the freezer well.

- Baked chicken breasts
- Brisket
- Casseroles
- Chili
- Enchiladas
- Meatloaf
- Pulled pork
- Shredded roast
- Soups
- Spaghetti sauce
- Stuffed peppers
- Tomato sauces
- Turkey

A Few Freezer-Unfriendly Foods

- Fruits and vegetables with a high water content, which become watery and limp when frozen (such as cucumber, watermelon, lettuce, or salad greens)
- Dishes that have yogurt, sour cream, milk, or light cream as their base. (These dairy products will likely separate when frozen.)
- Cooked pasta and macaroni, which may become rubbery when frozen

Sample Menus and More Recipes

As you've seen throughout this book, there is no "one-size-fits-all diet" for managing diabetes. There are a variety of eating patterns and approaches including a wide variety of foods and recipes. It's good to have options. Everyone is different. The end goal is finding what works for you to keep your blood glucose in range, and then doing more of that. Our hope is that you feel like you have an answer to the big question: **"What do I cook now?"** We also hope you are more confident about putting healthy eating into practice to help simplify life with diabetes and live your best life. Take it 1 meal, 1 day, 1 week at a time. Small changes add up!

Here are some sample menus and more recipes from Tami for breakfast, lunch, dinner, and snacks to help you get started on your journey to planning healthy meals and cooking more at home. The sample menus contain approximately 45 g carbohydrate per meal. This goal is intended to be a starting point and is a significant carbohydrate reduction for many people. Your diabetes health-care team may recommend a higher or lower carbohydrate goal based on a number of factors. You can see if what you're doing is "working" for you based on whether your blood glucose is in range or out of range when you monitor it.

The sample menus also include information on how the meal fills a healthy plate following the Diabetes Plate Method (described and discussed in Chapter 3) along with swift, simple tips for preparing the meal.

WHAT DO I EAT FOR . . . BREAKFAST?

Breakfast Menu 1

EATING PATTERNS THIS MENU ALIGNS WITH: **vegetarian, low-fat, low-carbohydrate**

- 1 *Bountiful Breakfast Sandwich* (page 262) made with *Easy Oven-Poached Eggs* (page 261)
- 4 oz low-sodium tomato juice
- Clementine orange
- Coffee or hot tea (unsweetened or using a low-calorie sweetener)

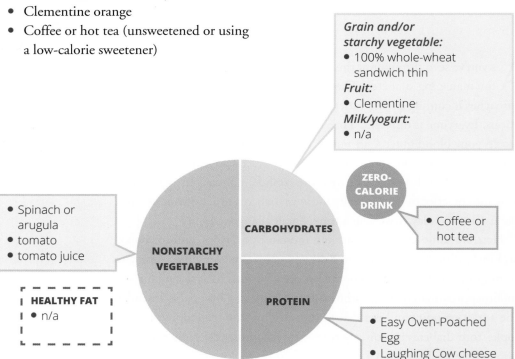

Grain and/or starchy vegetable:
- 100% whole-wheat sandwich thin

Fruit:
- Clementine

Milk/yogurt:
- n/a

CARBOHYDRATES

ZERO-CALORIE DRINK
- Coffee or hot tea

- Spinach or arugula
- tomato
- tomato juice

NONSTARCHY VEGETABLES

HEALTHY FAT
- n/a

PROTEIN
- Easy Oven-Poached Egg
- Laughing Cow cheese

SWIFT, SIMPLE TIPS

- Wrap the prepared sandwich in foil for breakfast on the run. And, eating the sandwich from the foil will hold everything together.
- Small cans of tomato juice are portable and easy to grab for a quick nonstarchy vegetable serving on the go.
- Clementines are also portable and pre-portioned.

EASY OVEN-POACHED EGGS

The following recipe instructions are for six eggs, but can easily be adjusted depending on how many eggs you would like to poach. This recipe is an example of batch-cooking poached eggs for future breakfasts and is used as a planned-over in the **Bountiful Breakfast Sandwich** *recipe on page 262.*

THIS RECIPE CAN FIT IN THE FOLLOWING EATING PATTERNS: **vegetarian, low-fat, low- and very-low-carbohydrate, DASH**

NUMBER OF SERVINGS: 6 | **SERVING SIZE:** 1 egg
PREP TIME: 5 minutes | **COOK TIME:** 16–18 minutes

INGREDIENTS

- 6 Tbsp water
- 6 large eggs
- Black pepper

INSTRUCTIONS

1. Preheat oven to 350°F.
2. In a muffin tin (nonstick works best), pour 1 Tbsp water in each of six muffin cups. (In a 12-cup tin, use the six cups in the middle of the tin for even cooking.)
3. Gently crack one egg into each water-filled tin. Top each with three shakes of black pepper.
4. Bake on the middle oven rack for 16–18 minutes. Smaller eggs may take 2–4 minutes less and extra-large eggs 2–4 minutes longer. The egg is done when the whites are opaque. If you want a hard-cooked yolk, test the doneness of the yolk by piercing it with a toothpick.
5. Using a spoon (a slotted spoon works best), run the spoon around the edge of each poached egg to loosen it and then scoop from the pan onto a paper towel to drain.

POINTER

- Extras reheat well in the microwave. Tami often poaches a few extra eggs to pull out for a quick breakfast later in the week.

CHOICES: 1 Medium-Fat Protein
BASIC NUTRITIONAL VALUES: **Calories** 70 | Calories from Fat 45 | **Total Fat** 5.0 g | Saturated Fat 1.6 g | Trans Fat 0.0 g | **Cholesterol** 185 mg | **Sodium** 70 mg | **Potassium** 70 mg | **Total Carbohydrate** 0 g | Dietary Fiber 0 g | Sugars 0 g | Added Sugars 0 g | **Protein** 6 g | **Phosphorus** 100 mg

BOUNTIFUL BREAKFAST SANDWICH

Rather than relying on the drive-through at a fast food restaurant for a breakfast sandwich on the go, try this make-at-home version that is much lower in carbohydrate, fat, calories, and sodium. It's quick to assemble if you have **Easy Oven-Poached Eggs** *(page 261) in the refrigerator.*

THIS RECIPE CAN FIT IN THE FOLLOWING EATING PATTERNS: **vegetarian, low-fat, low-carbohydrate**

NUMBER OF SERVINGS: 1 | **SERVING SIZE:** 1 sandwich
PREP TIME: 5 minutes | **COOK TIME:** 5 minutes

INGREDIENTS

- 1 made-ahead *Easy Oven-Poached Eggs* (see recipe on page 263)
- 1 100% whole-wheat precut sandwich thin (1 = 2 oz)
- 1 wedge (3/4 oz) white cheddar or spicy pepper jack low-fat spreadable cheese (such as Laughing Cow)
- 1/2 cup fresh spinach or arugula
- 1 slice of tomato

INSTRUCTIONS

1. Pull a pre-poached egg from the refrigerator and microwave 20–30 seconds to warm.
2. Toast sandwich thins.
3. Spread the cut side of both pieces of toasted sandwich thins with the spreadable cheese.
4. Place egg on bottom sandwich thin. Layer with tomato slice, spinach or arugula, and top sandwich thin.

CHOICES: 2 Starch, 1 Medium-Fat Protein

BASIC NUTRITIONAL VALUES: Calories 240 | Calories from Fat 70 | **Total Fat** 8.0 g | Saturated Fat 2.6 g | Trans Fat 0.1 g | **Cholesterol** 190 mg | **Sodium** 480 mg | **Potassium** 300 mg | **Total Carbohydrate** 29 g | Dietary Fiber 7 g | Sugars 5 g | Added Sugars 0 g | **Protein** 15 g | **Phosphorus** 420 mg

Timesaver Tip

- As noted in the Easy Oven-Poached Eggs recipe, oven-poach several eggs at one time to pull out for a quick breakfast on the go.

POINTER

- Try fresh pico de gallo instead of tomato to amp up the flavor. You can often purchase it premade in the refrigerated produce section.

Trick

- Wrap the prepared sandwich in foil for breakfast on the run. Eating the sandwich from the foil will hold everything together.

COOK'S SWAP

- Swap the sandwich thin for two Turkey Breakfast Patties with Fresh Pear (recipe on p. 49) for this recipe to also fit in a very-low-carbohydrate eating pattern. Keep in mind that this will change the nutrition values for the recipe.

BREAKFAST MENU 2

EATING PATTERNS THIS MENU ALIGNS WITH: vegetarian, vegan, low-fat, DASH, Mediterranean

- Heaping 1/2 cup *Cinnamon Steel-Cut Oats* (opposite page) topped with:
  - ○ 1 Tbsp unsalted almond butter
  - ○ 1 medium sliced fig or 1/2 cup fresh blueberries
  - ○ 1/2 tsp chia seeds
  - ○ 1/2 cup unsweetened vanilla almond milk
    (to drink or pour over oatmeal)
- Coffee or hot tea (unsweetened or sweetened with a low-calorie sweetener)

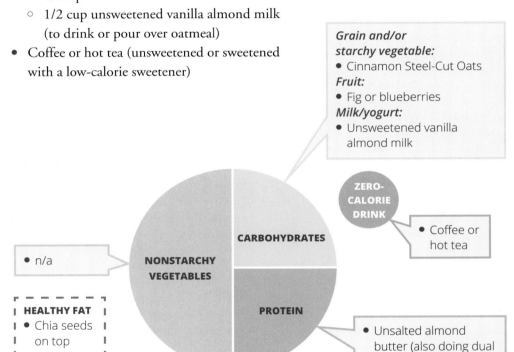

Grain and/or starchy vegetable:
- Cinnamon Steel-Cut Oats

Fruit:
- Fig or blueberries

Milk/yogurt:
- Unsweetened vanilla almond milk

ZERO-CALORIE DRINK
- Coffee or hot tea

CARBOHYDRATES

- n/a

NONSTARCHY VEGETABLES

HEALTHY FAT
- Chia seeds on top

PROTEIN

- Unsalted almond butter (also doing dual duty as a healthy fat)

SWIFT, SIMPLE TIPS

- Make a double or triple batch of oats and refrigerate in individual portions in microwavable containers or mugs to quickly reheat on busy mornings. Or freeze portions in muffin tins and then pop out and store in a resealable plastic freezer bag to grab for quick reheating.

CINNAMON STEEL-CUT OATS

This is a filling fiber-rich, plant-based, go-to breakfast for busy mornings. Steel-cut oats, a whole grain, come from the same grain as rolled oats and instant oats, but are the least processed. Steel-cut oats are left whole and cut into pieces with a steel mill so they take longer to cook and maintain a nuttier flavor and thicker, chewier texture.

***THIS RECIPE CAN FIT IN THE FOLLOWING EATING PATTERNS:* vegetarian, vegan, low- or very-low-fat, DASH, Mediterranean**

NUMBER OF SERVINGS: 2 | **SERVING SIZE:** 1/4 cup uncooked oats (or heaping 1/2 cup cooked oats)

PREP TIME: 5 minutes | **COOK TIME:** 25 minutes

INGREDIENTS

- 1/2 cup unsweetened almond milk (the nutty flavor of almond milk complements the oats, but skim milk may be substituted)
- 1 cup water (plus additional to thin cooked oatmeal as desired)
- 1/2 cup steel-cut oats (such as Bob's Red Mill Steel Cut Oats)
- 1/4 tsp cinnamon

(Customize Your Oats, Prep Tips, Storage Tips, and Pointer on following page)

INSTRUCTIONS

1. Place all ingredients in a medium saucepan and stir to combine well. Bring to a boil over high heat and then immediately reduce the heat to low so that the oats are at a gentle simmer.

2. Let the oats gently simmer for 20 minutes, stirring occasionally and scraping along the bottom of the pan to prevent sticking (a heat-resistant scoop spatula works great). At this point, judge how chewy or creamy you'd like the oatmeal. For softer, creamier oats, continue cooking 5–10 more minutes, stirring every few minutes until the oatmeal is as tender as you like. If the oatmeal becomes thicker than you'd like, splash in a little extra water to thin it out to your desired consistency.

3. Remove the oatmeal from the heat. Oats will continue to thicken as they cool (stir in water or almond milk to thin if desired).

CHOICES: 2 Starch, 1/2 Fat

BASIC NUTRITIONAL VALUES: Calories 180 | Calories from Fat 20 | **Total Fat** 2.5 g | Saturated Fat 0.0 g | Trans Fat 0.0 g | **Cholesterol** 0 mg | **Sodium** 30 mg | **Potassium** 170 mg | **Total Carbohydrate** 31 g | Dietary Fiber 4 g | Sugars 1 g | Added Sugars 0 g | **Protein** 6 g | **Phosphorus** 235 mg

Customize Your Oats

You can customize your bowl with any variety of toppings. The following are a few ideas. One of Tami's favorite topping combinations is 1 Tbsp unsalted almond butter or peanut butter, 1 Tbsp fig butter for sweetness (or any other fruit spread), and 1/2 tsp chia seeds (sprinkle on top for crunch). That topping combo adds about 15 g carbohydrate. A few favorite toppings:

- Nut butter (almond or peanut)
- Fruit butter/spread
- Fresh berries or sliced bananas
- Fat-free Greek or Icelandic yogurt
- Toasted unsalted walnuts

- Sliced unsalted almonds
- Unsalted pistachios
- Chia seeds
- Ground flax seeds

PREP TIPS

- **The liquid-to-oats ratio is important.** The rule is three to four parts liquid to one part oats—depending on how thick you'd like them to be (less liquid = thicker oatmeal; more liquid = thinner oatmeal). The 1/2 cup cooked serving may "expand" with reheating as the oats soak up liquid added to thin them.
- **To switch up the flavor**, instead of cinnamon, try ground cloves, nutmeg, ginger, allspice, or pumpkin pie spice.
- **How to cook in a slow cooker.** Start by at least doubling this recipe. Then increase liquid to a 1:4 ratio, cooking in a 4- to 6-quart slow cooker. Stir well, cover with lid, and cook on low for 7–8 hours or overnight.

Storage Tips

- **How to store extras:** Double or triple the recipe to make extra and refrigerate or freeze in individual microwave-safe containers for quick reheating on busy mornings. Cooked oats can be refrigerated for 4–5 days or frozen for up to 3 months in an airtight container. (You can microwave frozen oats straight from the freezer.)

POINTER   How to reheat

- The cooked oats thicken with chilling. Reheat gently in the microwave in a microwave-safe container or on the stove. Add an extra splash of liquid to thin oats back to the desired consistency, stirring a couple of times during reheating.

BREAKFAST MENU 3

EATING PATTERNS THIS MENU ALIGNS WITH: Low-fat, low-carbohydrate, DASH, Mediterranean

- 1 slice *Avocado and Tomato Toast with Grated Egg* (page 268)
- 1 cup fat-free vanilla Greek yogurt with
- 1 cup raspberries
- Coffee or hot tea (unsweetened or sweetened with a low-calorie sweetener)

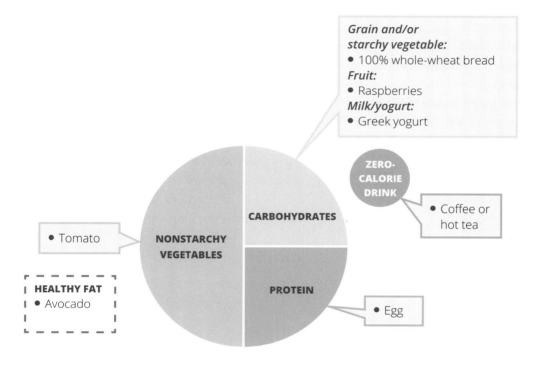

Grain and/or
starchy vegetable:
- 100% whole-wheat bread

Fruit:
- Raspberries

Milk/yogurt:
- Greek yogurt

ZERO-CALORIE DRINK
- Coffee or hot tea

CARBOHYDRATES

NONSTARCHY VEGETABLES
- Tomato

PROTEIN
- Egg

HEALTHY FAT
- Avocado

SWIFT, SIMPLE TIPS

- Boil several eggs at once and store in the refrigerator. Tami often even goes ahead and grates the egg and refrigerates it in a resealable plastic bag.
- Toast the bread while slicing the avocado and tomato.

AVOCADO AND TOMATO TOAST WITH GRATED EGG

This satisfying recipe is colorful and visually appealing, with the grated egg resembling shredded cheese. It starts the day with whole grains and fiber from the toast, healthy fats from the avocado, and lean protein from the boiled egg.

THIS RECIPE CAN FIT IN THE FOLLOWING EATING PATTERNS: low-carbohydrate, DASH, Mediterranean

---

NUMBER OF SERVINGS: 2 | **SERVING SIZE:** 1 open-faced sandwich
PREP TIME: 5 minutes | **COOK TIME:** 20 minutes

INGREDIENTS

- 2 slices 100% whole-wheat bread
- 2 tsp trans fat–free buttery spread (such as Smart Balance)
- 1 avocado, peeled, pitted, and sliced
- 1/8 tsp garlic powder
- 1 medium tomato, sliced
- 2 hardboiled eggs, peeled
- 1/8 tsp freshly ground black pepper

INSTRUCTIONS

1. Toast the bread.
2. Spread each slice with 1 tsp buttery spread.
3. Layer each toast with half of the avocado. Sprinkle evenly with garlic powder.
4. Top each with half of the tomato slices.
5. Use a grater with large holes (like a box grater) to grate one egg over each toast. The grated egg will look like shredded cheese. If concerned about the yolk, just leave out one or both yolks. Alternately, the egg can be finely diced.
6. Top each toast with half of the black pepper.

CHOICES: 1 Starch, 1 Nonstarchy Vegetable, 1 Medium-Fat Protein, 3 Fat

BASIC NUTRITIONAL VALUES: Calories 300 | Calories from Fat 180 | **Total Fat** 20.0 g | Saturated Fat 4.2 g | Trans Fat 0.0 g | **Cholesterol** 185 mg | **Sodium** 240 mg | **Potassium** 680 mg | **Total Carbohydrate** 22 g | Dietary Fiber 8 g | Sugars 4 g | Added Sugars 0 g | **Protein** 12 g | **Phosphorus** 215 mg

Timesaver Tip

Boil and peel the eggs ahead of time and then refrigerate to grab for quick assembly of the toast. Or grate the eggs ahead of time and store in a resealable plastic bag in the refrigerator.

COOK'S SWAPS

- Swap the buttery spread for a nondairy buttery spread for this recipe to also fit in a vegetarian eating pattern.
- Forego the buttered toast and layer toppings on a plate for this recipe to also fit in a very-low-carbohydrate or paleo eating pattern.

POINTER

- This is definitely fork-friendly fare.

PREP TIP

- As an alternative to the grated boiled egg, top the avocado with one of the *Easy Oven-Poached Eggs* (recipe on page 261.)

WHAT DO I EAT FOR . . . LUNCH?
LUNCH MENU 1

***EATING PATTERNS THIS MENU ALIGNS WITH:* low-fat, DASH, Mediterranean**

- ~1.5-oz 100% whole-wheat tortilla, spread with
  - 2 Tbsp hummus, and layered with
  - 2 oz turkey and
  - Diced tomato, spinach, and cucumber
- 3/4 cup *Cherry Berry Banana Smoothie* (page 271)
- Sparkling water with a twist of lime

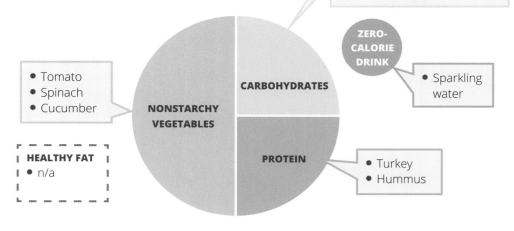

Grain and/or starchy vegetable:
- 100% whole-wheat tortilla

Fruit:
- Cherries, blueberries, banana (in smoothie)

Milk/yogurt:
- Greek yogurt, almond milk (in smoothie)

ZERO-CALORIE DRINK
- Sparkling water

CARBOHYDRATES

NONSTARCHY VEGETABLES
- Tomato
- Spinach
- Cucumber

HEALTHY FAT
- n/a

PROTEIN
- Turkey
- Hummus

SWIFT, SIMPLE TIPS
- Make a batch of the smoothies and freeze them in small jars to pull out and thaw in the microwave or at room temperature.
- When possible, purchase small portions of the veggies off the salad bar at the supermarket so no vegetable prep is required.

CHERRY BERRY BANANA SMOOTHIE

This simple smoothie uses fresh and unsweetened frozen fruit (over the sweetened variety), which helps fit in fruit yet manage carbohydrate. The fat-free Greek yogurt adds a little bit of protein without adding fat. And the blender does all the work!

THIS RECIPE CAN FIT IN THE FOLLOWING EATING PATTERNS: **low- or very-low-fat, DASH, Mediterranean**

NUMBER OF SERVINGS: 4 | **SERVING SIZE:** 3/4 cup
PREP TIME: 5 minutes | **COOK TIME:** NA

INGREDIENTS

- 1 1/2 cups unsweetened pitted frozen dark sweet cherries
- 1 cup unsweetened vanilla-flavored almond milk
- 1 (5.3-oz) carton fat-free blueberry Greek yogurt
- 1/2 cup frozen unsweetened blueberries
- 1 small banana, peeled and chopped into large pieces

INSTRUCTIONS

1. Combine all ingredients in a blender.
2. Cover and blend until smooth.
3. Enjoy right away or freeze for later use. (See four tips on freezing that follow.)

(Pointer, Trick, Prep Tips, Storage Tips, and Cook's Swap on following page)

CHOICES: 1 1/2 Fruit

BASIC NUTRITIONAL VALUES: Calories 100 | Calories from Fat 15 | **Total Fat** 1.5 g | Saturated Fat 0.2 g | Trans Fat 0.0 g | **Cholesterol** 2 mg | **Sodium** 55 mg | **Potassium** 300 mg | **Total Carbohydrate** 19 g | Dietary Fiber 3 g | Sugars 13 g | Added Sugars 0 g | **Protein** 4 g | **Phosphorus** 60 mg

POINTER

- While you can use fresh cherries or blueberries in this recipe, the frozen fruit is generally less expensive and gives the smoothie a frosty, creamy texture without diluting the smoothie with ice.

Trick

- Tami often tosses overly ripe unpeeled bananas in the freezer to save for smoothies. Just thaw slightly, peel, and use in smoothies like this one.

PREP TIPS

- Freezing smoothies is simple. Make a couple of different recipes and freeze to grab later in the week. **Here are 4 freezing tips that Tami has learned:**
  1. Use wide-mouthed, glass jars with lids (like mason jars).
  2. Pour in your portion, leaving at least 1 inch at the top so the liquid has room to expand.
  3. For best flavor, enjoy frozen smoothies within 1 week.
  4. To thaw, leave in the refrigerator overnight, or set out a few minutes (they thaw fairly quickly), or in a pinch, microwave on 50% power for 30–60 seconds or until desired consistency. Stir well and enjoy straight from the jar.

COOK'S SWAP

- Swap the Greek yogurt for a plant-based yogurt, and this recipe will then also fit in a vegetarian or vegan eating pattern.

LUNCH MENU 2

EATING PATTERNS THIS MENU ALIGNS WITH: **vegetarian, low-fat, low-carbohydrate, and DASH**

- 1 cup fresh spinach topped with sweet red pepper strips with
  - Olive oil and balsamic dressing
- 3 oz low-fat cheese
- 5 whole-wheat crackers
- 1/2 cup *Basic Banana Honey "Soft Serve"* (page 274)
- Iced water with an orange slice

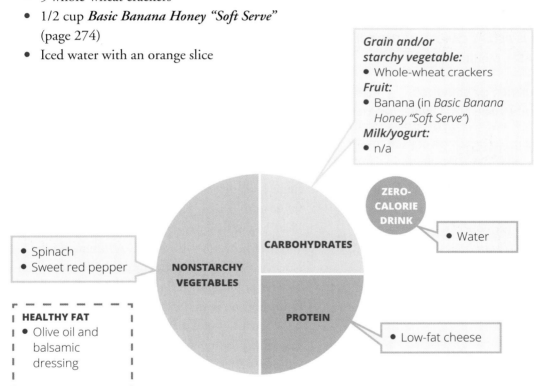

Grain and/or starchy vegetable:
- Whole-wheat crackers

Fruit:
- Banana (in *Basic Banana Honey "Soft Serve"*)

Milk/yogurt:
- n/a

ZERO-CALORIE DRINK
- Water

CARBOHYDRATES

NONSTARCHY VEGETABLES
- Spinach
- Sweet red pepper

HEALTHY FAT
- Olive oil and balsamic dressing

PROTEIN
- Low-fat cheese

SWIFT, SIMPLE TIPS

- Purchase a bag of ready-to-eat spinach and this meal comes together in minutes.
- Make a batch or two of *Basic Banana Honey "Soft Serve"* and keep on hand for a healthy sweet treat that works in a couple of fruit servings.

BANANA "SOFT SERVE" (3 WAYS)

This recipe is a plant-based, healthful alternative to traditional ice cream. It is a banana "soft serve" that is so simple to make, with the creaminess coming from frozen, blended bananas rather than rich dairy and sugar. And a 1/2-cup portion is an easy way to fit in a couple of fruit servings. There are three different versions and each is a treat. See Pointers following Version 3 for best results.

VERSION 1. BASIC BANANA HONEY "SOFT SERVE"

THIS RECIPE CAN FIT IN THE FOLLOWING EATING PATTERNS: vegetarian, low- or very-low-fat, DASH, Mediterranean

NUMBER OF SERVINGS: 3 | **SERVING SIZE:** 1/2 cup | **PREP TIME:** 10 minutes
COOK TIME: NA | **FREEZING TIME:** 3–4 hours

INGREDIENTS

- 3 very ripe bananas (about 7 inches in length; using ripe bananas is key for the recipe to turn out)
- 1 1/2 tsp honey

INSTRUCTIONS

1. Peel bananas and cut into 1-inch chunks Place in a single layer on an 8 × 8-inch or 9 × 13-inch pan and freeze until frozen solid (takes around 3–4 hours).
2. Place half of bananas in a blender or food processor and drizzle evenly with honey. Add remaining bananas, and pulse blender or food processor. Stop blender or food processor frequently and push chunks to the bottom with a spatula, as mixture will initially be very chunky and difficult to blend. Continue stopping, pushing mixture down with spatula, and pulse blending. With continued blending, the texture will become smooth and creamy, and the mixture will take on the consistency of soft-serve ice cream.
3. Store in an airtight container in the freezer. Before serving, soften at room temperature as you would ice cream, if desired.

CHOICES: 2 Fruit

BASIC NUTRITIONAL VALUES: Calories 110 | Calories from Fat 0 | **Total Fat** 0.0 g | Saturated Fat 0.0 g | Trans Fat 0.0 g | **Cholesterol** 0 mg | **Sodium** 0 mg | **Potassium** 405 mg | **Total Carbohydrate** 28 g | Dietary Fiber 3 g | Sugars 17 g | Added Sugars 3 g | **Protein** 1 g | **Phosphorus** 25 mg

VERSION 2. PEANUT BUTTER BANANA "SOFT SERVE"

THIS RECIPE CAN FIT IN THE FOLLOWING EATING PATTERNS: **vegetarian, vegan, DASH**

NUMBER OF SERVINGS: 3 | **SERVING SIZE:** 1/2 cup | **PREP TIME:** 10 minutes
COOK TIME: NA | **FREEZING TIME:** 3–4 hours

INGREDIENTS

- 3 very ripe bananas (about 7 inches in length; using ripe bananas is key for the recipe to turn out)
- 2 Tbsp peanut butter (crunchy or smooth; both work equally well)

INSTRUCTIONS

1. Peel bananas and cut into 1-inch chunks. Place in a single layer on an 8 × 8-inch or 9 × 13-inch pan and freeze until frozen solid (takes around 3–4 hours).
2. Place half of bananas in a blender or food processor, dollop with peanut butter, add remaining bananas, and pulse blender or food processor. Stop blender or food processor frequently and push chunks to the bottom with a spatula, as mixture will initially be very chunky and difficult to blend. Continue stopping, pushing mixture down with spatula, and pulse blending. With continued blending, the texture will become smooth and creamy, and the mixture will take on the consistency of soft-serve ice cream.
3. Store in an airtight container in the freezer. Before serving, soften at room temperature as you would ice cream, if desired.

COOK'S SWAPS

- Swap the peanut butter for almond butter for this recipe to fit in a paleo eating style.

CHOICES: 2 Fruit, 1 Fat
BASIC NUTRITIONAL VALUES: Calories 160 | Calories from Fat 50 | **Total Fat** 6.0 g | Saturated Fat 1.2 g | Trans Fat 0.0 g | **Cholesterol** 0 mg | **Sodium** 50 mg | **Potassium** 470 mg | **Total Carbohydrate** 28 g | Dietary Fiber 4 g | Sugars 15 g | Added Sugars 1 g | **Protein** 4 g | **Phosphorus** 65 mg

VERSION 3. CHOCOLATE CHIP BANANA "SOFT SERVE"

THIS RECIPE CAN FIT IN THE FOLLOWING EATING PATTERNS: low- or very-low-fat, DASH

NUMBER OF SERVINGS: 3 | **SERVING SIZE:** 1/2 cup | **PREP TIME:** 10 minutes
COOK TIME: NA | **FREEZING TIME:** 3–4 hours

INGREDIENTS

- 3 very ripe bananas (about 7 inches in length; using ripe bananas is key for the recipe to turn out)
- 1/4 tsp almond extract
- 1 Tbsp mini milk chocolate chips

INSTRUCTIONS

1. Peel bananas and cut into 1-inch chunks. Place in a single layer on an 8 × 8-inch or 9 × 13-inch pan and freeze until frozen solid (takes around 3–4 hours).

2. Place half of bananas in a blender or food processor, drizzle evenly with almond extract, add remaining bananas, and pulse blender or food processor. Stop blender or food processor frequently and push chunks to the bottom with a spatula, as mixture will initially be very chunky and difficult to blend. Continue stopping, pushing mixture down with spatula, and pulse blending. With continued blending, the texture will become smooth and creamy, and the mixture will take on the consistency of soft-serve ice cream. Stir in chocolate chips (do not blend).

3. Store in an airtight container in the freezer. Before serving, soften at room temperature as you would ice cream, if desired.

CHOICES: 2 Fruit

BASIC NUTRITIONAL VALUES: Calories 130 | Calories from Fat 20 | **Total Fat** 2.0 g | Saturated Fat 1.0 g | Trans Fat 0.0 g | **Cholesterol** 0 mg | **Sodium** 0 mg | **Potassium** 420 mg | **Total Carbohydrate** 29 g | Dietary Fiber 3 g | Sugars 16 g | Added Sugars 2 g | **Protein** 1 g | **Phosphorus** 30 mg

COOK'S SWAP

- Swap the mini milk chocolate chips for vegan mini chocolate chips to also fit in a vegetarian or vegan eating pattern.

POINTERS (for all 3 variations)

- Using ripe bananas is necessary for these recipes to turn out. We often put bananas that become overly ripe in the freezer to use for this purpose.
- If you find it a challenge to get a smooth consistency, just let the mixture soften a few minutes at room temperature and then blend again until smooth. Works every time!
- It's important to use mini chocolate chips to "spread" the chocolate throughout.

LUNCH MENU 3

EATING PATTERNS THIS MENU ALIGNS WITH: **low-fat, low-carbohydrate, DASH**

DIY superfoods salad bar selections (see page 145 for more on *Do-It-Yourself Superfoods Salad Bar*):

- 3 cups total chopped curly kale, broccoli florets, thinly sliced red onion, grape tomatoes
- 1/4 cup black beans
- 1/4 cup corn
- 3 oz roasted or grilled chicken, diced (or use extra portions of chicken marinated with *Mix & Match Chicken Marinade* on page 297 for *Chicken Southwest* on page 299)
- 1 Tbsp dried cherries, no sugar added
- 1/4 medium avocado, diced
- 2 Tbsp *Lemon Olive Oil Vinaigrette* (page 280)
- 8 oz *Lemony Spa Water* (page 37)

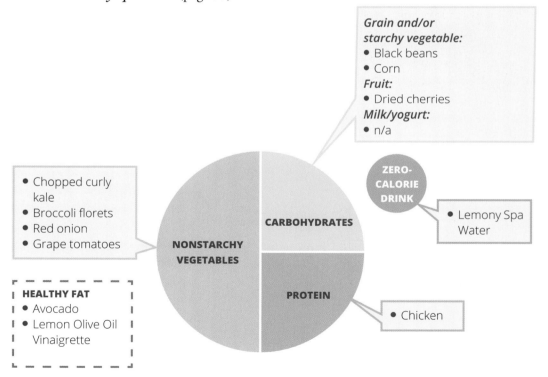

Grain and/or starchy vegetable:
- Black beans
- Corn

Fruit:
- Dried cherries

Milk/yogurt:
- n/a

ZERO-CALORIE DRINK
- Lemony Spa Water

- Chopped curly kale
- Broccoli florets
- Red onion
- Grape tomatoes

NONSTARCHY VEGETABLES

CARBOHYDRATES

PROTEIN
- Chicken

HEALTHY FAT
- Avocado
- Lemon Olive Oil Vinaigrette

SWIFT, SIMPLE TIPS

- Preassemble the DIY superfoods salad bar as described in the instructions on page 145.
- Prepare the vinaigrette ahead of time and store with the salad bar ingredients.
- Prepare the water ahead of time, not only to allow flavors to properly infuse, but to grab and go for a quick lunch. Alternately, you can add a squeeze of lemon and/or a slice of cucumber to a glass of iced water as a quick and flavorful alternative.

POINTER

- Swap marinated oven-baked diced tempeh as the protein in place of marinated grilled chicken to transform this meal into a vegetarian or vegan option.

LEMON OLIVE OIL VINAIGRETTE

This recipe is a simple and versatile vinaigrette-style dressing made with a healthy fat, olive oil, and with tang coming from fresh lemon juice. It can be used as a flavorful dressing but is also delicious drizzled over grilled or baked fish, steamed asparagus, fresh green beans, or roasted vegetables.

THIS RECIPE CAN FIT IN THE FOLLOWING EATING PATTERNS: vegetarian, vegan, low-fat, low- and very-low-carbohydrate, DASH, Mediterranean

NUMBER OF SERVINGS: 10 | **SERVING SIZE:** 1 Tbsp
PREP TIME: 5 minutes | **COOK TIME:** NA

INGREDIENTS

- 1/4 cup fresh-squeezed lemon juice (juice of about 2 lemons)
- 6 Tbsp olive oil
- 2 garlic cloves, finely minced or grated (or 2 tsp refrigerated fresh minced garlic or garlic "paste" in a tube)
- 1/4 tsp fresh ground black pepper
- 1/8 tsp kosher salt

INSTRUCTIONS

1. Place all ingredients in a small jar and shake to mix. Store in the refrigerator. Shake well before serving.

POINTER

- The flavor is best with fresh squeezed lemon juice (instead of bottled lemon juice) and fresh garlic. Do not substitute garlic powder.

CHOICES: 1 1/2 Fat

BASIC NUTRITIONAL VALUES: Calories 70 | Calories from Fat 70 | **Total Fat** 8.0 g | Saturated Fat 1.1 g | Trans Fat 0.0 g | **Cholesterol** 0 mg | **Sodium** 25 mg | **Potassium** 10 mg | **Total Carbohydrate** 1 g | Dietary Fiber 0 g | Sugars 0 g | Added Sugars 0 g | **Protein** 0 g | **Phosphorus** 0 mg

LUNCH MENU 4

EATING PATTERNS THIS MENU ALIGNS WITH: **low-fat, low-carbohydrate, Mediterranean**

- 1 cup *Fresh Mediterranean Quinoa Salad* (page 282)
- 1 2.5-oz foil packet/pouch salmon or tuna
- 1 cup diced watermelon
- Sparkling mineral water (such as Perrier or Pellegrino)

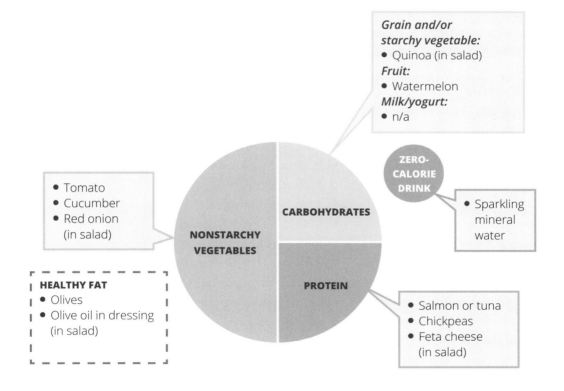

Grain and/or starchy vegetable:
- Quinoa (in salad)

Fruit:
- Watermelon

Milk/yogurt:
- n/a

ZERO-CALORIE DRINK
- Sparkling mineral water

CARBOHYDRATES

- Tomato
- Cucumber
- Red onion
  (in salad)

NONSTARCHY VEGETABLES

PROTEIN
- Salmon or tuna
- Chickpeas
- Feta cheese
  (in salad)

HEALTHY FAT
- Olives
- Olive oil in dressing
  (in salad)

SWIFT, SIMPLE TIPS

- To hasten assembly at mealtime, make the dressing ahead of time and store in an airtight contain in the refrigerator. Chop the vegetables when you have a few extra minutes and refrigerate.
- Purchase cubed watermelon rather than doing the work at home.

FRESH MEDITERRANEAN QUINOA SALAD

Packing in the flavors of the Mediterranean, a simple switch to reduced-fat feta cheese helps manage the fat in the salad ingredients. Cooking the quinoa in unsalted chicken stock helps manage the sodium. Flavor is pumped up in the dressing through red wine vinegar, fresh lemon juice, Dijon mustard, and fresh garlic and herbs, replacing salt and larger amounts of oil. This is a recipe that tastes as good the next day as when freshly made.

THIS RECIPE CAN FIT IN THE FOLLOWING EATING PATTERNS: low-fat, low-carbohydrate, Mediterranean

---

NUMBER OF SERVINGS: 5 | **SERVING SIZE:** 1 cup
PREP TIME: 30 minutes | **COOK TIME:** 20 minutes

INGREDIENTS

Salad

- 1 cup uncooked quinoa
- 2 cups unsalted chicken stock (or broth; the stock has a richer flavor)
- 1/2 cup canned drained no-salt-added chickpeas
- 1 cup grape or cherry tomatoes, quartered
- 1 cup diced cucumber (roughly a 6-inch cucumber peeled and diced in cubes the size of the chickpeas)
- 1/8 cup diced red onion
- 1/4 cup pitted Kalamata olives, chopped
- 1/4 cup crumbled reduced-fat feta cheese

Dressing

- 1 Tbsp olive oil
- 3 Tbsp red wine vinegar
- Juice of 1 fresh lemon (about 2 Tbsp juice)
- 1 tsp Dijon mustard
- 1 packed Tbsp fresh mint (or 1 tsp dried mint)
- 2 packed Tbsp fresh parsley (or 2 tsp dried parsley)
- 1 clove garlic, minced (or 1 tsp minced garlic)
- 1/4 tsp fresh coarse ground black pepper (less if not using coarse ground pepper)

(continued)

FRESH MEDITERRANEAN QUINOA SALAD (*continued*)

INSTRUCTIONS

1. Rinse uncooked quinoa thoroughly in a fine strainer under cold running water until water runs clear.
2. Combine quinoa and chicken stock in a medium saucepan and bring to a boil. Cover and lower heat to a simmer. Cook for about 15 minutes, or until all liquid is absorbed and quinoa is fluffy.
3. Transfer quinoa to a large bowl to cool.
4. Add chickpeas, tomatoes, cucumber, onion, olives, and Feta cheese.
5. Combine dressing ingredients in a small jar (like a small mason jar) and shake well to mix. Alternately combine in a small bowl and whisk to mix well.
6. Pour dressing over salad ingredients and toss gently to combine and coat well.

(Pointers, Trick, Cook's Swap, and Prep Tip on following page)

CHOICES: 1 1/2 Starch, 1 Nonstarchy Vegetable, 1 Lean Protein, 1 Fat

BASIC NUTRITIONAL VALUES: Calories 230 | Calories from Fat 70 | **Total Fat** 8.0 g | Saturated Fat 1.2 g | Trans Fat 0.0 g | **Cholesterol** 8 mg | **Sodium** 270 mg | **Potassium** 480 mg | **Total Carbohydrate** 32 g | Dietary Fiber 5 g | Sugars 5 g | Added Sugars 0 g | **Protein** 10 g | **Phosphorus** 255 mg

POINTERS

- Quinoa is a whole grain widely found in grocery stores and markets. It is usually located near rice and other grains.
- Quinoa is a nutritious option for gluten-free eating styles.
- Other varieties of beans and olives can be substituted for the chickpeas and Kalamata olives.
- This recipe is a favorite make-ahead salad, since the flavors blend with time and chilling. Stir well before serving. Because quinoa will soak up the dressing, add a splash of red wine vinegar or olive oil and toss gently to coat.

Trick

- The dressing minus the mint and parsley makes a tasty versatile vinaigrette for green salads or marinating chicken.

COOK'S SWAP

- Swap the unsalted chicken stock for unsalted vegetable stock for this recipe to also fit in a vegetarian eating pattern.

PREP TIP

- Tami likes to use small mason jars to shake up the dressing and then store in the refrigerator until ready to use. Just shake well again before adding to the salad.
- For dressing, do not use bottled lemon juice or garlic powder for best flavor.

WHAT DO I EAT FOR . . . DINNER?
DINNER MENU 1

EATING PATTERNS THIS MENU ALIGNS WITH: **low-fat, low-carbohydrate, DASH, Mediterranean**

- 1 *Salmon and Asparagus Foil Packets* (page 286)
- 1 cup *Roasted Carrots* (page 288)
- 1 cup mixed green salad with
  - 1/4 cup sliced strawberries and
  - 1 Tbsp sliced almonds with
  - 1 Tbsp vinaigrette dressing
- 1/2 cup wild rice
- Unsweetened or low-calorie sweetend iced tea

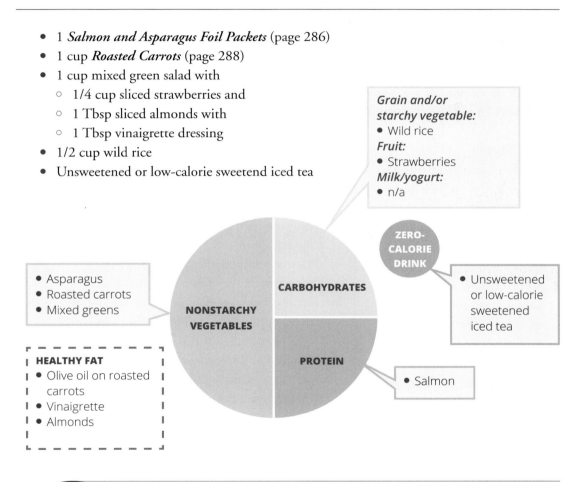

Grain and/or starchy vegetable:
- Wild rice

Fruit:
- Strawberries

Milk/yogurt:
- n/a

ZERO-CALORIE DRINK

- Unsweetened or low-calorie sweetened iced tea

CARBOHYDRATES

NONSTARCHY VEGETABLES

- Asparagus
- Roasted carrots
- Mixed greens

HEALTHY FAT
- Olive oil on roasted carrots
- Vinaigrette
- Almonds

PROTEIN

- Salmon

SWIFT, SIMPLE TIPS
- Purchase prepared ready-to-eat mixed salad greens.
- Purchase ready-to-heat precooked wild rice in shelf-stable packages.
- Purchase pre-portioned salmon fillets, so no weighing or cutting is required.

SALMON AND ASPARAGUS FOIL PACKETS

This is a basic no-fail way to prepare moist fish without any added fat. Fresh lemon juice, garlic, black pepper, and reduced-sodium soy sauce lend flavor. Even with a little honey balancing the flavors with a hint of sweetness, this recipe is low in carbohydrate. Clean up can't get much simpler, since the fish is baked in foil packets.

THIS RECIPE CAN FIT IN THE FOLLOWING EATING PATTERNS: **low- and very-low-carbohydrate, DASH, Mediterranean**

NUMBER OF SERVINGS: 4 | **SERVING SIZE:** 1 packet
PREP TIME: 15 minutes | **COOK TIME:** 12–15 minutes

INGREDIENTS

- 1 lb fresh asparagus, trimmed
- 4 sheets 12 × 18-inch heavy duty aluminum foil wrap
- 4 (4-oz) fillets skinless salmon
- 2 Tbsp reduced-sodium soy sauce
- 1 Tbsp freshly squeezed lemon juice (the juice from ~1/2 lemon)
- 1 Tbsp honey
- 1 tsp minced fresh garlic
- Coarse ground black pepper (need about 1/4 tsp in total)

INSTRUCTIONS

1. Preheat oven to 425°F.
2. Snap the tough ends off washed asparagus spears and discard. Set spears aside.
3. Spray the center of each foil sheet with nonstick cooking spray.
4. Place one salmon fillet in the center of each foil sheet and top with 1/4 of the asparagus.
5. In a small bowl or mug, combine the soy sauce, lemon juice, honey, and garlic. Stir to mix well. Spoon 1/4 of the mixture over each asparagus and salmon pile. Top each asparagus and salmon pile with one to two shakes of black pepper.
6. Bring up the sides of foil and fold the top over twice. Seal the ends, leaving room for air to circulate inside the packet. Place packets on a baking sheet.
7. Bake 12–15 minutes (salmon will become opaque when cooked). Take care opening the packets, since moisture creates steam during cooking that could burn you.

CHOICES: 1/2 Carbohydrate, 3 Lean Protein, 1 Fat

BASIC NUTRITIONAL VALUES: Calories 210 | Calories from Fat 80 | **Total Fat** 9.0 g | Saturated Fat 1.9 g | Trans Fat 0.0 g | **Cholesterol** 60 mg | **Sodium** 350 mg | **Potassium** 770 mg | **Total Carbohydrate** 8 g | Dietary Fiber 1 g | Sugars 6 g | Added Sugars 4 g | **Protein** 24 g | **Phosphorus** 335 mg

POINTERS

- To keep this recipe simple, buy individually frozen 4-oz salmon fillets.
- Frozen asparagus spears can be used when fresh aren't in season (although fresh asparagus has a much better taste and texture).
- To add a little spice to this recipe, after baking, try a drizzle of sriracha over the salmon.
- These foil packets are great for grilling too. Grill over medium-low heat. Cover grill and cook for 10–13 minutes, rotating packets a half turn after about 6 minutes.

Timesaver Tip

- Minced fresh garlic in a jar is a quick alternative to mincing a fresh garlic clove. For best flavor, don't substitute garlic powder.

ROASTED CARROTS

This is a simple, basic recipe with only four ingredients. Roasting brings out the natural sweetness in the flavor of the carrots. Learn more tips for roasting vegetables on page 151.

THIS RECIPE CAN FIT IN THE FOLLOWING EATING PATTERNS: All

NUMBER OF SERVINGS: 8 | **SERVING SIZE:** 1/2 cup cooked
PREP TIME: 10 minutes | **COOK TIME:** 25–30 minutes

INGREDIENTS

- 2 lb baby carrots
- 2 Tbsp olive oil
- 1/4 tsp kosher (or coarse ground) salt
- 1/2 tsp coarse ground black pepper

INSTRUCTIONS

1. Preheat oven to 425°F.
2. Slice the baby carrots in half lengthwise.
3. Place carrots in a 1-gallon resealable plastic bag. Drizzle in olive oil. Sprinkle salt and pepper evenly over carrots.
4. Shake bag and massage carrots to coat well with oil and seasonings.
5. Transfer carrots to a baking sheet lined with a sheet of parchment paper. Spread carrots out in a single layer.
6. Place tray on middle oven rack and roast for 25–30 minutes, or until the edges are lightly browned and carrots are tender when pierced with a fork. Stir once or twice to help carrots brown evenly. Keep an eye on them during the final 10 minutes so they don't burn. Depending on the texture you prefer, longer roasting time makes the carrots more tender while shorter roasting time leaves the carrots more firm.

CHOICES: 2 Nonstarchy Vegetable, 1/2 Fat
BASIC NUTRITIONAL VALUES: Calories 80 | Calories from Fat 30 | **Total Fat** 3.5 g | Saturated Fat 0.5 g | Trans Fat 0.0 g | **Cholesterol** 0 mg | **Sodium** 140 mg | **Potassium** 370 mg | **Total Carbohydrate** 11 g | Dietary Fiber 3 g | Sugars 5 g | Added Sugars 0 g | **Protein** 1 g | **Phosphorus** 40 mg

Timesaver Tips

- Use baby carrots to keep this recipe simple, and they're the perfect size for roasting. Or you can peel and chop whole carrots into 1 1/2-inch-long chunks. They key is to make all of the pieces about the same size for even cooking.
- While we use parchment paper or foil to line the baking pan when roasting vegetables for easy cleanup, alternately you can spray a nonstick baking pan with cooking spray.

POINTER

- Depending on your preference for black pepper and heat, you may want to start with 1/4 tsp black pepper, see how it tastes, and then add the other 1/4 tsp after roasting. Sprinkle over carrots evenly and toss in.

DINNER MENU 2

EATING PATTERNS THIS MENU ALIGNS WITH: low-carbohydrate

- 1 serving **Bell Pepper Pizza Poppers** (page 291)
- 2 cups chopped romaine lettuce tossed with
  - 2 Tbsp light Caesar dressing
- 1 (5.3-oz) fat-free lemon Greek yogurt
- Sparkling water

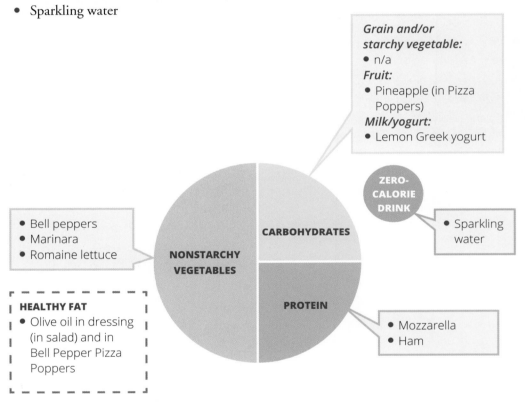

Grain and/or starchy vegetable:
- n/a

Fruit:
- Pineapple (in Pizza Poppers)

Milk/yogurt:
- Lemon Greek yogurt

ZERO-CALORIE DRINK
- Sparkling water

CARBOHYDRATES

NONSTARCHY VEGETABLES
- Bell peppers
- Marinara
- Romaine lettuce

HEALTHY FAT
- Olive oil in dressing (in salad) and in Bell Pepper Pizza Poppers

PROTEIN
- Mozzarella
- Ham

SWIFT, SIMPLE TIP
- Purchase prepared ready-to-eat chopped romaine to save time. Then the salad can be quickly assembled while the Bell Pepper Pizza Poppers are baking.

BELL PEPPER PIZZA POPPERS

A take on a "Hawaiian-style" pizza, these delicious pizza poppers are much lower in carbohydrate than a traditional pizza, with bell pepper serving as the "crust" in place of a dough crust. Using a lower-sodium sauce and reduced-sodium ham keeps the sodium within a reasonable range. And when you eat this recipe, you fit in two nonstarchy vegetable servings in a flavorful way!

THIS RECIPE CAN FIT IN THE FOLLOWING EATING PATTERN: low-carbohydrate

---

NUMBER OF SERVINGS: 2 | **SERVING SIZE:** 2 halves
PREP TIME: 15 minutes | **COOK TIME:** 15–20 minutes

INGREDIENTS

- 2 red, yellow, or orange bell peppers, halved lengthwise and cored
- 1 tsp olive oil
- Freshly ground black pepper
- 1/2 cup low-sodium marinara sauce without added sugar (such as The Silver Palate or Victoria)
- 2/3 cup shredded part-skim mozzarella cheese
- 1/4 cup diced lean reduced-sodium ham (such as Boar's Head)
- 1/4 cup drained pineapple tidbits packed in juice

INSTRUCTIONS

1. Preheat oven to 350°F.
2. Dry pepper halves well.
3. Place pepper halves cut-side-up on a baking sheet with sides. Drizzle the edge of the peppers with olive oil (allowing it to run down the outside of the peppers) then rock peppers back and forth in the oil to coat the outside.
4. Season peppers to taste with black pepper.
5. Spoon marinara sauce into each pepper half. Sprinkle with mozzarella and top each with ham and pineapple.
6. Bake for 15–20 minutes on the middle oven rack, until the peppers are crisp-tender when poked with a fork and the cheese is melted. You may move the tray to the top rack during the last 5 minutes of cooking to roast edges of peppers slightly. Depending on the size of the peppers, they may take a few minutes less to cook, or a few minutes more.

(Pointers and Cook's Swap on following page)

CHOICES: 1/2 Carbohydrate, 2 Nonstarchy Vegetable, 1 Lean Protein, 2 Fat
BASIC NUTRITIONAL VALUES: Calories 220 | Calories from Fat 100 | **Total Fat** 11.0 g | Saturated Fat 4.5 g | Trans Fat 0.0 g | **Cholesterol** 30 mg | **Sodium** 420 mg | **Potassium** 600 mg | **Total Carbohydrate** 18 g | Dietary Fiber 4 g | Sugars 12 g | Added Sugars 0 g | **Protein** 14 g | **Phosphorus** 265 mg

POINTERS

- While green bell peppers can also be used in this recipe, the red, yellow, and orange peppers are sweeter and blend well with the other flavors.
- If you have Kroger grocery stores in your area, the Private Selection Heirloom vine-ripened tomato sauce is flavorful and fresh-tasting without added sugar.
- Swap in other favorite pizza toppings to mix up the flavors.

COOK'S SWAP

- Swap the part-skim mozzarella cheese for dairy-free mozzarella shreds and the ham for a vegan ham alternative to also fit in a vegetarian or vegan eating pattern.

DINNER MENU 3

EATING PATTERNS THIS MENU ALIGNS WITH: vegetarian, low- or very-low-fat, DASH

- 1 3/4 cup *Hoppin' John* (page 294)
- 1 cup unsweetened almond milk

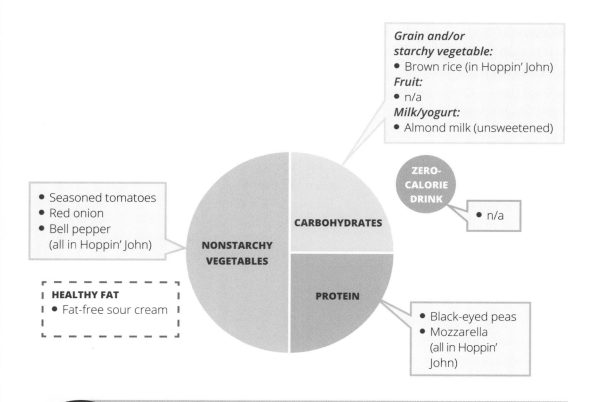

Grain and/or starchy vegetable:
- Brown rice (in Hoppin' John)

Fruit:
- n/a

Milk/yogurt:
- Almond milk (unsweetened)

ZERO-CALORIE DRINK
- n/a

CARBOHYDRATES

- Seasoned tomatoes
- Red onion
- Bell pepper
  (all in Hoppin' John)

NONSTARCHY VEGETABLES

HEALTHY FAT
- Fat-free sour cream

PROTEIN

- Black-eyed peas
- Mozzarella
  (all in Hoppin' John)

SWIFT, SIMPLE TIPS

- When possible, purchase diced onion and pepper off the supermarket salad bar to make this recipe preparation even faster.

HOPPIN' JOHN

This plant-based recipe is a flavorful way to fit in a hefty dose of fiber. The use of reduced-sodium canned black-eyed peas and quick-heat brown rice keeps preparation simple and quick.

THIS RECIPE CAN FIT IN THE FOLLOWING EATING PATTERNS: vegetarian, low- or very-low-fat, DASH

NUMBER OF SERVINGS: 5 | **SERVING SIZE:** 1 3/4 cups
PREP TIME: 15 minutes | **COOK TIME:** 15 minutes

INGREDIENTS

- 2 (15-oz) cans no-salt-added black-eyed peas (rinse and drain peas, if a no-salt-added version is unavailable)
- 1 (14.5-oz) can diced tomatoes, seasoned with basil, garlic, and oregano, drained (such as Del Monte brand)
- 1 bag boil-in-bag brown rice *or* 1 (8.8-oz) microwavable pouch fully cooked brown rice (such as Uncle Ben's Ready Rice)

- 3/4 cup finely shredded part-skim mozzarella (finely shredded provides more ample coverage than a regular shred)
- 1 1/4 cups coarsely chopped red onion
- 1 1/4 cups coarsely chopped green bell pepper
- 1/4 cup fat-free sour cream (or fat-free plain Greek yogurt)

(continued)

COOK'S SWAPS

- Swap the shredded mozzarella for non-dairy mozzarella-style shreds and the fat-free sour cream for a dairy-free sour cream alternative to also fit in a vegan eating pattern.

HOPPIN' JOHN (*continued*)

INSTRUCTIONS

1. Combine black-eyed peas and drained tomatoes in a pan, stirring gently to combine. Warm over low heat, gently stirring periodically.
2. Meanwhile, cook rice according to package directions, omitting any salt. If using boil-in-bag variety, drain well.
3. In an 8 × 12-inch serving dish, or platter of equal size, layer the rice and evenly top with black-eyed pea and tomato mixture. Sprinkle evenly with cheese, onion, and bell pepper. Top with small dollops of sour cream (or Greek yogurt).

PREP TIPS

- Plain, unseasoned diced tomatoes can be used instead of tomatoes seasoned with basil, garlic, and oregano.
- Use a combination of red, orange, and green bell peppers for a colorful plate.
- If not following a vegetarian eating pattern, diced cooked chicken makes a tasty addition. Just warm the cooked chicken in the pan with the beans.

Trick

- Add a splash of heat with a couple dashes of hot sauce.

CHOICES: 2 1/2 Starch, 2 Nonstarchy Vegetable, 1 Lean Protein

BASIC NUTRITIONAL VALUES: Calories 280 | Calories from Fat 40 | **Total Fat** 4.5 g | Saturated Fat 2.1 g | Trans Fat 0.0 g | **Cholesterol** 10 mg | **Sodium** 290 mg | **Potassium** 590 mg | **Total Carbohydrate** 49 g | Dietary Fiber 8 g | Sugars 7 g | Added Sugars 0 g | **Protein** 16 g | **Phosphorus** 290 mg

DINNER MENU 4

***EATING PATTERNS THIS MENU ALIGNS WITH:* low-carbohydrate, DASH**

- 1 serving ***Chicken Southwest*** (page 299) made with ***Mix & Match Basic Chicken Marinade*** (page 297)
- 1 cup grilled or sautéed zucchini and onions
- 1/4 oz square bittersweet chocolate with 1/2 tsp nut butter
- Water with slice of lemon

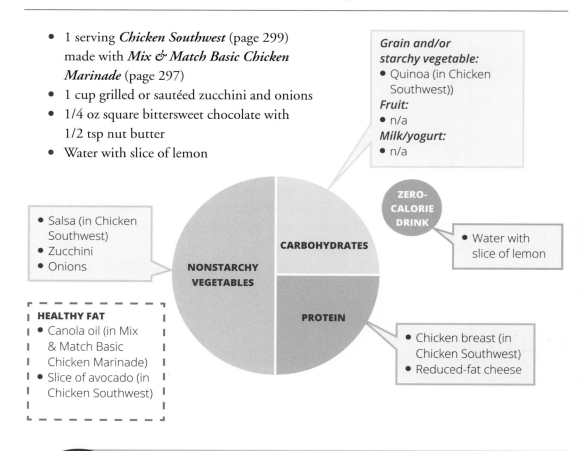

Grain and/or starchy vegetable:
- Quinoa (in Chicken Southwest))

Fruit:
- n/a

Milk/yogurt:
- n/a

ZERO-CALORIE DRINK
- Water with slice of lemon

CARBOHYDRATES

NONSTARCHY VEGETABLES
- Salsa (in Chicken Southwest)
- Zucchini
- Onions

HEALTHY FAT
- Canola oil (in Mix & Match Basic Chicken Marinade)
- Slice of avocado (in Chicken Southwest)

PROTEIN
- Chicken breast (in Chicken Southwest)
- Reduced-fat cheese

SWIFT, SIMPLE TIPS

- The day before, prep marinade and let the chicken marinate overnight so it's ready to go.
- Cut zucchini and onion into chunks (about the same size for even cooking) earlier in the day and store in a container or resealable plastic bag in the refrigerator to speed up mealtime preparation.
- While the grill is hot to grill the chicken, grill zucchini and onion chunks on a skewer, sealed in a foil packet, or in a disposable foil pan on the grill grate.

MIX & MATCH BASIC CHICKEN MARINADE

This versatile marinade is a recipe in Tami's family that has been enjoyed for years. Flavor combinations can easily be mixed up by making swaps in the citrus juice and herbs, which lend flavor without added sodium. In comparison, bottled marinades are typically loaded with sodium. This marinade is enough to marinate six 4-oz chicken breasts. **Note on yield:** *this recipe makes a total of 10 Tbsp, but we recommend discarding the remaining 4 Tbsp after marinating is complete in the interest of food safety.*

THIS RECIPE CAN FIT IN THE FOLLOWING EATING PATTERNS: vegetarian and vegan (marinade only), low- and very-low-carbohydrate, DASH, Mediterranean

NUMBER OF SERVINGS: 6 | **SERVING SIZE:** 1 Tbsp
PREP TIME: 5 minutes

8 Juice and herb combinations

1. Lime juice and cilantro
2. Lime juice and parsley
3. Lemon juice and parsley
4. Lemon juice and chives
5. Lemon juice and dill
6. Lemon juice and thyme
7. Lemon juice and rosemary
8. Lemon juice and basil

INGREDIENTS

- 1/4 cup fresh squeezed citrus juice (lemon or lime) (this will take about two lemons or limes)
- 1/4 cup olive oil or canola oil
- 1 tsp fresh minced garlic
- 2 Tbsp fresh herbs (such as basil, chives, cilantro, dill, parsley, rosemary, or thyme)

INSTRUCTIONS

1. In a 1-gallon resealable plastic bag, combine all marinade ingredients. Seal and shake to mix.

(How to Use Marinade, Timesaver Tip, Pointer, and Box on following page)

CHOICES: 1 Fat

BASIC NUTRITIONAL VALUES: Calories 50 | Calories from Fat 45 | **Total Fat** 5.0 g | Saturated Fat 0.7 g | Trans Fat 0.0 g | **Cholesterol** 0 mg | **Sodium** 0 mg | **Potassium** 10 mg | **Total Carbohydrate** 1 g | Dietary Fiber 0 g | Sugars 0 g | Added Sugars 0 g | **Protein** 0 g | **Phosphorus** 0 mg

How to Use Marinade

- Add chicken breasts to the resealable plastic bag containing the marinade. Tightly seal bag. Turn several times to coat chicken well. Place bag in a pan in case of any leaks. Refrigerate chicken at least 4 hours (turning bag to recoat chicken once or twice). Grill or bake chicken to 165°F and juices run clear.

Timesaver Tip

- For the fresh herbs, we often use the "paste" versions, which can be purchased in a tube in the refrigerated produce section. Leftover pastes last much longer than fresh herbs.

POINTER

- Use fresh-squeezed lemon or lime juice instead of a bottled version. The flavor will be much better.

This Recipe Will Help Put "Planned Overs" into Practice

To make the most of our time in the kitchen, we often double the marinade recipe or do two different juice/herb combinations, each in a different bag. Then we plan to use the chicken throughout the week in two or three different meals as "planned overs."

Planned-Overs Example: Double the lime juice and cilantro marinade (which lends a Mexican or southwest flavor) and plan to include the chicken in 3 different ways for 3 different meals.

1. *Chicken Southwest*: See recipe on page 299.
2. **Chopped salad:** Chopped romaine lettuce, canned black beans (rinsed and drained), frozen corn (thawed), diced tomato, diced jicama, and green onions drizzled with salsa or vinaigrette.
3. **Chicken nachos:** Baked tortilla chips (such as Tostitos Oven Baked Scoops) layered with warmed fat-free refried beans, warmed diced or shredded chicken, shredded lettuce, diced tomato, diced avocado, a sprinkle of reduced-fat shredded Mexican style cheese, and salsa.

CHICKEN SOUTHWEST

Incorporating the **Mix & Match Basic Chicken Marinade** *on page 297, this recipe is nearly a meal in itself—including lean protein, whole-grain quinoa, and healthy fat from the avocado.*

THIS RECIPE CAN FIT IN THE FOLLOWING EATING PATTERNS: low-carbohydrate, DASH

NUMBER OF SERVINGS: 6 | **SERVING SIZE:** 1 chicken breast, 1/2 cup cooked quinoa, 2 Tbsp cheese and salsa, 1 slice avocado | **PREP TIME:** 10 minutes
MARINATING TIME: 4 hours | **COOK TIME:** approximately 10 minutes

INGREDIENTS
Marinade

- 1/4 cup fresh-squeezed lime juice
- 1/4 cup canola oil
- 1 tsp fresh minced garlic
- 2 Tbsp chopped fresh cilantro

OTHER INGREDIENTS

- 6 4-oz boneless, skinless chicken breasts
- 3/4 cup shredded reduced-fat Mexican-style cheese
- 3 cups hot cooked quinoa
- 3/4 cup thick salsa, heated
- 1 avocado, sliced into six slices

INSTRUCTIONS
TO MARINATE CHICKEN

1. In a 1-gallon resealable plastic bag, combine all marinade ingredients. Seal and shake to mix.
2. Add chicken breasts. Tightly seal bag.
3. Turn several times to coat chicken well. Place bag in a pan in case of any leaks. Refrigerate chicken at least 4 hours (turning bag to recoat chicken once or twice).

(continued)

(Timesaver Tip and Trick on following page)

CHOICES: 1 1/2 Starch, 1 Nonstarchy Vegetable, 4 Lean Protein, 2 Fat
BASIC NUTRITIONAL VALUES: Calories 390 | Calories from Fat 150 | **Total Fat** 17.0 g | Saturated Fat 3.8 g | Trans Fat 0.0 g | **Cholesterol** 70 mg | **Sodium** 350 mg | **Potassium** 590 mg | **Total Carbohydrate** 29 g | Dietary Fiber 6 g | Sugars 5 g | Added Sugars 0 g | **Protein** 34 g | **Phosphorus** 430 mg

CHICKEN SOUTHWEST (*continued*)

TO PREPARE CHICKEN

1.   Prepare grill for medium-high heat (350–450°F).
2.   Remove chicken from marinade. Discard remaining marinade.
3.   Place chicken on grill. Grill 5 minutes. Turn chicken over and continue grilling until chicken reaches 165°F and juices run clear (roughly 4–6 minutes). (Alternately, bake chicken at 350°F for 25–30 minutes or until chicken reaches 165°F and juices run clear.)
4.   During the last 2–3 minutes of cooking, sprinkle each chicken breast with 2 Tbsp cheese.

TO SERVE

1.   Place 1/2 cup cooked quinoa on plate.
2.   Top with chicken breast.
3.   Then top with 2 Tbsp salsa and 1 slice avocado.

Timesaver Tip

- Try ready-to-serve microwavable quinoa.

Trick

- Try mixing in chopped green chili peppers with the salsa for even more flavor.

DINNER MENU 5

EATING PATTERNS THIS MENU ALIGNS WITH: low-fat, low-carbohydrate, DASH

- 3 oz lean grilled steak (such as flat iron)
- 1 cup *Garlic Roasted Brussels Sprouts* (page 302)
- 1 medium (~6 oz) baked sweet potato with
  - 2 tsp trans fat–free buttery spread
- Iced water

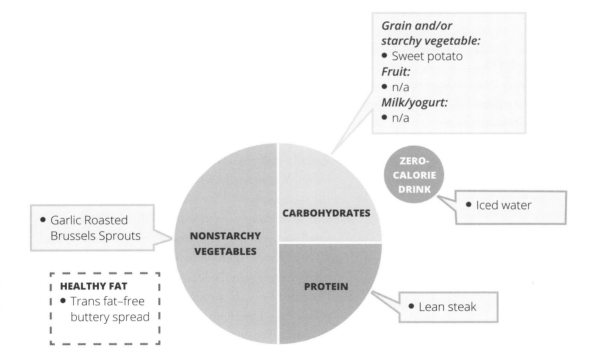

Grain and/or starchy vegetable:
- Sweet potato

Fruit:
- n/a

Milk/yogurt:
- n/a

ZERO-CALORIE DRINK
- Iced water

CARBOHYDRATES

- Garlic Roasted Brussels Sprouts

NONSTARCHY VEGETABLES

HEALTHY FAT
- Trans fat–free buttery spread

PROTEIN
- Lean steak

SWIFT, SIMPLE TIP

- One of our favorite time-saving tips is to microwave a potato for about 3 minutes to warm it up, and then it can finish baking alongside the tray of Brussels sprouts. We find that oven-baked potatoes have a different texture than potatoes cooked fully in the microwave.

GARLIC ROASTED BRUSSELS SPROUTS

This is another basic four-ingredient recipe that can help you fit in more nonstarchy vegetables in a flavorful way. Many people who don't like Brussels sprouts find they enjoy them roasted. Roasting mellows the strong, bitter taste. Garlic and sriracha add a burst of seasoning. Learn more tips for roasting vegetables on page 151.

THIS RECIPE CAN FIT IN THE FOLLOWING EATING PATTERNS: All

NUMBER OF SERVINGS: 8 | **SERVING SIZE:** 1 cup cooked
PREP TIME: 15 minutes | **COOK TIME:** 25–30 minutes

INGREDIENTS

- 2 lb fresh Brussels sprouts
- 2 Tbsp olive oil
- 1 tsp sriracha sauce
- 2 tsp fresh minced garlic

INSTRUCTIONS

1. Preheat oven to 425°F.
2. Wash the Brussels sprouts in a colander and dry well, patting off the moisture with a clean dishtowel or paper towel.
3. Remove and discard any discolored or withered leaves. You may choose to trim off the dry cut edge of the sprouts also.
4. Cut Brussels sprouts in half lengthwise (if they are small sprouts, you may choose to leave them whole). We usually cut them in half regardless because we prefer more roasted edges.
5. Place dry Brussels sprouts in a 1-gallon resealable plastic bag. Drizzle in olive oil and sriracha sauce. Sprinkle in garlic.
6. Shake bag and massage Brussels sprouts to coat well with oil and seasonings.

(continued)

CHOICES: 2 Nonstarchy Vegetable, 1/2 Fat
BASIC NUTRITIONAL VALUES: Calories 70 | Calories from Fat 35 | **Total Fat** 4.0 g | Saturated Fat 0.6 g | Trans Fat 0.0 g | **Cholesterol** 0 mg | **Sodium** 35 mg | **Potassium** 360 mg | **Total Carbohydrate** 8 g | Dietary Fiber 3 g | Sugars 2 g | Added Sugars 0 g | **Protein** 3 g | **Phosphorus** 65 mg

GARLIC ROASTED BRUSSELS SPROUTS (*continued*)

7. Transfer Brussels sprouts to a baking sheet lined with a sheet of parchment paper. Spread sprouts out in a single layer. This is important for even roasting.

8. Place tray on an upper (not top) oven rack and roast for 25–30 minutes, or until the edges are lightly browned and sprouts are tender when pierced with a fork. Stir once or twice to help sprouts brown evenly. Keep an eye on them during the final 5–10 minutes so they don't burn. Depending on the texture you prefer, you may want to roast a few minutes longer for larger Brussels sprouts.

Timesaver Tips

- While we use parchment paper or foil to line the baking pan when roasting vegetables for easy cleanup, alternately, you can spray a nonstick baking pan with cooking spray.
- Minced fresh garlic in a jar is a quick alternative to mincing a fresh garlic clove.
- Purchase ready-to-use pre-cut Brussels sprouts.

POINTER

- If you're not a fan of sriracha sauce, leave it out and sprinkle Brussels sprouts with coarse ground pepper after they're spread out on the baking sheet.

DINNER MENU 6

EATING PATTERNS THIS MENU ALIGNS WITH: low-carbohydrate, DASH, Mediterranean

- 1 serving *Teriyaki Salmon and Broccoli Sheet Pan for Two* (page 305)
- 1/2 cup fresh pineapple
- Unsweetened or low-calorie sweetened green tea

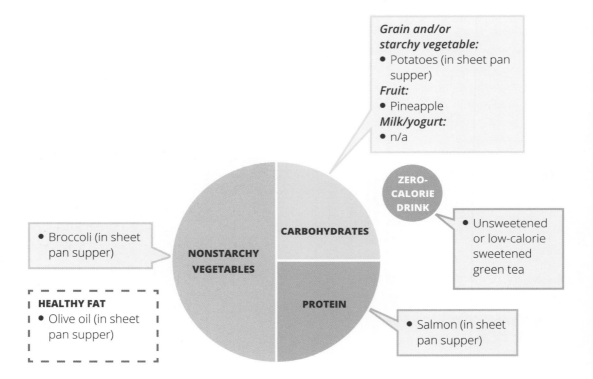

Grain and/or starchy vegetable:
- Potatoes (in sheet pan supper)

Fruit:
- Pineapple

Milk/yogurt:
- n/a

CARBOHYDRATES

ZERO-CALORIE DRINK
- Unsweetened or low-calorie sweetened green tea

- Broccoli (in sheet pan supper)

NONSTARCHY VEGETABLES

HEALTHY FAT
- Olive oil (in sheet pan supper)

PROTEIN

- Salmon (in sheet pan supper)

SWIFT, SIMPLE TIPS

- Purchase pre-portioned salmon fillets.
- Purchase a bag of fresh broccoli florets to save time—no chopping needed.
- Purchase fresh pineapple chunks in the produce section to save time peeling a pineapple.

TERIYAKI SALMON AND BROCCOLI SHEET PAN FOR TWO

This flavorful, colorful sheet pan supper is rich in potassium, fits in a fish serving with healthy omega-3 fats, and contains Mediterranean-style vegetables and herbs.

THIS RECIPE CAN FIT IN THE FOLLOWING EATING PATTERNS: low-carbohydrate, DASH, Mediterranean

---

NUMBER OF SERVINGS: 2 | **SERVING SIZE:** 4-oz salmon fillet, 1/2 the potatoes, 1/2 the broccoli
PREP TIME: 20 minutes | **COOK TIME:** 45–50 minutes

INGREDIENTS

- 2 4-oz salmon fillets (about 1 1/2 inches thick)
- 2 Tbsp reduced-sodium teriyaki sauce
- 12 oz (about 3 cups) fingerling potatoes, dried well and halved lengthwise (Tami likes to use a combination of purple, yellow, and white that are sold together in a small bag.)
- 3 Tbsp olive oil, divided
- 2 Tbsp fresh rosemary leaves (or 1–2 tsp dried rosemary)
- Freshly ground black pepper (3/8 tsp in total, divided)
- 4 cups broccoli florets (approximately 1 medium head of broccoli)
- 1 tsp minced garlic

INSTRUCTIONS

1. Place salmon in a resealable plastic bag with the teriyaki sauce and shake gently to coat well. (Alternately, salmon can be placed in a single layer in a dish or baking pan and coated evenly with the teriyaki sauce.) Set in refrigerator to marinate while prepping remaining ingredients.
2. Preheat oven to 450°F.
3. Line a rimmed baking sheet with parchment paper.
4. Place the potatoes, 1 1/2 Tbsp olive oil, and rosemary leaves in a second resealable plastic bag and shake to coat well. (Alternately, place the potatoes on one end of the baking sheet, drizzle with the olive oil, sprinkle with rosemary leaves, and toss with hands to coat well.) Place the potatoes in a single layer on one end of the baking sheet and sprinkle with 1/4 tsp freshly ground coarse black pepper (adjust pepper to suit your taste).
5. Bake until the potatoes begin to soften, about 20 minutes.

(continued)

(Timesaver Tips, Cook's Swap, and Prep Tips on following page)

CHOICES: 2 Starch, 2 Nonstarchy Vegetable, 3 Lean Protein, 4 Fat
BASIC NUTRITIONAL VALUES: Calories 520 | Calories from Fat 260 | **Total Fat** 29.0 g | Saturated Fat 4.8 g | Trans Fat 0.0 g | **Cholesterol** 60 mg | **Sodium** 380 mg | **Potassium** 1580 mg | **Total Carbohydrate** 38 g | Dietary Fiber 8 g | Sugars 5 g | Added Sugars 0 g | **Protein** 30 g | **Phosphorus** 485 mg

TERIYAKI SALMON AND BROCCOLI SHEET PAN FOR TWO (*continued*)

6. While the potatoes are roasting, place the broccoli in a third resealable plastic bag (or large bowl) and add garlic. Drizzle with the remaining 1 1/2 Tbsp olive oil. Shake and massage to coat well.
7. Reduce oven heat to 425°F.
8. Remove the baking sheet from the oven and put the broccoli in the center. Sprinkle with 1/8 tsp freshly coarse ground black pepper.
9. Return the baking sheet to the oven for 15 minutes.
10. Remove the baking sheet from the oven and add the salmon fillets on the other empty end, skin side down. Pour juices in the bag over the salmon fillets.
11. Return to the oven for 10–12 minutes, or until salmon flakes easily with a fork (if the fillets are thinner, cooking may take 2 or 3 minutes less).

Timesaver Tips

- Lining the baking pan with parchment paper makes for easy cleanup and prevents the ingredients from sticking to the pan.
- We're fans of using resealable plastic bags to coat each type of food with seasonings for ease and quick cleanup.

COOK'S SWAP

- Swap the potatoes for cauliflower florets or carrot chunks for this recipe to also fit in a very-low-carbohydrate eating pattern.

PREP TIPS

- Regular-size potatoes can be used instead of the small fingerling potatoes. Just cut into strips about 1-inch wide and thick and 2–3 inches long. Similar size pieces are essential to allow for even roasting.
- Here are a few ways to mix up the flavors of this sheet pan supper:
  - *Salmon seasoning:* Swap barbecue sauce, olive oil and lemon juice, or vinaigrette dressing in place of teriyaki sauce.
  - *Potato seasoning:* Swap thyme, tarragon, lemon pepper, or another salt-free seasoning blend in place of the rosemary. Or omit herb seasoning altogether.

WHAT DO I EAT FOR . . . SNACKS?

For most women, 15 g carbohydrate at a snack is appropriate; for most men, 15–30 g carbohydrate is appropriate. Check with your diabetes health-care team to find the amount of carbohydrate that's right for you.

7 Smart 15-Gram Carbohydrate Snacks

- 3/4 cup *Lean Green Pineapple Smoothie* (page 309)
- One (6-inch) corn tortilla sprinkled lightly with reduced-fat cheddar, heated, and topped with fresh salsa
- 1/2 cup cottage cheese with 1/2 cup sliced fresh peaches (or canned in juice or water)
- 12 grapes with 2 Tbsp *Hint of Maple Dip* (page 311)
- 3 cups Parmesan peppered popcorn (air popped or light microwave popcorn sprinkled with black pepper and 1/8 cup Parmesan cheese)
- 2 cups jicama sticks with pesto for dipping
- Two medium fresh figs with 1 oz brie cheese

7 Smart 30-Gram Carbohydrate Snacks

- Yogurt parfait (1 cup light vanilla yogurt topped with 1/2 cup total of blueberries, sliced strawberries, and mandarin oranges in juice)
- 1 slice sprouted-grain bread topped with almond butter and 1/2 sliced banana
- 3 graham cracker squares with 1 cup fat-free milk
- 2 1/2 cups diced watermelon
- 9 reduced-fat Triscuits topped with sliced Canadian bacon and reduced-fat cheese slices (toast or microwave to melt cheese)
- 1/4 cup raisins and 12 cashews
- One small mango or 1 cup mango

LEAN GREEN PINEAPPLE SMOOTHIE

To make a smoothie that's more plant-based and lower in carbohydrate than many traditional smoothies, unsweetened vanilla-flavored almond milk is used in place of dairy milk. Additional creaminess and calcium comes from fat-free Greek (or Icelandic) yogurt, which is naturally lower in carbohydrate and higher in protein. Frozen pineapple adds sweetness. Fresh baby spinach lends a nonstarchy vegetable and pleasing light green color to this smoothie.

THIS RECIPE CAN FIT IN THE FOLLOWING EATING PATTERNS: vegetarian, low- or very-low-fat, low-carbohydrate, DASH, Mediterranean

NUMBER OF SERVINGS: 4 | **SERVING SIZE:** 3/4 cup
PREP TIME: 5 minutes | **COOK TIME:** NA

INGREDIENTS

- 1 cup unsweetened vanilla-flavored almond milk
- 2 cups raw baby spinach
- 2 (5.3-oz) containers fat-free vanilla Greek (or Icelandic) yogurt
- 2 cups unsweetened frozen diced pineapple
- 3 large ice cubes
- 4 dashes ground cinnamon

INSTRUCTIONS

1. Combine almond milk, spinach, yogurt, pineapple, and ice cubes in blender.
2. Cover and blend until smooth.
3. Pour into four glasses and top each with a dash of ground cinnamon.
4. Enjoy right away or freeze for later use. (See four freezing tips on page 310.)

(Timesaver Tip, Pointers, Prep Tips, and Cook's Swap on following page)

CHOICES: 1 Fruit, 1 Lean Protein
BASIC NUTRITIONAL VALUES: Calories 90 | Calories from Fat 10 | **Total Fat** 1.0 g | Saturated Fat 0.1 g | Trans Fat 0.0 g | **Cholesterol** 1 mg | **Sodium** 80 mg | **Potassium** 290 mg | **Total Carbohydrate** 16 g | Dietary Fiber 2 g | Sugars 12 g | Added Sugars 0 g | **Protein** 7 g | **Phosphorus** 120 mg

Timesaver Tip

- Buy prewashed, bagged baby spinach for this smoothie to keep it quick.

POINTERS

- If you desire a sweeter flavor, add your favorite low-calorie sweetener and give the blender a couple of pulses to mix.
- If you plan to freeze this smoothie to enjoy later, omit the ice when blending.

PREP TIPS

- Freezing smoothies is simple. Make a couple of different recipes and freeze to grab later in the week. **Here are 4 freezing tips that Tami has learned:**
  1. Use wide-mouthed, glass jars with lids (like mason jars).
  2. Pour in your portion, leaving at least 1 inch at the top so the liquid has room to expand.
  3. For the best flavor, enjoy frozen smoothies within 1 week.
  4. To thaw, leave in the refrigerator overnight, or set out a few minutes (they thaw fairly quickly), or in a pinch, microwave on 50% power for 30–60 seconds or until desired consistency. Stir well and enjoy straight from the jar.

COOK'S SWAP

- Swap the fat-free vanilla Greek or Icelandic yogurt for a nondairy vanilla yogurt for this recipe to also fit in a vegan eating pattern.

HINT OF MAPLE DIP

This recipe is a much lower-calorie, lower-fat, and lower-carbohydrate option to traditional cream cheese–based fruit dip, with the creaminess coming from fat-free vanilla Greek yogurt and light whipped topping. A combination of extracts and cinnamon lend sweetness without carbohydrate.

THIS RECIPE CAN FIT IN THE FOLLOWING EATING PATTERNS: **vegetarian, low- or very-low-fat, low- or very-low-carbohydrate, DASH**

NUMBER OF SERVINGS: 6 | **SERVING SIZE:** 2 Tbsp
PREP TIME: 5 minutes | **COOK TIME:** NA

INGREDIENTS

- 1/2 cup fat-free vanilla Greek yogurt
- 1/2 cup light whipped topping (such as light Cool Whip)
- 1/8 tsp maple extract
- 1/8 tsp almond extract
- 1 dash ground cinnamon

INSTRUCTIONS

1. Combine all ingredients in a bowl and whisk to mix well.

(Pointers and Tricks on following page)

CHOICES: Free

BASIC NUTRITIONAL VALUES: Calories 25 | Calories from Fat 10 | **Total Fat** 1.0 g | Saturated Fat 0.7 g | Trans Fat 0.0 g | **Cholesterol** 0 mg | **Sodium** 10 mg | **Potassium** 25 mg | **Total Carbohydrate** 3 g | Dietary Fiber 0 g | Sugars 2 g | Added Sugars 1 g | **Protein** 2 g | **Phosphorus** 35 mg

POINTERS

- Fruits that pair well with this dip include grapes, apple slices, pear slices, and strawberries.
- This dip is versatile in that it's easy to switch up flavors by adding more extract to further intensify flavor or using different extracts. Start with 1/8 tsp extract and increase by another 1/8 tsp of the same or a different flavor. You could swap in lemon, orange, or strawberry to pair with angel food cake. Or add vanilla, coconut, or coffee extract to pair this "dip" as a topping for oats, for instance. The extracts are carbohydrate- and calorie-free.

Tricks

- To prevent apple and pear slices from browning, dip them in lemon, lime, or orange juice and drain well.
- This "dip" can also serve as a tasty topping for waffles or pancakes.

Index